Radical Dreamers

Radical Dreamers

Race, Choice, and the Failure of American Education

JOSEPH P. VITERITTI

OXFORD
UNIVERSITY PRESS

Oxford University Press is a department of the University of Oxford.
It furthers the University's objective of excellence in research, scholarship,
and education by publishing worldwide. Oxford is a registered trade mark of
Oxford University Press in the UK and in certain other countries.

Published in the United States of America by Oxford University Press
198 Madison Avenue, New York, NY 10016, United States of America.

CIP data is on file at the Library of Congress.

ISBN 9780197827109

DOI: 10.1093/oso/9780197827109.001.0001

Printed by Sheridan Books, Inc., United States of America

The manufacturer's authorized representative in the EU for product safety is
Oxford University Press España S.A., Parque Empresarial San Fernando de Henares,
Avenida de Castilla, 2 – 28830 Madrid (www.oup.es/en or product.safety@oup.com).
OUP España S.A. also acts as importer into Spain of products made by the manufacturer.

Contents

Preface

Between 2022 and 2024, twelve states enacted new laws that enable parents to send their children to private and religious schools at public expense. Twenty-three states passed measures to broaden existing laws.[1] By the spring of 2025, twenty-nine states had introduced ninety-eight bills that either would expand, revise or limit private school choice.[2] These statutes are the most recent chapter in the story of the school choice movement that began in the mid-1990s when Black activists in Milwaukee and Cleveland aligned themselves with Republican legislators and religious leaders to create programs that would give their children better options than the failing public schools where they were routinely assigned.

The recent legislation championed by Republicans and religious conservatives was initially prompted by culture wars over the treatment of race, sex, and gender in the classroom.[3] Among the most controversial topics is critical race theory (CRT), which holds that racism is a systemic and perpetual feature of US society. Across-the-board declines in academic achievement evident since the COVID-19 pandemic further fed wide disillusion with public schools and demands for alternatives. Results from tests administered by the National Assessment for Educational Progress (NAEP), commonly referred to as the Nation's Report Card, released in 2022 showed that performance in reading and math was down in a majority of states since 2019.[4] The drop in math was the largest ever recorded.

Any hopes for a postpandemic recovery were dashed earlier this year when the NAEP scores for 2024 were released. Reading scores for the fourth and eighth grades declined from the previous round of tests, compounding losses first recorded in prepandemic 2019. The percentage of eighth graders reading below the basic level was the largest in history; the percentage of eighth graders who scored below basic in math was the largest in twenty years. The only bright spot in the 2024 scores appeared in fourth-grade math, where there was a two-point gain that followed a five-point decline from 2019 to 2022. That improvement was mostly driven by higher-performing students. There was no significant change in eighth-grade math in 2024.[5] Especially concerned with the reading results, Commissioner Peggy G. Carr of the National Center for Education Statistics lamented, "This is not just a pandemic story. Our nation is facing complex challenges in reading."[6]

A closer look at the 2024 test results revealed a deeper crisis in American education defined by race. Black student test scores remained the lowest of all racial/ethnic groups in both subjects and in both grades when compared to Asians and whites. Hispanic students scored the second lowest, having fallen three points in eighth-grade math since 2022. Lower-performing students struggled the most in reading. In both the fourth and eighth grades, scores in the tenth and twenty-fifth percentiles were lower than NAEP's first reading assessment from 1992.[7]

These disparities in academic performance are part of a larger story of America's failed journey that began seventy-one years ago when a unanimous US Supreme Court in *Brown v. Board of Education* (1954) outlawed racial segregation in schools and ruled that "education is a right that must be made available to all on equal terms."[8] Today, race and class remain the most reliable predictors of education achievement in America, and our public schools continue to be segregated.

Seven decades after *Brown*, it's about time we had an honest conversation about education in America and where we have gone wrong. The school choice issue provides an excellent lens for exploring that history and exposing the roles played by competing forces on both the left and the right sides of the political spectrum to perpetuate our failure.

Looking back some thirty years, when Black activists were finally able to eke out victories for parental choice programs in Milwaukee, Cleveland, and eventually Washington, DC, that targeted their children as the intended beneficiaries, we find that they did so over staunch opposition from teachers' unions and a formidable alliance of groups commonly identified with the liberal left. When laws were successfully passed, the same liberal coalition effectively lobbied to underfund the programs, even though the programs were specifically designed to benefit disadvantaged populations. They did the same with charter schools, which are public schools of choice that disproportionately enroll students of color who had been struggling in regular public schools.

The recent round of legislation advanced by those on the political right has taken choice to a different place. It has ushered in a new era of universal choice, whereby choice in the form of vouchers or education savings accounts (ESAs) is given to all children, not just those with limited incomes or other vulnerable characteristics. By April of 2025, seventeen states across the nation were providing universal eligibility; as recently as 2021, there were none.[9] There are more to come.

The reelection of Donald Trump to the White House and Republican control of both houses of Congress will energize the stampede toward universal choice, even though the states control most education policy. Less than two weeks after taking office, Trump issued an executive order that could repurpose federal funding to that end, while encouraging states to adopt universal choice programs that would be available to all students.[10] As universal plans that are on the rise broaden the political base for choice, they undermine the progressive redistributive intent of the earlier movement.

When more families are able to afford tuition at private and parochial schools, it functions to enhance the choices available to school admissions officers rather than parents. That does not play well for underperforming students who are handicapped by years of struggle in chronically failing public schools. The new choice initiatives have the effect of helping families that don't need it and underfunding those that do. Choice programs have an even more regressive effect when they do not pay the entire cost of tuition, subsidizing better-off families and neglecting those with fewer resources who can't make the payments. All this is happening while Trump's Secretary of Education is in the process of dismantling the US Department of Education (DOE). The DOE administers the federal Elementary and Secondary Education Act (ESEA) program that allocates funding to low-income school districts and other programs that target vulnerable students.

If you want to read a story that validates the essential components of critical race theory, stick with this one. Consider it the backstory to a contemporary movement that has gained traction with the rise of Donald Trump and a wave of policy making that compounds past injustices. Let this chronicle of the political battles over school choice serve as a lens for observing a larger picture of America's failed seventy-one-year journey towards educational equality. And allow the major characters that I am about to introduce breathe life into that narrative as you learn about their efforts to transform the dream of educational equality into a reality for all children.

* * *

I could pat myself on the back for coming up with an original idea—call it "the politics of racial surrogacy"—to explain what has happened, except that it is not all that original. I have been a conscientious student of history and policy who has had the opportunity to learn from four extraordinary individuals who have played key roles in shaping more than a half-century of debate and with whom I have been an occasional collaborator and an admiring friend. Their personal stories animate this history and present it on a human scale. I write as a witness.

Despite our discouraging history, I believe that there is hope going forward for a political compromise in favor of targeted choice for the poor and working poor beyond the limits of ongoing disagreement between those on the left and right. On the one hand, universal choice will drive education costs to a level that neither conservative politicians nor their budgets will be able to sustain. On the other hand, Democrats can no longer defend policies that sustain failure and confine students of color to underperforming public schools. Before getting to that, we first need to take a closer look at where we have been and how we could do better.

The book is organized into three parts. Part 1 includes two short introductory chapters. Part 2, "Critical Thinkers," constitutes the bulk of the book, devoting chapters to each of four major characters, although their stories intersperse throughout the volume, establishing their relationships to each other and a host of other significant actors. Two short supplementary chapters (6 and 9) complete the narratives of those they immediately follow. Part 3 includes a concluding chapter and an addendum that summarizes the existing empirical research on school choice through the end of 2024.

Acknowledgments

As will become evident when you begin to turn the remaining pages, this entire project is an expression of gratitude to individuals from whom I have learned over a long career in education, beginning with the four whose luminous lives drive the narrative: Jack Coons, Ron Edmonds, Howard Fuller and Diane Ravitch. Their stories are brought together by their productive interaction with two other influential figures – Derrick Bell and James Coleman – whose names could not be omitted from any serious attempt to chronicle our nation's long struggle with the dynamics of race and schooling. Add to them a host of other players whose perseverance, against all odds, pointed the way towards more just outcomes: including, Babette Edwards, Fannie Lewis, Deborah McGriff, and Annette (Polly) Williams.

I would not have a story to tell if my teacher and mentor, Frank Macchiarola, had not invited me to join his team when he took charge of the New York City public school system many years ago, or if Bud Spillane did not invite me to apply what I learned from Frank to help with his efforts to lead the public schools in Boston. As I tell my students, the best way to learn something well is to work beside someone who does it well.

Bill Rojas and Joseph Skerrett were the other half of our "Gang of Four" at 110 Livingston Street who would regularly convene in Ron's office to think through instructional strategies that would best serve our students. I was later pleased to head west with Bill in 1992 to assist with his transition when he was appointed Superintendent of Schools in San Francisco. Joe was a member of the Spillane transition team in Boston. A cultural powerhouse in his own right, it was Joe who introduced me to Alvin Ailey and Dance Theater of Harlem and a range treasures across the arts that were then foreign to me.

I would not have a venue to tell this story if not for my collaboration with the fine folks at Oxford University Press. Once again, my wise and affable editor, Dave McBride, took an immediate interest in the project and provided his usual sound advice about what was needed to convert a rough manuscript into a published book. I was fortunate that when Dave left OUP to pursue a new opportunity, he turned my project over to Angela Chnapko who put the final pieces in place. I also thank Alexcee Bechthold who ushered me through production and Rajalakshmi Ezhumalai for navigating the editorial process. My very able publicist, Gretchen Crary, worked prodigiously to make sure that what we produced would reach an attentive audience.

Tess Gutierrez, a graduate student in urban policy and planning at Hunter College, helped get the project off to an early start by digging up research that would help me frame the book and continued to share her imaginative ideas through the very end while tending to her own career. Over the past few years, Colleen Denmon, an honors student at Hunter, became a true partner in this endeavor right through her first year at Cornell Law School, providing research, analysis, light editing, and sound substantive feedback. I would never have met Colleen and several other students who have worked with me on previous book projects if not for Hunter College's phenomenal pre-law advisor Elise Jaffe.

I would not be at Hunter College at all if I had not been personally recruited by its former president Jennifer Raab; nor would I have been as productive without her unwavering support for my research. Provost Manoj Pardasani has remained a consistent source of encouragement, all while serving through a transition period of three different presidencies at the college in a matter of a few years. I look forward to further collaboration with President Nancy Cantor, whose decades of experience have equipped her well to deal with the unprecedented assault we are now experiencing in higher education.

My foremost gratitude goes to my wife, Rosemary Salomone, who was with me throughout the entire experience I have written about in these pages. In addition to the much-appreciated moral support she provided, it was absolutely fabulous to have someone around the house who is a respected education scholar, constitutional law professor, and prize-winning author to offer words of advice throughout the entire endeavor.

PART I
INTRODUCTION

1

What's This About?

I had been out of the conversation for some time. Nearly ten years had passed since I had written on the politics that drive American education. I thought I had said what I had to say—at least for a while—and occupied myself with other intellectual pursuits. Then in late 2019, I was contacted by John Ross of the Institute for Justice (IJ), a libertarian public-interest law firm that was in the process of bringing a landmark case before the US Supreme Court. Ross invited me to participate in a podcast he was producing about the case.

Espinoza v. Montana involved the controversial issue of school choice.[1] As I suggested in the preface to this book, choice concerns a debate over the use of government funds to pay for the educational costs of children whose parents decide to send them to schools outside the jurisdiction of their local public school districts. One level of choice involves charter schools, which are public schools run by private parties or organizations. A more contentious form of choice concerns subsidizing the education of children who attend private schools. Most controversial of all is the use of public money to pay the tuition of students at religious schools through scholarships, vouchers, tax credits, or other means.

Espinoza was about the latter. A Latina mother in Montana was challenging a state law that prohibited her from using a state-supported private school scholarship at a religious school she wanted her daughter to attend. Dick Komer, a very capable litigator with a long record of experience in this area of the law, was brought out of retirement by IJ to argue the case before the high court. I had known Dick for years. He and other attorneys who had argued school-choice cases before federal and state courts regularly cited my research to bolster their arguments. My book *Choosing Equality* and one of my law review articles on the subject were eventually cited in Justice Samuel Alito's concurring opinion when the court handed down its decision favoring the grieved mother in *Espinoza*.[2]

In the previous book, I outlined a plan supporting charter schools and a system of private school choice that targeted low-income students who were stuck in underperforming public schools. It called for equal funding

Radical Dreamers. Joseph P. Viteritti, Oxford University Press. © Oxford University Press (2025).
DOI: 10.1093/oso/9780197827109.003.0001

for students who attended public, charter, and private schools participating in public choice programs and for performance-based standards that would be enforced as a condition of public funding. Participating private and religious schools would not be permitted to charge tuition above the amount of the public scholarship. Faculty and students at charter schools and private schools would be afforded the same basic rights as those in public schools. Religious schools would be permitted and expected to maintain their faith-based traditions. Scholarship students attending those institutions would be excused from participating in religious services if they chose.[3] The book was very much aligned with the progressive orientation of school choice programs that had been implemented at the time in Milwaukee, Cleveland, and Washington, DC, and at charter schools throughout the country designed to steer resources and opportunities into underresourced communities.

My familiarity with the attorneys at IJ dated back at least to 1999, when I gave expert testimony for the State of Ohio in another landmark case that would reach the Supreme Court in 2002 (*Zelman v. Simmons-Harris*).[4] There the court ruled that allowing low-income parents in Cleveland to use state-supported scholarships to attend religious schools does not violate the establishment clause of the First Amendment. While distracted for many years by my writing on city politics, I always assumed that I would return to the topic of education. I had an idea (some would call it a theory) that I wanted to develop—the *politics of racial surrogacy*—to help explain why we do such a shameful job educating low-income children, a disproportionate number of whom are Black and Brown. Choice figures largely in my conception of racial surrogacy, not only as an issue of contention on the battlefields of education politics, but also as a window for exposing the premises and pitfalls underlying that politics.

It was during my conversation with John Ross, when he flew up from Washington in November 2019 to record the podcast in my New York office, that I decided how to frame this new book.[5] On the one hand, I was encouraged by the way the Supreme Court had expanded the range of educational options available to less advantaged families whose children were routinely consigned to chronically failing public schools. On the other, I was growing increasingly uncomfortable with the way the court had begun to redefine the scope of religious freedom.

I was pleased to play a very small part in lowering the high wall that stood between poor children and a decent education while it set impenetrable boundaries between church and state; I had not signed up for a campaign to topple the wall completely. The First Amendment jurisprudence emerging from a newly reconstituted Supreme Court is part of a larger conservative shift that is having a particularly damaging effect on the rights of women and members of the LGBTQ+ community. Beyond the legal issues, many choice advocates already had begun to support versions of the policy that undermined the progressive objectives that originally attracted me to the cause. A reform measure originally adopted in places like Milwaukee and Cleveland to address the needs of underserved students is being reshaped to provide financial assistance to a wider range of students that could effectively limit the choices available to the more needy ones.

Prompted by Ross's queries, I began to ask myself how I arrived at the position I had taken in several books and dozens of essays in policy journals, law reviews, anthologies, and more popular venues. After some reflection, I did what any self-respecting and responsible academic would do: I pointed to other people. This book is actually an extended acknowledgment and note of gratitude to several activist-scholars who shaped my thinking about schools over a long career in education.

There are four individuals in particular: the late Ronald R. Edmonds, John E. (Jack) Coons, Diane Ravitch, and Howard Fuller. This book is very much about them. I consider each one of them a friend, and I've worked especially closely with two. Collectively they have had a decisive impact on the way I came to understand education policy and how we might alter it to better extend its benefits to all children. That should not be surprising. Each of these individuals has had a major influence for decades on the way school advocates and scholars have thought about equality of opportunity in education. A close reading of their material reveals that they also influenced one another. Tracing the trajectory of their work sheds light on our nation's long struggle to provide a good education for every child and where we are today in that never-ending journey. While choice is the entry point for this examination, these people's careers serve to introduce us to a larger range of post-*Brown* issues, including desegregation, integration, fiscal equity, community control, and competency standards.

Let me make some brief introductions:

I don't believe I ever had a conversation with *Ron Edmonds* about the issue of school choice as defined here to include both public and nonpublic schools. Nor, as far as I know, had he ever written about it. For that reason, I do not presume to know how he would view it. I include him in this retrospective because it was he who introduced me to the world of education policy and set the parameters for how I would contemplate it on a larger scale. He trained my eye to critically examine well-intentioned practices that did not meet the needs or priorities of disadvantaged families. Through my association with him I began to develop the basic elements for the politics of racial surrogacy.

Before his untimely death in 1983 at the age of forty-eight, Ron Edmonds served as deputy chancellor of schools in New York City and was the force behind what became known as the effective schools movement. Through his research and advocacy, he defied major figures in the education establishment—like James Coleman of the University of Chicago, and his more senior colleague at Harvard, Christopher Jencks—whose data-driven research held that schools were incapable of overcoming the home-borne social deficits of Black families to educate their children effectively.[6] As a Black educator, Ron also admonished civil rights attorneys, most of whom were white then, to get beyond their singular preoccupation with racial integration and to focus more intently on changes in schools that would bring all children, regardless of race or class, to acceptable levels of academic proficiency.[7] His own field-based research was designed to demonstrate how that could be done.[8]

As a young law professor in 1971, *Jack Coons* helped launch a revolution in American education that would change the way states approach the distribution of funds to schools. Collaborating with two former law students who themselves would become leading lights in the legal academy, Jack's team argued a case that challenged the school finance system of California as being discriminatory against families who lived in communities with a low property tax base. They showed that the state's school finance system had no rhyme or reason to it. As a result, the state could spend more or less money on students with greater needs than it did on those who were privileged, violating any reasonable standard of equity or efficacy. Notwithstanding all the rhetoric heard across the country about educational equality at the time, California was not unique among the states. The landmark *Serrano v. Priest* case was the first in a long string of lawsuits that propelled a nationwide school finance reform movement reaching across forty-eight states.[9] That campaign is ongoing.

Jack and his colleagues developed a plan to restructure state school finance systems designed to maximize equity and maintain local control of education decision-making.[10] Their scheme could also empower families to spend public education dollars as they saw fit, allowing them to select schools they believed best met the needs of their own children.[11] This marked the beginning of the school choice movement, or at least an aspect of it targeting students from less privileged families. It became the driving passion of Jack's long career. There were other early proponents of progressive voucher experiments, including Christopher Jencks, but Coons and his collaborators carried the idea forward.[12] Jack was also instrumental in explaining the value of choice beyond its utility as a tool to improve academic achievement, conceiving it as a basic democratic value that affirms human dignity and agency. Now with emeritus status from the University of California at Berkeley and into his nineties, he continues to write vigorously on the topic.

Diane Ravitch has no peer in contemporary American education. If you are reading this book, you probably already know who Diane Ravitch is. The first volume of her more recent trilogy was a best seller.[13] Her personal blog, which she curates almost daily, has drawn more than forty million reads and four hundred thousand comments. As contemporary education historians go, Diane Ravitch is a superstar. I consider my eight-year collaboration with her a highlight of my career. Seeing my name appear below hers on four separate book jackets has been a point of professional pride.

Whatever Ravitch does commands attention. When *Left Back*, her 555-page critique of progressive educators appeared in the year 2000,[14] it merited lengthy, if not altogether agreeable reviews, in the *New York Times Book Review*, the *New York Review of Books* and the *New Yorker*. The *Times* reprinted an entire chapter. Diane's work has a way of stirring controversy, and it suits her temperament just fine. She is clear and self-assured about her views, and she will tell you why she thinks you're wrong without seeming to lift a finger.

As I contemplated Diane's place in the present project, I concluded that I should divide her legacy into two separate chapters in the "Critical Thinkers" section of the book to recognize that, in retrospect, there are two Diane Ravitches. After the publication of *Left Back*, her three subsequent books refuted just about everything she had stood for throughout the earlier part of her career, including the work we did together. Other former collaborators of Ravitch got angry with her. I took the reversal at face value as Diane being Diane and speaking her own mind. Although I have not changed my mind about school choice, I find myself agreeing with much of what Ravitch says about the general direction of education in our country today, which is consistent with what I learned from Ron Edmonds.

Howard Fuller finally brought me home to where I am now in understanding why this long march toward education equality never seems to reach its destination. It is one thing to grasp a topic intellectually and another to feel it in your bones. I never worked closely with Howard as I did with Ron or Diane, but I have known him for more than thirty years and we have spoken a lot since I began this project. Listening to a Black man who has been deeply involved in what he calls "the struggle" discuss the failure of American education is a different sort of lesson. It is personal. It conveys a certain pain and hopelessness, even anger. It evokes sympathy, if not empathy, beyond an intellectual understanding of what is at stake.

As was Ron, Howard is passionate about his work and unambiguous about his mission. Howard is all about improving the educational opportunities of Black and Brown children. He is a man who has had a full career as a Black Power activist, who worked in government—by happenstance became the superintendent of schools in Milwaukee—and then returned to activism after his four-year tenure as a school administrator.[15] His cause is school choice, or as he would correct me in saying it, "student choice." For Howard, choice is about power, specifically Black Power. He is not shy when it comes to talking about race. He will tell you that if we want to be honest, race is central to the conversation about American education.

From his upbringing in the Deep South and through his impactful work, Howard's story personifies, like no other in the book, the struggle of Black people, not only to better educate their children, but also to have a seat at the table in determining how that would be done. Influenced by Ron Edmonds and Jack Coons, Fuller saw education both from inside the system and from the distant corners occupied by marginalized people. He dedicated his life to the goal of giving voice to Black parents, first in an attempt at community control and later, when that failed, through school choice.

I include two additional principal characters in this chronicle, not because I knew them personally, but because of the way their scholarship blended so valuably with that of the other four—not to mention their own larger influence on our thinking about race and schooling. One is *James Coleman*; the other is *Derrick Bell*. Coleman, in my mind, is the most consequential education scholar of the twentieth century. It would constitute scholarly negligence to attempt to tell this story without him. He serves as both a protagonist and a foil in the narrative. Ron Edmonds devoted much of his career to refuting Coleman. Jack Coons played a role influencing Coleman and changing his mind about school policy. Diane Ravitch did more than anyone to explain that change in a way that made him more compatible with Edmonds's thinking.

Derrick Bell is considered by many the father of critical race theory. Bell and Edmonds were colleagues at Harvard. An underappreciated part of Edmonds's legacy that I intend to remedy in these pages is the influence he had on Bell's thinking about race and schools. All four of our main characters in this book show up in Bell's writing. Howard Fuller stands out, not only as a friend to Bell and co-activist; Fuller's career is a case study that illustrates in dramatic detail the premises and implications of Bell's vision as it pertains to politics, race, and schooling in America. As you read further, you will meet other players who round out this story of how America has frustrated well-intentioned efforts to provide all of our children with decent schools.

A common characteristic shared by all the principal actors is a painful honesty that drives people like them to tell others what they do not want to hear regardless of the consequences. They challenge our basic assumptions and force us to deal with the implications of our own conclusions. That quality of character is what enables them to help change the stubborn course of history. It inevitably involves them in controversy. It can lead to hostility, misrepresentation, and isolation. Such treatment never seems to deter their determination. Instead it motivates, sustains, and concentrates their actions.

I suppose I should mention that none of my leading characters is the product of privileged backgrounds. Ravitch, one of eight children from a Jewish family, attended segregated public schools in Houston, and was the only one among our main characters to benefit from what might be considered an elite education (Wellesley and Columbia). I believe their humble beginnings endowed them with a certain appreciation for the plight of marginalized people. I know it granted them credibility with me that nourished our friendships.

I hope these opening pages give you, the reader, a sense of what this project is about. In some respects, it is a primer on how one learns, more specifically how I learned from my engagement with an unusual group of individuals whom I grew to know and trust. As you get to know them, you will gain insight into how they navigated the complex dynamics of race and politics and schools. You'll have an opportunity to confront these realities on their terms. It is a perilous undertaking, made no easier by the rhetoric applied in academic and policy circles over who the real progressives are in this ongoing conversation about fair and effective schooling. So we need to spend some time on the topic of political labeling and where it figures in the discussion.

This book explores key ideas that can shape collective action and public policy. I do not pretend that it is a complete review of the work of my favored four or that I agree with everything any one of them has ever said. If you believe that full accord is a prerequisite for beneficial collaboration, the pages ahead offer another important lesson for you. A most fascinating part of this tale is my discovery of their overlapping concerns and perspectives, only made more compelling by their connections to James Coleman and Derrick Bell.

In telling this story, I hope to advance our understanding of why we have failed to educate a large part of our student population and how we might do better. I also elaborate on what I believe to be the risks assumed by the way the US Supreme Court is now redrawing the boundaries between church and state as it takes up a broader range of issues. Finally I share my concerns about how some proponents of choice have altered aspects of its policy design that inadvertently undermine its more progressive attributes and possibilities.

Notwithstanding my enormous debt to each and every one of my four subjects, I bear full responsibility for my conclusions.

* * *

Let me say something here about the prospect of a white man writing a book about race in twenty-first-century America. The question is a worthy one. This is not a how-to guide for people of color. It is a book about what I learned over the course of a long career in urban education, with some of the most important lessons derived from people who do not look like me and who had more personal stakes in the outcome than I. This book is directed at white activists on the left and the right, some of whom, while often well-intentioned, have difficulty distinguishing between what they want for the future of education and what is best for others. My message to them is to let people decide for themselves what is in their own best interest and allow them to act on it.

2

Once upon an Idea

My first glimpse at urban education writ large came in 1978 when my dissertation adviser and mentor, Frank Macchiarola, became chancellor of schools in New York City and asked me to join his senior staff at 110 Livingston Street in downtown Brooklyn. Macchiarola appointed me his special assistant for management and put me in charge of a newly created Chancellor's Office of Policy Analysis, Research, and Planning. That is where I met Ron Edmonds, who was recruited from Harvard to become the deputy chancellor for instruction and was charged to serve as the principal architect of our education agenda. As our relationship grew into a friendship, Ron became my unofficial tutor on the issues.

I had not intended to stay in education administration. My goal was to enter university teaching and research. I wanted to write about what I had learned from my experience in helping to run the largest public school system in the country. I got that opportunity before my third year was up at Livingston Street when the National Institute of Education awarded me a grant to write a book, which I took to the Harvard Graduate School of Education.

The book I wrote, *Across the River*, included chapters on five issue areas: the raging battles over the school budget, the implementation of competency standards for teaching and learning, attempts to improve instructional and support services for students with special needs, confrontations over racial integration, and tensions with the powerful teachers' union then led by the legendary Albert Shanker.[1] Ron and I had both left 110 Livingston Street by the time I got into the thick of the writing, and he had relocated to East Lansing to take a tenured faculty position at Michigan State University. He and I would chat by phone as I wrote, and he read drafts of the chapters. The book was in production when he suddenly passed away during the summer of 1983 and was published that November.

The project was nearing completion when we had our last discussion about it. I was searching for a theoretical link that could tie my findings and conclusions together. Given the five episodes I had chronicled in great detail,

Radical Dreamers. Joseph P. Viteritti, Oxford University Press. © Oxford University Press (2025).
DOI: 10.1093/oso/9780197827109.003.0002

how might I succinctly describe the challenge facing an urban school super-intendent navigating a tumultuous political environment to make the system more responsive to the needs of the mostly Black and Brown students occu-pying its classrooms? Almost impulsively, Ron threw out a suggestion that I explore the institutional tension between constituents and clients.

The idea was simple yet illuminating. The *clients* of public schools are those children in its care, a disproportionate number of whom come from economically disadvantaged families whose parents do not wield political power. The *constituents* are those influential individuals and organizations to whom the leadership is politically accountable, whose interests may or may not coincide with those of the clients. That dichotomy between constituent and client goes a long way in explaining why public schools have historically failed to educate so many Black, Brown, and low-income students. I adopted the idea as an analytic tool. It fit well within the academic framework of the book. I reviewed the literature on public organizational environments and incorporated the concept into an "Addendum for Social Scientists."[2]

Ron Edmonds played a prominent role in the story I told about our time at 110 Livingston Street because his thinking provided an intellectual founda-tion for our policy agenda. I did not realize at the time that Ron had applied the dichotomy concept he handed off to me so casually as a tool to struc-ture his own writing about race. I discovered that soon after he passed away, when I was asked to speak at several memorial services in New York and to write a piece for a special issue of *Social Policy* honoring his impactful life.[3] Those bleak assignments took me back to Ron's written work, much of which he had handed over to me during the course of our friendship.

Ron had discussed the "client-constituent dynamic" in an article that appeared in the *Black Law Journal* in 1974, where he took civil rights attor-neys to task for their focus on racial integration while neglecting the need for quality education. As he explained, "Clients are those on whose behalf the civil rights attorney brings a suit," while constituents are those "whom the civil rights attorney consults before fashioning relief in a class action."[4] He further elaborated, "The constituents of civil rights attorneys are 'liberal' whites and middle class blacks."[5]

Edmonds, who clearly opposed legal segregation, was convinced that most lower-class Black parents are more interested in getting their chil-dren a good education than using them as foot soldiers on the front lines of forced integration. Taking more direct aim at litigation that was ongoing, he insisted,

Attorneys are not trained to respond to clients who do not pay their fees. A class action suit serving only those who pay the attorney fee has the effect of permitting the fee-paying minority to impose its will on the majority of the class on whose behalf the suit is presumably brought.[6]

Asked to construct a general overview of Ron's work for the *Social Policy* festschrift with little space to do it, I did not discuss the constituent-client notion there either. Alan Gartner, the editor of the magazine and a friend of Ron's, had found an unpublished paper of Ron's from 1974 that would do it better. He included it at the end of the collection. In that essay, Ron applied the concept more broadly across social services. He advocated for reforms that would allow clients to be constituents and encourage service communities to participate in decision-making. As he would have it, "Being respectful of those being served is the minimal prerequisite to effective social service." He singled out educators who harbored "the widespread belief that pupil home life and social milieu are the principal causes of pupil performance." He further warned against educators who "reject a community's definition of schooling when the community does not fulfill the educator's cultural expectations of what a community should be."[7]

* * *

The year 2024 marked the seventieth anniversary of the landmark *Brown v. Board of Education* (1954) ruling handed down by the US Supreme Court. It was then that a unanimous court outlawed racial segregation and declared that education "is a right that must be made available to all on equal terms."[8] Some progress has been made toward that end over time, but not nearly enough. As a result of *Brown*, it is no longer legal to prohibit access to schools on the basis of one's racial identity—but schools remain segregated because of discriminatory residential patterns that define the demographics of public school districts.[9] Because of efforts by Jack Coons, his colleagues, and those who have followed in their footsteps, many state legislatures have been forced to take measures that reallocate educational resources in a more equitable way, and there is some evidence of a developing parity in spending among rich and poor districts.[10] The federal government and states have instituted compensatory education programs that provide more assistance to students in need, but rich school districts still spend more per student than poor school districts and the Trump administration is in the process of dismantling many of the redistributive programs that could be helpful.

With all that, reliable federal data continue to document throughout this prosperous nation significant gaps in learning that are consistently defined by race and class. If that indisputable information doesn't disturb you, this book may not be worth your time. If you plan to stay for the ride, then we need to return to where we began and ask how things got so bad. My late friend Ron Edmonds would say that we as a nation know what to do, we just do not have the will to do it. As a political scientist, I would turn more directly to politics by way of explanation. I was hoping that with the passage of forty years, I could take the analysis beyond constituents and clients.

Saying that we as a nation have done nothing is not fair. The truth is that we have not done enough and in some instances we have done the wrong things, however well intentioned we may or may not have been. In attempting to elaborate on the constituent-client dichotomy more clearly, I came up with the concept of racial surrogacy. Because the clients of the school system do not have sufficient power to demand meaningful change, they rely on more influential surrogates to advance their cause: that is, other people. That process takes matters just so far. Because surrogates have only a secondary investment in the clients' interests, their action doesn't usually take them far enough to satisfy those same clients' needs.

I initially thought I was on to an altogether original insight with the surrogate idea. Then one evening I was having dinner with Cheryl Wade, a friend and law school colleague of my wife's who teaches and writes about race.[11] As I explained to her how I intended to proceed with my project theoretically, she suggested that I take a look at the writing of the late Derrick Bell. I was familiar with Bell and had read some of his work, mostly because of his past relationship with Ron Edmonds. Bell was a contributor to the *Social Policy* symposium honoring Ron, but I did not know him personally.

Edmonds and Bell were colleagues at Harvard, where neither of them stayed. According to Edmonds's widow, Karen, they were also good personal friends, and the husbands and wives enjoyed a social relationship. Karen also revealed to me that when Ron had been taken to the hospital in Cambridge with a heart episode, Derrick was the first person to appear by his bedside the next morning.[12] It is not presumptuous to suggest that each had an impact on the other's thinking. I would not dare to speculate in which direction the influence flowed more generously, and I am fairly confident that neither of them would have cared much to promote such a contest.

Derrick Bell is one of the most influential scholars ever to enter the legal academy—as mentioned earlier, considered by many the father of critical race theory (CRT). One more interesting discovery I have made in undertaking this project is how Bell's agenda interacted not only with Ron's but also with those of the other three principal figures in this book. The more I proceeded through this project, the more Bell's voice appeared in the dialogue I had entered on race and schooling, even though I wasn't always aware it was his voice I was hearing. That's why he emerges as a fifth character in the book. He helps explain the why (we fail) and how (we succeed) questions that this project raises.

It is unfortunate that, as CRT has entered the mainstream of discussion, it has fallen prey to caricature from detractors and supporters on all sides of the controversy about its proper place in elementary and secondary schools. To move beyond that, I would recommend several serious investigations of Bell's foundational contributions to that tradition now available.[13] Here I focus on Bell himself.

* * *

In 1971, seventeen years after the US Supreme Court struck down racial discrimination in public schools, Derrick Bell became the first Black man to be awarded tenure at Harvard Law School. How might we explain that? Should we assume that there was not until then a single Black lawyer in the country who was capable of meeting Harvard's high intellectual standards? Or was it that Black men and women rarely populated the elite law school classes from which Harvard customarily recruited its faculty? Or was it outright prejudice?

A native of Pittsburgh, Bell had attended Duquesne University and the University of Pittsburgh Law School, thereby making his appointment unusual for two reasons. These were fine schools, but they did not reflect the kind of pedigree (a revolting but relevant term still in use at elite institutions) one would find on the Harvard Law faculty. Bell had previously taught at the University of Southern California, which also is a very fine school, but not part of the academic stratosphere that Harvard and a few other institutions jealously occupy.

As part of his teaching load, Bell developed a new course on civil rights that focused on race. It was the first of its kind at Harvard. It is difficult to imagine that by the early 1970s one of the leading law schools in the country did not have such a course among its regular offerings—or maybe not. In order to meet the topical requirements of the course, Bell wrote a textbook in 1973 that was like no other in the legal academy. *Race, Racism and*

American Law is foundational in the literature on critical race theory.[14] It holds as a basic premise, as does all of Bell's subsequent writing, that racism is an ordinary and permanent feature of American society.[15] Bell's claim that racism is not aberrational was viewed by many of his colleagues in the legal academe at the time as a radical statement. It still is by some. Should an individual be labeled a radical for so matter-of-factly uttering the truth? Or is it that cool and certain attitude that makes him a radical?

Bell originally had been hired by Harvard in 1969 as an untenured lecturer in response to student protests about the lack of diversity on the law school faculty. Prior to that, he had served in the US Department of Justice, spent six years with the NAACP (National Association for the Advancement of Colored People) Legal Defense Fund under the tutelage of Thurgood Marshall, and for a short time led the newly formed federal Office for Civil Rights within the Department of Health, Education, and Welfare. By the time he arrived in Cambridge, he had supervised hundreds of civil rights cases, most dealing with school desegregation.

In 1980, Bell left Harvard for a five-year stint as dean of the law school at the University of Oregon. After he returned to Harvard in 1986, he staged a five-day sit-in at his office to protest the law school's refusal to promote two colleagues who were teaching courses on race. In 1990, he took an unpaid leave of absence to protest Harvard's failure to tenure a woman of color on its more than sixty-member faculty. Harvard revoked Bell's tenure in 1992 after it had still not hired a minority woman and he had asked for an extension of his leave. It would not tenure a woman of color until 1998, when it hired the late Lani Guinier, an expert on election law. Bell spent the rest of his teaching career as a nontenured visiting professor at New York University Law School. Notwithstanding his strongly held views, Bell enjoyed a reputation as a gracious teacher who welcomed debate in his classroom. Diane Ravitch, who knew him well, described Bell to me as a "strong, kind, gentle man."[16]

The original edition of Bell's pathbreaking *Race, Racism and American Law* included a chapter outlining "Alternatives to Integrated Schools" by which "black children might receive the long-promised equal educational opportunity—in predominantly black schools."[17] It examined a number of initiatives that "for some black children . . . may prove quite functional."[18] The chapter included essays by other experts on four topics: community control, compensatory education, free schools, tuition vouchers, and equalized school funding. In addition to excerpts from Edmonds's work, Bell in several places referenced studies led by Jack Coons.[19] By this time, Coons had become a principal player in litigation to achieve equity in school funding and had emerged as an early proponent of school vouchers to provide alternatives for students who attended chronically failing public schools.

Before taking up these topics, I want to turn our attention to two seminal law review articles that, along with his textbook, established Derrick Bell's reputation as a leading scholar of critical theory and further explain his intellectual kinship to Ron Edmonds and the idea of racial surrogacy.

* * *

In 1976 Derrick Bell published "Serving Two Masters: Integration Ideals and Client Interests in School Desegregation Litigation" (hereafter "Two Masters") in the *Yale Law Journal*.[20] The article reviewed the "unique lawyer-client relationship" that evolved over more than two decades of civil rights litigation with particular attention to the work of the National Association for the Advancement of Colored People (NAACP) and its Legal Defense Fund (LDF). Bell's article begins with a long quote from what has become known as "The Freedom House Statement."

In 1974, a group of nearly two dozen Black leaders met at the Freedom House Institute on Schools and Education in the Roxbury section of Boston to draft a response to Phase II of the Boston School Committee's plan to desegregate the public schools.[21] Boston was the scene of one of the most violent confrontations over racial integration through busing that the country had experienced, where angry white parents shouted obscenities and heaved rocks at buses that carried Black children to school. In early 1975, the group of Black leaders submitted its statement to federal judge W. Arthur Garrity Jr., who was famously overseeing the case.

Although the group supported efforts to end discriminatory pupil placement, it insisted, "Any steps to achieve desegregation must be reviewed in light of the black community's interest in improved pupil performance as the primary characteristic of educational equity." The statement continued, "We think it neither necessary nor proper to endure the dislocations of desegregation without reasonable assurances that our children will instructionally profit."[22] Bell once again mentioned the Freedom House statement at the very beginning of the essay he had written in 1984 for the *Social Policy* symposium commemorating Ron Edmonds, where he complimented Ron as the principal author of the document and included a longer excerpt from it.[23]

In "Two Masters," Bell noted that Judge Garrity eventually had adopted several provisions designed to improve the quality of education for the aggrieved parties, but he also emphasized that these initiatives were more "the product of judicial initiative than civil rights advocacy."[24] He reported on meetings he attended with the Freedom House group and attorneys from the NAACP, where the former unsuccessfully attempted to get the latter to revise their objectives in response to the priorities of Black parents. The lawyers, according to Bell, instead wanted to increase busing efforts. He mentioned similar disagreements between "contributors and clients" in the Detroit and Atlanta desegregation cases, where federal judges incorporated provisions that focused on quality schooling.[25]

Citing Edmonds's work on constituents and clients, Bell elaborated on how these attorneys did not represent the best interests of their supposed clients, but instead responded to the demands of those middle-class Blacks and whites positioned to pay their fees. Bell pointed to the rise and decline of the Congress of Racial Equality (CORE) to illustrate "the fate of civil rights organizations relying on white support while espousing black self-reliance."[26] He challenged those who believe that the actual presence of white children in schools is a prerequisite to a sound education. He declared, "Those civil rights attorneys, regardless of race, whose commitment to integration is buoyed by doubts about the effectiveness of predominantly black schools should reconsider seriously the propriety of representing blacks."[27]

When Cheryl Wade suggested over dinner that evening that I look at Bell's work, she specifically referred to his *Harvard Law Review* article on the interest-convergence dilemma from 1980 and emailed it to me later that night.[28] It is not a hopeful piece of literature. It begins on a negative note when the author observes, "Most black children attend public schools that are both racially isolated and inferior." He cites demographic patterns, white flight, and the inability of the courts to effect meaningful social change as reasons to expect "further progress implementing *Brown* almost impossible."[29] Bell's interest-convergence theory holds, "The interest of blacks in achieving racial equality will be accommodated only when it converges with the interests of whites."[30]

What I call the "politics of surrogacy" is implicit in Bell's convergence theory, and we end up in the same discouraging place. Observing the imbalance of power between constituents and clients in American education, perhaps because I am a political scientist, I focus on the political dependency of the latter on the former and the vulnerability that such a relationship imposes on clients. Bell more clearly explains why the relationship can be expected to bear such disappointing results when the convergence of interests is so shallow from the start. He declares, "It is clear that racial equality is not deemed legitimate by large segments of the American people."[31] This is a bold statement for sure. In 1980, the statement was not only veracious; it was prophetic. Just look at where we are now in American education. In America, white liberals remain the perpetual surrogates of Black people, which may help explain things. Pay attention as this story proceeds. It doesn't end there.

As Bell moved further away from the NAACP ethos of forced racial integration, he perceived the *Brown* decision as largely symbolic. In his mind, *Brown* served the country's white power structure by demonstrating American democracy's superiority to communism in a cold war being fought for the hearts and minds of "third world" peoples. It reassured Black GIs who returned from World War II that America would deliver on its promises of equality and freedom. More practically speaking, many white entrepreneurs had come to realize that the rural South could make an easier, more profitable transition to an industrialized sunbelt when the legal battles over segregation of the races were finally done.

In all, according to Bell, much of the country's progress on race was fortuitous. Elaborating on the interest-convergence concept in a later publication, Bell contends, "Even when common interests lead to effective racial remedies, these actions will be abrogated when policy makers fear that the policy will threaten the superior social status of whites."[32] It did not take long. As Bell noted in previous work, *Brown II*—handed down a year after the original decision—denied an NAACP request for a general order requiring all school districts to desegregate.[33] Instead the court issued the "all deliberate speed" standard of guidance that returned cases back to the district courts and slowed implementation.[34] The point was to prioritize deliberation over speed. It was the court's way to acknowledge the resistance that would come from southern states and admit that it did not have the institutional capacity to force immediate changes. Legal scholars refer to this feeble disposition as "judicial restraint."

* * *

By the end of his prolific career, Derrick Bell had published a dozen books and more than one hundred articles. His writing cut across several genres, including fiction. His bestseller *Faces at the Bottom of the Well* includes a science fiction tale in which extraterrestrials land on Earth and offer our country gold, safe energy, and technological advances in return for its entire Black population.[35] I won't tell you how it ends. You can read it for yourself.

His *And We Are Not Saved* reads like a series of biblical parables.[36] Elsewhere, Bell wrote a hypothetical case for his law students in which the *Brown* court, acknowledging the "evils of segregation" in a patently racist society, rules in favor of the "separate but equal doctrine" with the explicit intention of enforcing equality.[37]

If one of my students asked me to recommend only one of Derrick Bell's publications, I would suggest *Silent Covenants*. Published in 2004, seven years before his death at the age of eighty, it was his last monograph. It continues the inquiry he began with his pioneering textbook, *Race, Racism and American Law* from 1973, analyzing the case law to demonstrate how the high court consistently retreated from the promise of *Brown*, a topic we revisit in later chapters. *Silent Covenants* elaborates on concepts that have been central to his thinking, including "Two Masters," interest convergence, and fortuity. It also updates the discussion he began in the textbook on alternatives to racial integration now framed in a chapter on "effective schools."[38] Let's compare the two.

The chapter in the original textbook includes a reprint of a 1972 document titled "Assumptions on the Value of Integrated Education for Blacks" from the proceedings of a National Policy Conference on Education for Blacks.[39] The author is Ron Edmonds, sounding themes now familiar to the reader concerning the primacy of good schools over schools that are artificially integrated. Edmonds also includes demands for open housing, equity in the distribution of resources, and parent access to educational decision-making.

A large portion of the chapter is devoted to schools controlled by the community, with particular attention given to a controversial experiment in community control that took place in Ocean Hill–Brownsville in Brooklyn in the late 1960s.[40] Here references are made to Charles Hamilton, a Columbia University political scientist, and Stokely Carmichael, who would go on to organize the Black Panther Party. In an excerpt from an essay in the *Harvard Education Review*, Hamilton explains how this new educational model "views the ghetto school as the focal point of community life."[41] A Carmichael quote in the Hamilton essay emphasizes the need for Black people to "control our institutions—our destinies."[42]

Carmichael and Hamilton were coauthors of one of the first and most influential books written on the topic of Black Power, a sign of the times in 1967 as racial minorities grew impatient with the slow progress of the civil rights movement and turned to more militant forms of activism.[43] I had read the book as a college student. The small Vintage paperback edition with black lettering printed across a white cover sits on my bookshelf today, its $1.95 price tag still showing (right next to the Kerner Commission report, which appeared a year later for $1.25).

Ocean Hill–Brownsville was one of three demonstration school districts set up by the New York City Board of Education to experiment with community control. (The others were located in Harlem and lower Manhattan.) The district had a locally elected school board, which chose its own chief administrator. Brooklyn exploded into turmoil in the spring of 1968 when District Administrator Rhody McCoy informed thirteen teachers, five assistant principals, and one principal that they were being removed from their positions and transferred to the central headquarters at 110 Livingston Street because they were deemed "unfit for service." All the personnel were white and most were Jewish, and they were removed without a formal hearing. The conflagration infuriated union president Albert Shanker and led to three citywide teachers' strikes that closed the schools, the final one lasting ten weeks. Charges of anti-Semitism and racism were slung back and forth, resulting in ruptured relations between the Black and Jewish communities in New York that would take years to heal.

What has been written about Ocean Hill–Brownsville could fill a small library. An early testament is presented in *The Great School Wars*, Diane Ravitch's magisterial history of the New York City public schools.[44] The book chronicles experiences with racism, segregation, demonstrations, boycotts, corruption scandals, and confrontations between proponents and opponents of community control. Ravitch observed how advocates had hoped that community control would lead to the ouster of stubborn bureaucrats and racist teachers, diversify the predominantly white core of professionals, improve the self-image of minority children, and give parents more voice.

At the time, however, Ravitch expressed doubts that, with such a poor record of political participation in minority neighborhoods, the decentralization plan eventually implemented would either increase parent involvement or reform the schools.[45] The system, once a showcase of excellence, had been showing signs of slippage in poorer communities throughout, regardless of race. Ravitch also noted how the architects of school decentralization had made a strategic error by placing all three demonstration districts in minority communities when the idea could have generated wider appeal.

A larger lesson can be drawn from the episode: It dramatically illustrates how the Black community was losing confidence in its public schools. Community control was not merely a demand for power; it was a desperate plea, after years of unfulfilled promises, to either provide children of color with a decent education or to let Black people do it on their own. A similar conflict over the establishment of a community-run school district would occur in Milwaukee, Wisconsin, in 1988, where Derrick Bell would meet Howard Fuller. It was a prelude to parental demands for school choice. More on that later.

* * *

With frustration growing, many leaders in the Black community, especially more militant organizers who had broken with the gradualist legal tactics pursued by the NAACP, would have settled for an arrangement that provided for truly "separate and equal schools." The problem was that "separate and equal" was a legal delusion that the *Brown* court helped to perpetuate. Calling for equalized funding in his law text from 1973, Bell cites research by Jack Coons and his colleagues showing "discrimination on the basis of wealth."[46]

Bell also traces the development of the *Serrano* case in California, where Jack and his colleagues argued for a more equitable distribution of education resources. Bell picks up the story again in *Silent Covenants*, and it does not have a happy ending. Jack's team did prevail in California, where the state court found that the finance system "invidiously discriminates against the poor."[47] Stymied by another landmark ruling involving Texas,[48] however, the case history of school finance also shows that when it comes to the tangible matter of education dollars, the US Supreme Court has abandoned its pledge in *Brown* declaring that education "is a right [that] must be made available to all on equal terms,"[49] claiming that school funding is not a federal concern.

As a legal scholar and litigator who entered the discussion on race in education through the courts, Bell was consistently disappointed. More and more, he found answers to the problem of inequality in schools themselves. As he lost faith in neighborhood public schools, he grew more inclined to look beyond their limits for solutions. Compensatory education programs like the federal government's Title I legislation enacted under President Lyndon Johnson's Great Society initiative to channel money into poorer school districts were positive gestures but not enough. They were not sufficient to either support the services that students needed nor to overcome the effects of inequitable funding at the state level.

Bell's textbook from 1973 covers two other alternatives to school integration. What he called "free schools" were small private institutions in poor areas supported by foundation grants, fundraising efforts, and sometimes public dollars. These schools were not free for everyone. Tuition was charged on a sliding scale, and only those students whose parents were unable to pay attended for free. Many of these schools began "deep in the black community." As an example, Bell mentioned a system of schools operated by Black Muslims that emphasized racial pride, self-discipline, and self–sufficiency. The implication here was that such virtues are not commonly celebrated in neighborhood public schools that Black students attend. Bell reports that students at the Muslim schools performed several grade levels above most Black teenagers who attended public schools.[50]

Bell also mentions tuition vouchers that are made available for students to attend private schools. Citing Jack Coons, he argues that for such programs to work, poor families would need to receive substantially larger grants than the more fortunate, which is rarely the case—to the point that students in such programs usually receive significantly less funding than their public school peers.[51] He notes that early experience with such programs indicated that they were not very effective, and he is correct. If he were to assess the efficacy of the more numerous programs that exist today, he could very well reach a similar conclusion, for reasons that would probably not surprise him, like inadequate funding or accountability.

* * *

Taking advantage of the passage of time and the lessons it brings, Bell's 2004 exploration of alternatives in *Silent Covenants* contains more detail. Following another allusion to school funding suits, he begins with a discussion of inner-city independent schools, where he draws heavily on an essay written by Gail Foster. Diane Ravitch and I originally had commissioned the essay for a book we assembled on city schools in New York.[52] Foster is an education scholar and entrepreneur who founded the National Association of Historically Black Independent Schools (HBIS) and the Toussaint Institute Fund. She is adamant in insisting that, despite what some people may believe, education is highly valued in the Black community.

Foster recalls that when many Black families finally admitted to themselves that they would have neither good schools in their communities nor enough control to change them, they decided to set up their own institutions with their own limited resources. Many were started by Black churches. She describes the network of independent institutions as low cost, private, and culturally affirming, bolstering high expectations for pupils. Her essay focuses on the need to develop psychologically healthy young people with positive role models in front of the classroom. HBI campuses house programs for students who need extra help, as well as gifted and talented programs for those who excel. Commenting on Foster's essay, Bell refers to a "crisis of self-hatred" that needed to be addressed.[53] Some of these institutions have converted from private to charter schools to facilitate more adequate funding.

When Bell delves into the charter school topic in *Silent Covenants*, he presents such schools as innovative institutions that give choices to all students, not just the wealthy. He rejects claims by charter opponents that the institutions will become bastions for middle-class families who are better prepared to work the system. He cites evidence that two-thirds of charter students nationwide are nonwhite and more than half are from low-income families. Charter critics raise concerns that charters will discriminate, become racially isolated, and drain resources from regular public schools. Bell was not moved by these claims. He was more concerned about data indicating that charters receive 15 percent less funding than other public schools. He cites Foster, who finds that charters and vouchers get consistently high marks in communities of color.[54]

Bell was well aware that "tuition voucher arrangements are probably the most controversial of educational alternatives to emerge in the last decade," but that they were also growing in popularity.[55] By then the Supreme Court, in the *Zelman* case, had found that awarding public scholarships for students to attend religious schools did not run afoul of the First Amendment. The court had not yet ruled on whether the states, applying state constitutional criteria, could discriminate against religious schools in administering such programs. Voucher opponents continued to claim that minority parents were being duped by advocates, that the real beneficiaries of such programs were private religious schools where enrollments were increasing. We might also count such church-based allies as surrogates, in that they were part of a larger coalition that originally supported targeted vouchers for poor minority students.

Bell acknowledged these criticisms. He also recognized arguments made by free-market advocates like economist Milton Friedman, who believed that the competition fostered by choice would provide an incentive for public schools to improve. He went on to describe the basic features of the voucher programs that had been started in Milwaukee and Cleveland, where public schools had been floundering for decades. Truth be told, the kinds of redistributive voucher programs implemented in these two cities are more aligned with the thinking of Jack Coons and Milwaukee's cofounder Howard Fuller than Milton Friedman, and they do not rely on a market-based rationale.

If I may elaborate on this point, let me reference the work of James Forman Jr., another leading legal scholar who covered similar ground as Bell in reviewing Black attempts to secure better educational opportunities, but who was more directly familiar with varied choice initiatives that later developed.[56] Forman is the son of the storied civil rights leader and intellectual whose name he carries. Now on the faculty of Yale Law School, he is also the author of a Pulitzer Prize–winning book on criminal justice.[57] Our paths crossed in the late 1990s because of his work in education, he having been a cofounder of the Maya Angelou Public Charter School in Washington, DC. In his extensive law review essay from 2005 on the secret history of school choice, Forman, like Bell, writes about free independent schools and demands for community control brought about by Black grievances with the public school bureaucracy, but he takes his analysis beyond these campaigns.[58]

Concentrating his inquiry on the progressive roots of choice, Forman reaches as far back as the Reconstruction era when freed slaves needed to create their own schools to get an education. He refers to these institutions outside of the public school system as an "important pre-curser [sic]" to the school choice movement. He ends his analysis covering more contemporary issues by distinguishing Milton Friedman–type market plans from progressive programs designed to promote educational opportunity for poor and minority children. He then outlines the moral arguments that underlie demands to extend real choice to parents beyond those who are privileged.[59] He describes the then ongoing conversation as "essential fifty years after *Brown*." In contemporary America, he argues, school choice does exist, and it is for the most part a function of family wealth that enables some to live in high-priced communities with good public schools or send their children to private schools. We explore these normative issues more carefully later through the work of Jack Coons.

Toward the end of Bell's chapter on alternatives in *Silent Covenants*, we find a section on Catholic schools. As choice critics claimed, the Catholic Church, whose inner city schools were losing enrollments and revenues, became a major player in the pro-choice movement, a convergence of interests if ever there was one. Bell is more taken in his discussion, though, with how many Black and Hispanic parents chose Catholic schools over public schools because of their more disciplined learning environments and better academic outcomes. He also observes that at one particular Catholic school in Milwaukee, where 80 percent of the students are not Catholic, the voucher covered most of the tuition.[60]

Unlike what we have seen in much of Derrick Bell's other writing, *Silent Covenants* does not include an excerpt from Ron Edmonds. Ron had already been gone for more than twenty years, but he was not forgotten. Bell mentions Ron in the first sentence of the book, under the "Acknowledgments," which reads,

> The maturing of my views about school desegregation owe much to my contact with the late Ronald R. Edmonds, who tirelessly urged that legal concepts of equality were not linked to and could prove barriers to effective schooling.[61]

PART II
CRITICAL THINKERS

3

Ron Edmonds

Effective Schools

What better place is there to begin a story about the failed promise of *Brown* than the New York City school system in the last quarter of the twentieth century? You already got a glimpse of it through the Ocean Hill–Brownsville episode featured by Derrick Bell, where Black parents, frustrated by racial and political isolation, unsuccessfully attempted to take control of their children's education. The system is the largest in the nation, with more than a million students in its care. Studying it is like an ambitious experiment that puts all of urban education under a giant microscope so that we are better able to observe its defining features. Seeing it through the eyes of Ron Edmonds brings it into sharper focus.

Unlike most of his predecessors as schools chancellor in New York, Frank Macchiarola had not worked his way up through the ranks of the school system, so he had no stake in maintaining it as it was. Nor did Mayor Edward Koch, who was able to help secure Macchiarola's appointment in 1978 by its seven-person governing body, the New York City's Board of Education. Koch understood that a rebound of New York's ailing public school system was crucial to the fiscal recovery of the city that had nearly gone bankrupt a few years earlier. At the time of his selection, Macchiarola was vice president and a professor of political science at the Graduate Center of the City University of New York. He had previously served as deputy director of the state Emergency Financial Control Board that oversaw the finances of the city during the early years of the fiscal crisis and instituted reforms to improve its management. The new schools chief had earned a good reputation at the state and local levels of government and handled politics skillfully.

The circumstances facing the new administration did not promise an easy run. It already was a time of declining national confidence in public education. An annual Gallup survey of parental confidence in schools taken in 1979 revealed a mean score of 2.38 on a possible scale of 5. From 1975 to 1978, sixteen school superintendents had been replaced in the nation's

Radical Dreamers. Joseph P. Viteritti, Oxford University Press. © Oxford University Press (2025).
DOI: 10.1093/oso/9780197827109.003.0003

twenty-eight largest urban districts. Between 1955 and 1975, the population of racial "minorities" attending New York City schools had increased from 28 percent to 68 percent and their families were more economically vulnerable.[1] These data were not just a snapshot of the times but also a portrait of the future, not to mention our present circumstances.

The huge calcified central school headquarters located at 110 Livingston Street in Brooklyn was the stuff of legend. David Rogers had begun his penetrating study of the institution as an examination of desegregation policy. Once he got into it, he realized that he actually was writing a massive case study of organizational inefficiency and ineptitude, calling the system a "model of bureaucratic pathology."[2] During the first press conference after his selection, Macchiarola, in the presence of outgoing chancellor Irving Anker, joked that the reputation of 110 Livingston Street was so bad that he had looked into changing its address to 114 Livingston Street.

Appointed in April to take office in July, Macchiarola had time to prepare for his entry. He set up a transition team of eight outsiders to the school system who would go on to take top staff positions in his administration. He asked Alan Gartner, his university colleague and the editor of the journal *Social Policy*, to plan a conference to assess school system needs and discuss an agenda. The two-day meeting held at the upstate New York Sterling Forest Conference Center in May 1978 included academic experts, public school advocates, and representatives of organized labor.

A highlight of the Sterling Forest conference was a talk by Ron Edmonds, then a Harvard-based researcher whom none of the group other than Gartner had previously met. In a deliberate and systematic presentation, Edmonds laid out his research on how to design effective schools for disadvantaged urban communities. He further explained the social significance of its evidence of success in a national climate so clouded by despair. It was a refreshing contrast to the can't-be-done attitude that would greet us at Livingston Street. A few days later, Macchiarola invited Edmonds to join us as his senior assistant for instruction. His position was soon elevated to deputy chancellor.

It did not take long for the clash of cultures between the old guard and the new team to become apparent. During the first meeting of the chancellor's top staff that July, Macchiarola suggested that we might put out a public document outlining our philosophy, plans, and goals. By this time, the chancellor had invited several seasoned administrators from the prior administration to stay on, hoping that their familiarity with the machinery of the bureaucracy would help with the implementation of new programs. One of them took exception to the chancellor's suggestion, especially the last point.

Drawing on years of experience inside the system, the veteran administrator warned that setting specific goals for educational outcomes over which we had little control was a sure formula for failure that would lead to public embarrassment. He further remarked that the factors inhibiting success in city classrooms were social in nature—elaborating that there was only so much to be expected from the population placed at our doorstep. At that point, a very exasperated Ron Edmonds spoke up to explain that such an attitude was a large part of the problem we faced. After a spirited ninety-minute discussion, the chancellor closed the meeting remarking that if he really thought we could not do much to improve learning, he would not have taken the job. Edmonds concurred and added, "If we don't believe in our students, we ought not to be here."

* * *

These conversations were not new to Ron Edmonds. He had heard them before at the highest levels of discourse among university scholars who were widely respected as national leaders in the field of education policy. He had spent a considerable part of his professional career contradicting what they had to say. The first of these was James Coleman, the esteemed sociologist from the University of Chicago.

Shortly after the passage of the Civil Rights Act of 1964, US commissioner of education Francis Keppel, in compliance with the law, asked Coleman (then at Johns Hopkins) to undertake a study to examine "the lack of educational opportunities for individuals by reason of race, color or national origin."[3] At the time, the Coleman Report was one of the largest social science projects in American history. It involved the evaluation of 570,000 students, 60,000 teachers, and facilities at 4,000 schools. It examined the relationship between educational inputs (staff, resources, and facilities) and educational outcomes measured by student performance on basic skills tests.

Coleman and his colleagues' findings included the following:

1. Most Black and white students attend racially segregated schools.
2. The measured characteristics and resources of schools are equal between Black and white institutions.

3. The measured characteristics of schools have little impact on Black and white student performance on standardized tests.
4. The presence of classmates from affluent backgrounds had a positive impact on student performance.

The major conclusion of the report was that a student's home environment has a more significant bearing on academic achievement than what goes on in school.

The report had profound public policy implications. Although it lent credibility to ongoing efforts to integrate schools, it cast doubts on compensatory education programs that would channel additional resources into high-poverty communities. As might be expected, it led to more studies and reanalysis.[4]

In 1972 Christopher Jencks and a group of his colleagues at the Harvard Graduate School of Education reanalyzed the data from the Coleman Report. Their well-funded research, published under the title *Inequality*, confirmed that school conditions had little effect on pupil performance.[5] The authors went so far as to claim that school administrators and teachers had no idea what to do to improve test scores. Again pointing to family background as a critical variable determining educational success, Jencks and his colleagues proposed that nothing less than a redistribution of wealth through an economic restructuring of society would bring about an equalization of opportunity.

As the back cover of the paperback edition attests, the book was a media triumph. The *New York Times Book Review* found it "startling" and "impressive," declaring, "[Jencks] makes a revolutionary case for restructuring not education but society." *Newsweek* approvingly observed, "*Inequality* says things that many Americans do not want to hear. It will most certainly annoy traditional educators by suggesting that schools are an ineffective force." The *Christian Science Monitor* predicted, "This book will influence American educational policies for years to come." Even the *American School Board Journal* found, "*Inequality* is likely to have as much effect on education as anything written in the last 50 years."

Given the improbability that a major economic revolution would occur in the foreseeable future, Jencks's study was even more discouraging than Coleman's in undermining the role that schools could play in fostering a just society. What was intended as a radical critique of American class and social structure became a rationale for conservative public policy. Why invest more in schools if educators don't know what to do to make improvements? The accumulated wisdom derived from this thickening line of studies can be summarized in three words: "Schools don't matter."

However unintended it may have been, there was a more pernicious subtext to the message that Coleman and Jencks were conveying. In 1969, psychologist Arthur Jensen published an article in the *Harvard Educational Review* that tied academic achievement to native intelligence. Criticizing costly compensatory education programs, Jensen argued that intelligence is a product of genetic inheritance, suggesting that low-performing students were naturally inferior.[6] I hesitate to even repeat such an offensive claim in the present text, but one needs to hear it in order to understand what motivated the work of Ron Edmonds and what he was facing.

Ron's most full-throated response appeared in a symposium that was published as a special edition of the *Harvard Educational Review* called, "Perspectives on *Inequality*: A Reassessment of the Effect of Family and Schooling in America."[7] It was occasioned by the publication of Jencks's *Inequality* a year earlier. On October 6, 1972, the Carnegie Corporation invited ten Black social scientists to meet in New York City to discuss the research that was emerging.[8] Each had independently read and analyzed the material. They decided to prepare critical reviews of the works under consideration as a way to "interrupt the ethnocentrism that presently characterizes corporate and foundation subsidy of social science."[9] When the Harvard journal invited representatives of the group to prepare commentary in November, it chose Ron Edmonds to incorporate their reactions in a single essay. The piece was published under the title "A Black Response to Christopher Jencks's *Inequality* and Certain Other Issues."[10]

* * *

Edmonds began his response by explaining how Jencks and others have shifted the stakes of schooling by blaming failure on the students and their families. As he put it, rather than holding educators responsible for successful outcomes, Jencks, "intentionally or inadvertently," serves to take them "off the hook."[11] Edmonds then reached back into history to express concerns about how the current research may be used, linking it to "a long line of scholarly productions that somehow appear to impede the progress being made by minorities or to buttress a major antidemocratic move by government or other social institutions."[12]

Edmonds embarked on his history tour by first recalling the work of Professor William Graham Sumner of Yale, who in 1906 claimed that egalitarianism could not work in America because "society's engrained mores and folkways" would inevitably split a possible union between poor whites and newly emancipated Blacks. Citing Darwin, who held that society advances through a "natural law" of "survival of the fittest," the Yale professor argued that it would be easier for the nation to "forget about equality and accept as natural that the Freedmen and their children become landless peasants or maids and janitors." Edmonds then referred to the Army Alpha intelligence tests administered during World War I, which found that "blacks were less brainy than whites."[13]

Turning to more contemporary research, Edmonds then ticks off a list of scholars "based at the nation's most prominent centers of learning," including Coleman and Jencks, who "all seem to reach the conclusion that blacks and lower class people are about where they ought to be in the society—at the bottom—and that efforts to move them or let them move themselves are futile."[14] Comparing Jencks and his colleagues to Jensen, Edmonds accuses them of implying that "the black 'deficit' in IQ could well have a genetic basis!" He specifically quotes a sentence on page 83 of their book stating, "Given the wide range of other physical differences between ethnic groups, such a difference in IQ gene types is certainly conceivable."[15]

While agreeing with Jencks that the country needs fundamental social change, Edmonds predicted that Jencks's book and its "sister studies" would turn back the clock on civil rights and equal opportunity advances that occurred in the 1960s, especially if we write off schools. Here again, he quotes directly from *Inequality*, which reads, "Children with affluent parents want more education than children with poor parents. . . . Those who want a lot should get a lot and those who want very little should get very little." This leads Edmonds to infer, "Schools share the larger society's distaste for the poor." He continues, "By grade 9, the cultural autocracy that characterizes schools has persuaded the average poor child that the school doesn't like him, or his condition, except that he is prepared to behave in ways that make him seem affluent."[16] Edmonds calls for an approach to education that would have schools appreciate and respond to a variety of cultures that children bring with them. He mentions some "fledgling instances of minority community control" as rare examples of such an approach.[17]

Among the nine other contributors to the Harvard symposium was Kenneth Clark. Clark was the African American psychologist from City

College in New York whose expert testimony on how segregation is psychologically damaging to Black children led a unanimous US Supreme Court in *Brown* to prohibit laws that would restrict access to schools on the basis of race. Like Edmonds, Clark denounced references to "cultural deprivation" and "genetic inferiority" and the negative effects the research would have on school policy.[18] He alluded to the futility of ongoing school finance suits like the *Serrano* case that Jack Coons was arguing, if we are to accept the notion that school resources do not affect instructional outcomes. He also offered an additional insight worthy of consideration, especially in light of the wide attention Jencks's *Inequality* received in the media.

Clark, ordinarily reserved in his commentary, deplored the "glib, journalistic, smart-alecky manner" in which the research was presented. He denounced the authors for exploiting Madison Avenue advertising techniques so that by the time other social scientists had an opportunity to review the study, "the general public, including policy makers, were quoting Jencks's questionable findings as if they were sacred writ." He called out this "new fashionable and most disturbing approach" supported by a prestigious university that "confuses scientific validation with mass publicity."[19]

In his own contribution to the symposium, Christopher Jencks emphasized that the main objective of the study was to demonstrate that "equalizing opportunity, especially educational opportunity, would not do much to reduce economic inequality or alleviate poverty."[20] Although his essay was supposed to be a response to the full range of commentary presented in the symposium, much of it was directed at Edmonds—as were the bulk of Edmonds's remarks, purportedly provoked by a larger body of literature, focused on Jencks. The most heat was generated around the controversial topic of genetics. Jencks wrote, "It is depressing to find Edmonds claiming that since we say it is conceivable that genetic differences between blacks and whites account for part of the test score gap, our position is indistinguishable from Jensen."[21]

Edmonds and Jencks were talking at cross-purposes here. Armed with data and a prestigious university affiliation, Jencks's team thought of themselves as experimental scientists exploring all possible explanations for disparate educational performance. They apparently did not understand that Kenneth Clark, Ron Edmonds, and the group of Black scholars Edmonds spoke for were offended by even posing a question involving genetics.

Maybe Jencks's team would have understood that better if their membership included more social scientists who looked like the population they were studying.

To make matters worse, this laboratory experiment was not isolated. As Clark indicated, there was a concerted public relations campaign attached to the release of the book. The findings had serious potential consequences. Diane Ravitch made similar critical remarks about the publicity around its release in a review she wrote for *Commentary*. Referring to a popular movie at the time, she wrote that the book was promoted "like the *Love Story* of social science."[22]

Beyond the policy implications, this was the kind of conversation that could confirm or contribute to harmful racial stereotyping. Recall the *Newsweek* commentator mentioned earlier who praised the Jencks project because it "says things that many Americans do not want to hear." Perhaps it said some things that too many Americans really believed but were reluctant to say out loud. Ron Edmonds and other school reformers were trying to overcome deep-seated beliefs like these.

Negative images of Black people were at the heart of Edmonds's and others' reaction to school integration campaigns. Writing elsewhere on the issue of desegregation planning, Edmonds quotes extensively from Stokely Carmichael and Charles Hamilton's book *Black Power*:

> [Integration] is based on complete acceptance of the fact that in order to have a decent house of education, black people must move into a white neighborhood or send their children to a white neighborhood or send their children to a white school. This reinforces among both blacks and whites the idea that "white" is automatically superior and "black" by definition inferior.[23]

This sentiment led many Black activists to call for community control of their own schools, as they did in Ocean Hill–Brownsville—the same sentiment that led educators like Gail Foster to grow a network of Black independent schools, the same sentiment that led critical thinkers like Ron Edmonds and Derrick Bell to call for alternative policies that empowered underserved people and let them take matters into their own hands, thereby establishing them as the effective *constituents* of the system. However well-intentioned integrationists may have been, their programs could actually function to reinforce the minority status of Black people and undermine their voice in the policymaking process. Writing in the same article just quoted, Edmonds cites the work of his Harvard colleague Charles Willie, a Black sociologist who served as a court-appointed master in the Boston desegregation case. Analyzing the Massachusetts Racial Imbalance Act, Willie concluded,

> The law itself could be described as racist because it declared illegal, and therefore not in the public interest, any school which had a majority black student body. The principle enunciated is that it is not in the public interest for whites to be in a minority in any Massachusetts schools, hardly a valid educational principle.[24]

Willie would later become the architect of a desegregation plan that utilized public school choice.

Despite the momentum that the Coleman Report gave to racial integration, it is notable that the courts did not faithfully follow its finding with the implementation of busing programs. The Coleman Report had found that the presence of classmates from "affluent" backgrounds had a positive effect on low performers. Most Black children were bused into white working-class neighborhoods like South Boston where the schools were experiencing their own problems. Few whites, especially the affluent, were sent into Black neighborhoods. Very wealthy whites stood aloof from the commotion over busing because they sent their children to private schools that poor families could not afford.

Boston's Brahmans, many Harvard-credentialed, watched from a distance without umbrage as "Southie" (South Boston) exploded. Perhaps racial turmoil was preferable to class warfare. One can go back at least as far as the musings of Yale professor William Graham Sumner in 1906 for examples where privileged commentators placed the causes and burdens of segregation on the white working class. As Derrick Bell and other scholars have observed, the white working class was threatened by desegregation because of fears that it would eliminate the only advantage they had over the Black people with whom they shared the bottom tier of the economic ladder.[25] Policy, however, was dominated by political and economic elites.

* * *

Although Ron Edmonds dedicated his career to improving the education opportunities of Black children, he was well aware of how income and class can be limiting factors.[26] Of modest beginnings himself, Ron was born and raised in Ypsilanti, Michigan, a segregated Black community near Ann Arbor. One of four children raised by their mother, he was the first in his family to attend college. His twin brother, Donald, had left school when he was seventeen. As a part-time student who worked his way through the University of Michigan, Ron was eligible for the draft, which interrupted his studies for two years.

While working in a children's psychiatric hospital to support his studies after being discharged from the military, he met Karen Anderson, a nurse who had also graduated from Michigan. She had been engaged to a man with a promising architectural career ahead of him. But she was taken with this charming Black man with piercing blue eyes who had served as an honor guard at the Tomb of the Unknown Soldier in Arlington, Virginia. The couple defied anti-miscegenation laws effective in sixteen states and decided to get married. They developed a close group of friends composed of interracial couples who called themselves the Salt and Pepper Club.

Edmonds began his professional career in 1964 as a high school teacher in Ann Arbor after graduating from college and earning a master's degree in history from Eastern Michigan University. He was especially dedicated to working with kids who, like his own brother, were in danger of dropping out. After teaching history for four years, he became the school district's first human relations director at the age of thirty-three. On the day of his selection Edmonds declared, "The public school community has shown ignorance and insensitivity to children who don't fit the picture of the average middle class student."[27] He was speaking from personal experience, being the product of a modest upbringing in the town of Ypsilanti. The young school administrator called for the hiring of more Black teachers, adding that it would do both white and Black students good if the janitors were not the only Black adults they saw at school.

Over two and one-half years on the job, Edmonds developed a Black studies collection in the library, created a Black Studies Center for teacher training, and oversaw the development of a Negro History course that he encouraged all students to take regardless of race. He prepared a memorandum to the school board suggesting that in order to improve race relations in the district, there would need to be a set of shared goals and commitments among central administrators that was lacking. In his second year Edmonds established a Committee on Equal Education Opportunity that reported directly to the school board. Its role was to act as "citizen-parent critics of the Ann Arbor Public Schools," to recommend new policies and practices for improvement, and to maintain lines of communication.[28]

In 1970, Edmonds left to take a position as assistant superintendent for urban affairs in the Michigan Department of Education. As his career advanced, Ron became more interested in applied research. He discovered the work of George Weber, who was one of the first empirical researchers to explicitly challenge the findings of the Coleman Report. Weber had studied four schools in New York, Kansas City, and Los Angeles that successfully taught reading to poor Black students. He proceeded to document characteristics, strategies, and practices the schools followed that distinguished them from other urban schools. Much to Edmonds's liking, Weber concluded, "Their success shows that failure in beginning reading typical of inner city schools is the fault not of the children or their backgrounds, but of the schools."[29]

Weber's study was followed by others, all of which Ron regularly cited as instructive in the evolution of his own thinking.[30] In 1977, Wilbur Brookover and Lawrence Lezotte of Michigan State University completed a comparison of six improving and two declining schools in their state, again affirming the previous scholarship.[31]

Edmonds had a stake in the latter project because it built on "cost effectiveness" and "elementary school climate" surveys that the Michigan Department of Education had been conducting since the early 1970s. He and Lezotte became collaborators. By 1973, Ron had left Michigan to continue his studies at the Harvard Graduate School of Education. When the director for the Center for Urban Studies there took a leave, he was given the opportunity to serve as its director and granted the title of lecturer, which was an untenured position. Ron would use his post as a podium for his research on effective schools, challenging the work of Coleman, Jencks, and the latter's colleagues at Harvard. It was a bold move for an untenured faculty member.

While at Harvard, a close colleague at the education school informed Ron that he had no chance for permanent position there as a tenured professor because he did not hold a doctorate. Jencks did not have a doctorate either (except for honorary ones later in his career), but he remained there and went on to a named professorship at the Kennedy School of Government. Why the difference? Perhaps it was because Jencks sported a prep school pedigree and two Harvard degrees. What's your guess? He, no doubt, has had a prolific career. He was an early advocate for vouchers, too early for it to matter.[32] Ron eventually departed Harvard for a tenured position at Michigan State.

Ron's project at Harvard was called "The Search for Effective Schools: The Identification and Analysis of Schools That Are Instructionally Effective for Poor Children."[33] In 1974, he and Lezotte published a report on twenty elementary schools in Detroit's Model Cities neighborhood with a predominantly Black and poor population. A random sample of test scores for twenty-five hundred of ten thousand students at the twenty schools revealed that eight were effective at teaching math, nine were effective at teaching reading, and five were effective teaching both.[34] A second phase of the project, completed by his Harvard colleague John Frederiksen, involved a database that was larger and richer, incorporating a reanalysis of Coleman's Equal Educational Opportunity Survey. That phase found fifty-five effective schools in the northeast quadrant that were able to sever the relationship between academic performance and family background.[35] Edmonds and Frederiksen followed this with an on-site study of five effective schools in Lansing, Michigan, to better understand what made them thrive.[36]

Ron's work on effective schools was not just descriptive. It was prescriptive and normative, designed to buttress a philosophical position. The goal was to identify characteristics of effective schools that could be replicated in poor communities across the country. Analyzing the condition of underperforming schools, Ron was acutely aware of critical factors pertaining to both race and class. In an essay for a book edited by Derrick Bell in 1980, Ron wrote, "Analysis of achievement that focuses on race to the exclusion of class misses the true import of the educational tragedy that presently characterizes most public schooling for Black children."[37] The volume, *Shades of Brown*, was a result of a conference that Bell had convened at Harvard Law School. Ron's essay provides a good overview of his work on the limitations of integration and the emphasis on effective schools.

Drawing on the research of those who preceded him and his own empirical findings, Edmonds summarized five ingredients of successful schooling. They included

1. Strong principal leadership.
2. A climate of high expectations in which no student is permitted to fall below a minimum but efficacious level of achievement.
3. An atmosphere that is orderly and conducive to instruction without being rigid.

4. Shared priorities placing pupil acquisition of basic skills over all other school activities.
5. A formal means by which pupil progress is frequently and regularly monitored.

The most important of these variables is the second. It suggests that professionals at successful schools believe in the basic abilities of their students and accept the responsibility for having them reach their potential. It should not be mistaken for a naïve assumption that each and every student can excel at the highest level, but it sets minimum standards for basic skills in reading and math that students should acquire by the time they complete school so that they can continue on to higher education if they choose, become productive citizens, and earn a decent living. As Edmonds spelled out in the Bell collection, "One of the cardinal characteristics of effective schools is that they are as anxious to avoid things that don't work as they are committed to implanting things that do."[38] He believed schools could work. His scholarship was a rebuke to those social scientists who assembled mountains of data to argue that "schools don't matter."

This was the message that Ron Edmonds delivered to the incoming New York City schools chancellor and his staff at the Sterling Forest Conference Center in upstate New York in the spring of 1978. He hardly represented himself as a dispassionate academic. He was a man on a mission, an individual with a deeper cause concerning the role of education in a just society. His message was well received.

* * *

The incoming schools chancellor, Frank Macchiarola, had his own message to convey. It was unambiguous and consistent with Ron's, allowing them to make common cause with little difficulty. At his swearing-in at the end of June, Macchiarola spoke out against the "garrison mentality" and "defensive attitude" so evident at Livingston Street and declared,

We cannot take the line that kids aren't what they used to be as an excuse for not doing the job, because the children we have in our schools are the same children that we had thirty years ago. They may have different faces, and they may have different needs, and they may come from different backgrounds, but they are our children and we have a responsibility to them as we have them.[39]

Ron Edmonds had four words that captured his philosophy: *All children can learn.* It became his calling card as he spoke across the country to advance the effective schools movement. It became the Macchiarola administration's anthem as it endeavored to translate his philosophy into practice.

I earlier referred to Ron as my tutor on education policy, but as the most knowledgeable person on our team regarding matters of elementary and secondary instruction, he assumed the role as everybody's teacher. The chancellor, an academic with a PhD and a law degree from Columbia who had chaired his children's local school board in Brooklyn, encouraged it. Some took to it better than others. At times, Ron could come off as opinionated because he was. He was articulate and erudite and wanted you to know it. He would never use a small word in a sentence when a larger one would do. He would never be dismissed because of his humble roots or the color of his skin. Having just completed graduate school when I joined the staff, access to Ron was like experiencing an immersive postdoc course of study. We would talk and argue and go out for drinks at the end of the day and move ahead. My future wife and I became friends with him and his family.

At one early meeting of the chancellor's staff, as we were becoming comfortable in our new roles, Ron handed out an annotated reading list. Written in the form of a memo from Ron Edmonds to the chancellor's staff, it began, "The attached 'Bibliography on Education' is my suggestion of those books and articles which when read will make you fully up to date on the most important and outstanding issues in urban education."[40] The first book on the list was Derrick Bell's *Race, Racism and American Law.* It might have seemed odd to some for Ron to recommend a law textbook. As he explained in the notation, however, this comprehensive book on the "historic American interaction between race and law" was meant to serve more as a resource rather than something to be read from cover to cover. So many issues we faced had legal implications, and so it was with race.

Ron's list also included the Coleman Report. The notation next to it explained that it was included because "Joe V. asked me if 'both sides of the question' were presented in my recommendations." He continued, "Questions worth asking don't have two-sided answers but in deference to Joe's sense of fairness you are invited to pursue the original, notorious, ill-conceived and poorly executed EEOS." Invested in the literature on equality in graduate school, I had already read Coleman. I wanted us to discuss it now with Ron Edmonds in the room because he had more to say about it than anyone I ever had met and I was reading his work on effective schools at the time.

Ron's annotation for Christopher Jencks's *Inequality*, also on the list, was no more charitable. He described it as, "C. Jencks' perverse and perverted discussion of the interaction between American schooling and economic and social inequality." He again added, "I cannot recommend this book but consistent with Joe V.'s interest in various sides to one-sided questions, the book is included."

At the end of the list was a book on Black colleges in America.[41] There Ron noted, "It probably shouldn't be here except that I co-authored (with Charles Willie) the book and it just came out." He continued, "Taken as a whole the book describes how the best black colleges successfully prepare under-educated black adolescents for successful college work." Then came the real commentary, which read, "The book will be most useful to you if you plan to be president of a liberal arts college, whose liberalized admissions resembles a revolving door."

The book most certainly did belong on the list. Along with his other commentary, Ron's memorandum to the chancellor's staff put on vivid display all at once Ron's sarcasm, frustration, and humor. He was a serious man who in the company of friends liked to laugh at you, himself, and others. He could do it without losing a beat to remind you what he was about.

* * *

By the late 1970s, school integration was no longer central to debates about education in New York. Population changes and segregated housing functioned to guarantee that schools remained racially segregated without breaking the law. Most Black leaders had come to accept that reality, either out of resignation or predilection. Nor would changing the racial composition of schools or classrooms be a priority of the new administration. Ron Edmonds was clear about that when he, as the top Black official in the school system, was asked the question by a reporter from the *New York Times*, and he explained, "The New York City schools are predominantly minority—we accept that. It is not our intention to do anything (beyond what is already being done) to alter the racial composition of buildings or boroughs. Our energies are fixed on raising achievement."[42]

The new chancellor and his senior advisor did understand the difference between what lawyers call *de jure* segregation and *de facto* segregation. One is an intentional product of policy or practice that is illegal; the other is not. The administration did not want to replicate the ugly experience of school busing that Ron had witnessed in Boston, but it would not tolerate attempts to exclude students from school facilities because of their race.[43]

On the first day of school after Macchiarola took office, thirty Black parents staged a four-day sit-in at IS 231 in Rosedale, Queens, to protest the opening of an annex to the school that was populated mostly by white students. The local school board had claimed that the annex was needed to deal with overcrowding, but the US Office for Civil Rights and a federal administrative court found that the action violated the Civil Rights Act of 1964. It was deemed purposeful segregation.

Rosedale was a classic case study of the dichotomy between *constituents* and *clients*, where a 6–3 white majority of the local community school board made policy for a local district where a majority of the pupil clients were African American.[44] After three years of confrontations that involved more sit-ins, school boycotts, mixed messages by the federal and state courts, marches around city hall and borough hall, demonstrations by white parents at the chancellor's home, and intervention by the state commissioner of education, Macchiarola suspended the local school board and dispatched one of his staff members to close down the segregated annex. I mention this case here so that the reader will not mistake the administration's or Ron's disinclination to forcefully integrate schools for a tolerance of purposeful discrimination.

* * *

Ron Edmonds did not involve himself in Rosedale. He had other priorities. Pardon me in advance for getting a bit into the weeds here on the pedagogy of urban schooling.[45] There are many weeds among the flowers in such places. A closer look at Ron's initiatives reveals a timeless case study of how we can interrupt generations of sustained failure and the systemic political constraints that prevail when decision makers ignore the interests of a powerless clientele. School choice is a worthy goal, but we cannot give up on reforming the neighborhood public schools where the great majority of our children are educated.

Coming to New York allowed Edmonds to extend his Search for Effective Schools research and apply it to a practical setting. With generous support from the Carnegie Corporation, the Ford Foundation, and the New York Foundation, the School Improvement Project (SIP) was an attempt to help participating schools better their performance by replicating the factors Ron had associated with effective instruction elsewhere. He first developed case studies of nine elementary schools in order to validate his findings from Detroit and East Lansing. A year later, he selected ten elementary schools to incorporate the research-based formula for effectiveness. The program was voluntary with complete buy-in from the principals and staff.

Planning committees were set up at each school comprising principals, teachers, parents, supervisors, and paraprofessionals. Technical assistance, training, and other support services were brought in from the chancellor's office. By the third year, seven of the original ten schools had implemented their improvement plans and nine additional schools joined the project. In January 1980, the New York Urban Coalition launched a similar project with support from the chancellor's office. This Local School Development Project (LSDP) involved thirty-seven elementary and middle schools that had volunteered to join. Although there were subtle differences between SIP and LSDP, they were both envisioned as school-based efforts designed to improve instruction based on Ron's research. While Edmonds had identified strong local leadership as a key ingredient of success, "strong" did not assume a hierarchic or autocratic organizational style. To the contrary, widespread participation of all stakeholders was essential.

The administration gave an early hint of the overall direction in which it was moving with the creation of its Transitional Class Program. Macchiarola persuaded the city council to fund 489 remedial classes for students in grades 1 through 3 who did not meet minimum levels of proficiency in basic skills. These reduced-size (fifteen to twenty students maximum), ungraded classes with specially qualified teachers were introduced as an alternative to how low-performing students in urban schools are often taught. As the program description noted, such students usually are either left back or advanced to the next grade without the proper skills to thrive. The longer they stay in school, the further they fall behind. Ron Edmonds called this phenomenon the "accumulated deficits of inferior instruction." The program, hindered by early administrative problems in the field, proved a modest success. It was eliminated after two years, when the city council, responding to a budget crisis, cut the funding.

For those on the central school board and other constituents who were paying attention, the Transitional Class Program was a clear statement of how the administration intended to raise academic standards. Focusing on the early grades was key, as Ron's remarks suggested, to stem failure in the younger years. And note his choice of words, referring to "inferior instruction" instead of "inferior students" as the culprit of failure, signaling a shift in the emerging conversation at Livingston Street and beyond.

The New York State Board of Regents was already in the process of proposing new and higher test-based standards for high school graduation. A major force behind this move was Dr. Kenneth Clark, the renowned psychologist who had given testimony in the *Brown* case and the only Black member of the powerful state board. Almost immediately after the first set of state tests was administered, however, the Puerto Rican Legal Defense Fund filed a complaint with the US Office for Civil Rights alleging that the tests had a disparate impact on Hispanic students, which they did. The organization was joined in the complaint by the state teachers' union and the school boards association. The next round of state tests was slated to be more demanding.

When Macchiarola was asked to testify at a Regents hearing to address the new standards, he voiced opposition to the "hastily and ill-considered implementation of what is, potentially, an extremely useful educational strategy."[46] He further explained that he was not opposed to new competency standards as a matter of principle. He was concerned that the state was imposing new requirements on graduating students without properly preparing them to pass. He mentioned the absence of a curriculum that was aligned with the test and the need for remedial programs to help students who failed. He recommended that high school standards be phased in and integrated with a more comprehensive approach to promotion in the lower grades that Ron Edmonds was developing.

After the Regents refused to heed the chancellor's recommendations, Macchiarola threatened to ignore the new policy. That only hardened their resolve to install what they trumpeted as "the highest diploma standards for foundation skills in the country." Macchiarola eventually complied by establishing his own Regents Competency Test Task Force. It was charged with creating a new high school curriculum aligned with the tests. It would also create training programs for staff and remedial programs for students who did not do well. He did continue to protest, asserting, "My model has been reversed. . . . We have been asked to administer tests in the absence of validated standards and a curriculum."[47]

The lost battle with the Regents in 1980 offered a dramatic example of how public school systems implement higher academic standards without providing adequate supports for either educators or students. In the end, the standards do become punitive rather than functioning as constructive instruments for student growth.

Ron Edmonds designed an alternative model for the promotional policy Macchiarola had promised in the lower grades. What Ron produced with wide consultation in the education community was exemplary and could still be applied today as a guide to improve teaching and learning in urban school systems that are underperforming. Unfortunately, such guidelines are rarely followed in public schools. We will see that story unfold in a later chapter where Diane Ravitch takes reformers to task for the way standards were implemented during the George W. Bush and Obama administrations.

* * *

As noted earlier, Ron Edmonds's retort to the "schools-don't-matter" perspective that had gained credibility in the lofty towers of academia was, "All children can learn." The corollary to his assertion among educators on the ground was, "All children must be taught." The promotional policy he put forward consciously reflected the essential ingredients he identified in successful schools. This began with a fundamental belief in the educability of all children regardless of race or class and a commitment to assure that they completed their studies with the basic skills they needed to succeed in life.

In order to abide by that commitment, student progress had to be monitored regularly. The best way to do that is through the responsible use of standardized tests. Testing remains as controversial today as it was forty-five years ago when Kenneth Clark proposed an upgrade for high school graduation requirements in New York state, yet testing is essential in education. Even critics of these tools like to cite standardized test scores to prove a point of argument, or to criticize and praise competing strategies as they see fit. Many defenders of the status quo would prefer to dismiss the tests when results prove that entire urban school systems are not properly serving generations of Black and Brown students. If we do not admit failure, we will never remedy it for the real clients of the public school: the children in the classrooms. This consistent repetition of failure in urban schools is what motivated Kenneth Clark to call for change. He had witnessed it repeatedly since the day he stood before the *Brown* court in 1954 to demand racial justice.

As the debate around the state standards demonstrated, the point was not whether to test, but how. The policy Ron Edmonds designed had five basic features:

1. A citywide standard curriculum
2. A testing program
3. Clearly defined promotional standards
4. Promotional gates
5. A remedial program

Let me highlight some key elements of the strategy to explain what to do and not to do when attempting to hone the skills of students who have not been properly served. Many of the pertinent issues have already come to the surface in our discussions so far of transitional classes and state standards. Once again, staff training was provided to support new curricula materials and remedial instruction. Accommodations were made for students in special education and bilingual education using criteria applied for promotion from grade to grade. Class size was reduced in first grade to get all students off to a good start. Community districts were permitted to establish their own criteria for promotion in all grades except 4 and 7, which were designated "gate grades." In these two grades, promotional criteria were enforced as a check on local policies. Students who failed to meet the standards in the gate grades were held over and placed in remedial classes.

The new program was greeted with much skepticism among school personnel who did not trust Livingston Street to provide the needed supports. Who could blame them? Established advocacy groups like the United Parents Association and Advocates for Children—both of which were longtime surrogates for the underserved and composed mostly of white, middle-class activists—opposed the program outright.

There was considerable support within the minority community, however. Rev. Carl Flemister, executive director of the American Baptist Churches of Metropolitan New York, made a public statement endorsing the program. He and the ministers, allied with Dr. Clark from the beginning, saw the program as a means to guarantee the quality instruction their Black congregations desired. There was a clear racial split among the community superintendents who had been selected by locally elected boards. Alfred Melov, president of the Citywide Association of Community Superintendents, had indicated to me in a private interview when I was researching my earlier book, "Minority superintendents are supportive. It's the white, middle-class liberals that are opponents."[48] Hadn't we seen this movie before? We would certainly see it again, repeatedly, with regard to issues of equity and reform.

Nearly all the major media outlets in the city endorsed the proposed changes as a way to end social promotion and rescue public education from decline. While expressing some reservations, the *New York Times*, following an editorial board meeting with Macchiarola and Edmonds, printed a statement repeating Ron's findings: "There is some evidence . . . confirming that the most effective schools in poor neighborhoods set high academic standards and keep evaluating their pupils' progress."[49] The business community endorsed the policy, hoping it could help generate a more qualified workforce. The most important source of support came from Sandra Feldman, the new president of the United Federation of Teachers, whose union was deeply involved in the program's planning and design.

When the central Board of Education finally approved the policy in November 1979, it had removed funding for the remedial program, claiming that high standards should not be held hostage to funding. Macchiarola and Edmonds felt betrayed, and the last-minute change made them look like liars to those who had been promised proper supports. Macchiarola was able to transfer a portion of federal and state funding to cover some of the gap, but there was still concern that the mayor's office might not appropriate sufficient funding to cover the remaining remediation costs. After considerable thought, Macchiarola communicated to city hall that he would resign rather than implement the program without a remedial component to assist weaker students. That would have been a disaster for Mayor Ed Koch, who was facing his first reelection campaign in 1981. Koch got the message, and Macchiarola got the money.

The problem is a recurring one in public education. Politicians like to give lip service to programs that have merit, but they don't always deliver the resources needed to make them succeed. When the chancellor announced the state reading scores in the spring of 1981, they showed that NYC schoolchildren in grades 2 through 9 had moved above the national average for the first time in a decade. Math scores had also improved and barely missed the mark. The scores continued to reveal a racial gap in achievement, but the rate of improvement since 1979 was higher in economically disadvantaged communities where Black and Brown children resided. Schools participating in Ron Edmonds's SIP and LSDP programs also excelled. Subsequent analysis indicated that students who attended a six-week remediation program that summer were more likely to advance a grade.[50]

* * *

Ron Edmonds left New York in February 1981. By the time I got to Harvard that spring as a visiting lecturer in the Graduate School of Education, he and his family were in the process of relocating to East Lansing. Not long after I arrived, a new school superintendent was being installed in Boston. Robert "Bud" Spillane had previously served as superintendent in five urban school districts, including the predominantly Black districts of Roosevelt on Long Island and New Rochelle in Westchester County, New York. He was deputy commissioner of education for New York state when chosen. He knew few people in Boston, needed help, and asked me to run his transition. I had never met Spillane before, but we had traveled in the same education circles and he was impressed by what Macchiarola's team had accomplished in New York City.

Chairing a transition demands a quick study of what your principal (in this case, Spillane) is about to face and what he or she should do under the circumstances. The most tangible product is an action plan filled with findings and policy recommendations. Before you can do that, you need to meet with key constituents—and hopefully clients—in the city. In Boston that meant a whirlwind of university presidents, business executives, advocates, community folk, parents, school administrators, and union leaders. Since I knew little about Boston other than what I had read, I kept in regular contact with Ron, who put me in touch with people who could be helpful.

The school board in Boston was still polarized along racial lines, although a Black man, John Bryant, was now chair. A member from South Boston named Elvira "Pixie" Palladino continued to harbor resentment over the desegregation plans that the iconic federal judge W. Arthur Garrity Jr. still presided over. Pixie had her own way of conveying her disapproval of liberal politics. She displayed a bust in her office of the late President John F. Kennedy, a Boston native. You had to look hard to determine whose image it was, though, because it was placed in the corner facing the wall like a misbehaved child, so you could only see the back of its head.

A more revealing introduction to Boston took place at city hall when Bud had his first meeting with Mayor Kevin White. White was originally elected in 1967 after a nasty contest against Louise Day Hicks, a staunch opponent of school busing. He had run as a liberal Democrat, in the image of the then-progressive New York Republican mayor John Lindsay. Both supported the creation of neighborhood city halls to bring government closer to the people, and both insinuated themselves into the racially explosive issues of school politics. By the time we met White in 1981, he had been so burned by the school wars that he wanted nothing to do with education—much as Lindsay had been bruised when he supported community control in Ocean Hill–Brownsville.

White told Spillane in no uncertain terms that education was so painful in Boston, he would be crazy as mayor to get involved. It was a losing cause, a political liability. As he further explained, the public schools were run by a popularly elected board that chose its leadership and was ultimately responsible for the mess Bud was inheriting. The only formal role the mayor played in education was to work with the city council to provide funding, of which there was little. The powerful business community had already given up on the public school system, abandoning it as a high-profile battleground for racial politics. The still healthy Catholic schools provided the mayor's constituents with a viable alternative. The same parochial schools were also beginning to serve Boston's growing Black community and doing a decent job.

White essentially instructed Spillane, "Nice to meet you, don't come back, and don't ask for anything." The mayor actually used more colorful language, and Spillane responded in kind. If you were in the room listening to these two bare-knuckled white-haired Irishmen go at it for an hour, you might fear that someone could get hurt. Despite the discouraging exchange, White and Spillane actually connected. Over time, I believe they grew to like each other, only the way men like that can genuinely like each other.

When Kevin White spoke of the disastrous budget situation in Boston, he wasn't talking malarkey. The city had suffered such an economic downturn the year before that municipal workers had to forgo two weeks of pay. With the powerful business community turning its back on schools, Bud Spillane had his work cut out for him.

While working on the project, I also came to know Robert Peterkin, whose counsel I solicited throughout the process. Bob was a senior aide in the administration of the former Boston Superintendent, Robert Wood. A confident Black educator familiar with Boston's political landscape. Bob would go on to serve as a top deputy under Spillane before his appointment as superintendent of schools in Cambridge, Massachusetts, and then Milwaukee. You'll hear more about him later.

Following six weeks of intense work, our sixty-eight-page transition report recommended many of the policies that we had implemented in New York, including curriculum reform, testing, instructional support, a standards-based promotional policy, and remediation.[51] The report also covered special education, bilingual instruction, vocational and occupational instruction, staff development, and a reorganization plan that would fuel schools with support services. Its major contribution, I believe, was philosophical. We discussed how the school system had lost its focus on children as learners. We demanded that not only children but teachers, principals, and administrators must be held accountable for performance. We called for a better use of resources yet indicated that additional spending would still be required. Ron Edmonds's fingerprints were all over the document.

Bud was supportive of the direction we took. He wanted to get beyond the battles over busing and concentrate on "instruction, instruction, and instruction." The incoming superintendent publicly registered his enthusiasm for our approach when hc gave a speech in late August to an assembly of principals, headmasters, and other key personnel at West Roxbury High School. After a brief introduction, he shouted,

> First, let me give you my philosophy of education. It can be stated so quickly that if you are not listening carefully you may miss it: **All Children Can Learn**. As simple as it sounds, this philosophy is something of a turnaround from the conventional wisdom of the last two decades, which has made excuses for why many children cannot learn in school.[52]

Nearly a decade after Ron Edmonds had drafted the Freedom House Statement urging school administrators and Judge Garrity to emphasize learning, Boston now had a superintendent willing to insist that improved instruction is an essential feature of school desegregation and racial equity. Ron Edmonds may have moved to Michigan, but he was still being heard in Boston. His four memorable words and their meaning were carefully laced throughout our transition report. Many leaders in the Black community recognized them and knew from where they came. The plan was well received by the school board, the press, and the greater school community.

Bud Spillane would go on to have a successful, if not easy, run in Boston.[53] A long, lanky man with blue eyes whose crop of white hair was usually combed straight back, Spillane had charm and swagger. If he had been born in Montana instead of Massachusetts, he might have ridden into Boston on a black stallion. Nicknamed "Six-Gun Spillane" and the "Velvet Hammer," he acted quickly to remove underperforming teachers and administrators and close failing schools. When threatened with budget cuts, he publicly declared, "I've got to go to war over that." He restored confidence in a declining system and gained support for his efforts in political and corporate circles. By the end of his four-year term, he had earned a national reputation as an innovator who put kids first and made effective schools a priority of Boston.

* * *

The last time I saw Ron Edmonds was in the spring of 1983. The family was returning to Cambridge because Danny, their teenage son, had one more visit with his orthodontist to remove his braces. A highlight of the trip was a visit to Peking Gardens, their favorite Chinese restaurant in Lexington near their former home, which hosted an elaborate buffet banquet on Tuesday evenings. Ron asked my then-future wife and me to join them. The kids were very excited that evening, and Karen seemed relieved that the big move was behind them. Ron walked us through the delectable offerings laid across a long banquet table along the wall, describing each dish in elaborate detail, attesting to their distinct allures as someone who had sampled each and every one on multiple occasions.

We also had some planning to do that evening. Ron and his family enjoyed spending time on Cape Cod during the summer, as did we. Karen, he, and their two children were partial to Wellfleet and its freshwater ponds. We tended to stay in North Truro, near Provincetown's national seashore and its extraordinary array of restaurants. The two locations were close enough so that we could meet and spend time together.

We arrived that July a few days before the rest. We were about to go out for a late breakfast one morning when we got a call from another friend who was planning to join us. He told me that they would not be coming. Ron had been taken to the hospital with a heart attack and was in intensive care. He never recovered. He was forty-eight years of age.

* * *

In the course of my research for this book, I had occasion to talk with Deborah McGriff, whom I had known since my tour of duty with the New York City schools. As a young college graduate from Virginia then, McGriff had relocated to New York because she wanted to work in a large urban school district and dedicate herself to the needs of underserved children of color. She taught in Brooklyn's Fort Greene, not far from Ocean Hill–Brownsville, and had become impressed with Ron Edmonds's work on effective schools. She would carry it with her though an extraordinary career as one of the nation's leading practitioners of school reform.

When Ron passed away in 1983, Deborah was instrumental in establishing the Ronald Edmonds Learning Center that is located in MS 113 on Adelphi Street in Brooklyn across from a park that also bears Ron Edmonds's name. In accordance with Ron's philosophy, the center is dedicated to providing the instructional supports needed to maintain high educational standards for the students in its care. A second Ron Edmonds Learning Center (RELC II) has since opened in Brooklyn's District 17, not far from the original facility.

During one of my conversations with her in 2022, Deborah mentioned that she had a friend in California who lived across the street from Ron's son Daniel. The last time I had seen "Danny" was in 1983, the day the young teenager had his braces removed and we dined in Lexington. Deborah offered to get word to Daniel about the project and passed on my contact information to him. He called me the same day. He was now semiretired from a successful career in the health field and had a husband along with two college-age children of his own. We had a warm conversation over the phone lightened with a few laughs about a beaten-up Italian sports car I used to drive that he swore I promised to give him when he was old enough to get a license. We agreed when we spoke that we would bring our families together again the next time he visited his mother and sister who were still living in Massachusetts.

That visit occurred very shortly thereafter in the summer of 2022, when Daniel, his mother Karen, his sister Kristin, and her two sons drove down from the Boston area to spend a day at our home in New York. It was a joyful reunion, and we exchanged more stories about Ron. Kristin was planning, later that day, to take her two boys to visit the Ronald Edmonds Playground located across from the learning center at MS 113 that also bore her father's name.

Karen shared one particular detail about Ron and his twin brother, Donald, that was especially enlightening. Ron, she told us, had always claimed that his brother, who worked as a laborer and never attended college, was the smarter of the two. He thought it was important for people to know that and would never hesitate to say so. Now I had finally gotten it. Now I appreciated why Ron became so visibly irritated when folks dismissed people who looked like him as uneducable. Now I better understood why he dedicated his professional life endeavoring to prove otherwise.

4

John "Jack" Coons

Simple Justice and Dignity

Once I decided to write this book, Jack Coons was among the first people with whom I spoke. I had known Jack for more than twenty-five years. We first met in April 1996 when my wife invited him to speak at her law school and the two of us had dinner with him the previous night. By then I was working with Diane Ravitch at New York University, and I had read his two important books on school finance reform and school choice.[1] If Diane Ravitch introduced me to the idea of school choice as an educational innovation, Jack Coons lodged it in a literature on law and policy I understood and appreciated. As someone who had begun a career working for public schools in New York, Boston, and by then San Francisco, I was not an easy convert to the choice cause.

Jack's pathbreaking work on behalf of school finance reform showed me that he cared about redistributive policies. His approach to school vouchers demonstrated how progressive principles could be applied to a conservative idea to enhance the role of not-so-privileged parents in their children's education. From Jack I learned about the bright line of demarcation within the choice camp between progressives like him who espouse targeted regulated choice and conservatives who adhere to Friedman's free-market principles. Although advocates from the left have supported choice, Jack gave it footing in the policy realm.

Over the next fifteen years, as I began to write on the subject, I became involved with a group of academics and advocates whom Jack had assembled to advance a progressive choice agenda. Our most memorable event occurred in 2005 when Jack had raised money to host a five-day meeting at the Christian Brothers Retreat and Conference Center, which is located on the grounds of a Napa Valley winery. The wine flowed as freely as the ideas in this lush enclave, which had the feel of a medieval monastery. The gathering was an ecumenical occasion in the sense that it included people of different persuasions from the school choice community. I got to spend

Radical Dreamers. Joseph P. Viteritti, Oxford University Press. © Oxford University Press (2025).
DOI: 10.1093/oso/9780197827109.003.0004

time with Terry Moe, whose book with John Chubb from 1990 did more to advance the market model of choice than anything written since Friedman's seminal article dating back to 1955.[2] Howard Fuller, who had put a progressive model of choice into practice in Milwaukee, was also there.

Despite the glorious setting, our first morning session got off to a gloomy start. Jack had planned to open the conference by publicly acknowledging John Walton, the philanthropist whose generous contribution had made our meeting under such delightful circumstances possible. Heir to the Walmart fortune, Walton was a politically connected proponent of choice programs that created new educational opportunities for low-income families. He had joined forces with Ted Forstmann, a New York financier, to develop a national scholarship program based in New York. He supported Howard Fuller's campaign to start an advocacy network composed entirely of Black leaders. Instead of celebrating John that morning, we mourned him. Just before we convened in the courtyard of the winery after breakfast, Jack had received word that John was killed when a plane he was piloting went down in Jackson, Wyoming. Howard told me he had just heard the tragic news right before Jack walked to the podium.

During the Napa conference, Jack urged us to found the American Center for School Choice. Our group would meet one or two times a year, usually in the faculty club at Berkeley. While there, I visited Jack's home and got to know his wife, Marylyn. Early on we organized an event on school choice at the National Press Club in Washington, DC that attracted an assortment of policy types from the executive and legislative branches and around the Beltway. We later hosted a convocation at the law school in Berkeley that was more academic in content. Our group, which also included Jack's colleague Steve Sugarman, did not have the impact their earlier activities had, but the effort helped keep the conversation moving in a certain direction on the policy front. The choice issue had gained traction in both political parties. We wanted to steer it in a leftward direction.

Jack had just turned ninety in 2019 when I called him about this project. He was as animated as ever. I soon learned that there were two new collections of Jack's work being assembled. Nicole Stelle Garnett, Rick Garnett, and Ernest Morrell of the University of Notre Dame Press were assembling a sampling of his more scholarly essays.[3] I had known Nicole and Rick, both law professors, for years from their work on education.[4] Ernest Morrell is a scholar who writes on race and has edited a very good book on the history of schooling in Harlem.[5]

Ron Matus of Step Up for Students was gathering a selection of Jack's shorter journalistic provocations published on his organization's blog.[6] I had never met but knew of Ron. His nonprofit organization administers a scholarship program in Florida that enables families to send their children to schools of their choice. I soon contacted these editors, who were kind enough to provide me with manuscript copies before their respective books went to press. I had also learned about an oral history that Jack had taped in 2015 for the university library at Berkeley.[7] Martin Meeker, the creator and interlocutor of the oral history, was likewise generous in sharing materials.

I was already familiar with some of the essays in the new collections. They and the oral history helped me fill in some biographical details as I wrote. Jack prepared an introductory chapter for each of the collections and a bibliographical essay for the Notre Dame book discussing the literature on choice.[8] I was pleased to read in the latter that, in his judgment, my policy position in *Choosing Equality* comes closer to his design of a working system of family choice than anything else he had seen. In this case, I can assure you the instruction flowed entirely in one direction.

* * *

Behind an "aw-shucks" demeanor that lays bare a modest soul, Jack Coons is a philosophical, faith-based man who believes that we all have a duty to make life better for those who are less fortunate. I consider him an accidental Catholic. His Irish mother, Marguerite Lavelle Eddins, was born on a Kentucky farm into a nominally Catholic family that was only occasionally observant. As Jack explains in the oral history project he recorded for the university library at Berkeley, she was one of five sisters who together managed to pile up thirteen divorces among them.[9] That's not very Catholic. Marguerite's first marriage was to a non-Catholic man named Oren. After they separated and put their two children in an orphanage for a while, she married William Coons, an ambivalent Protestant.

Marguerite's new husband, who had been born on a farm in Missouri, made an ample living selling kerosene stoves and eventually running his own store. Marguerite and Oren had split up their kids, she taking the girl and he the boy. Jack was the youngest of three boys she and Coons had together. Throughout her marriage to Coons, Marguerite did her best to remain a practicing Catholic. When Oren finally passed, Marguerite, released from her marriage vows in the eyes of the church, snuck Daddy Coons off to the

Catholic rectory for a proper wedding, allowing her to put that "dirty secret" behind her. According to Jack, the old man became a deathbed convert to Catholicism.[10]

After he had spent just one year of public school in Duluth, Minnesota, Marguerite put Jack in Catholic school where he remained through high school. That is where he absorbed the teaching and traditions of "the Romans," as he would call them. Young boys and girls got equal servings of God and grammar for a mere two dollars a month in tuition. Jack and I shared that kind of educational experience, but with different results—in part because I grew up in Brooklyn, New York, more so because my family was not that religious.

I feel indebted to the hardworking nuns and brothers who introduced me to learning. Like many others brought up in the faith, however, I was unable to reconcile myself with the scope and depth of the pedophile scandal. It was an absolute betrayal of trust. In lighter moments, I tell friends that there were two things we knew would always be there for us growing up in old Brooklyn, our Dodgers and our church.

I continue to have difficulty with some of the church's teaching, especially with its treatment of women and members of the LGBTQ+ community. If there is an enduring lesson Jack and I share from our common Catholic upbringing, however, it is an attitude toward poverty. One piece of Scripture that has stuck with me reads, "It is easier for a camel to pass through the eye of a needle than for a rich man to enter the Kingdom of God." In this passage from the Gospel according to Matthew, Jesus is advising a wealthy man to give his possessions to the poor in order to be saved. That biblical parable is the indelible mark of my Catholic education. Its message was well received by the throngs of devoted Irish immigrants in our parish whose men worked the docks by day and women cleaned Manhattan offices by night.

* * *

After high school, young Jack initially enrolled at Duluth State Teachers College, but when he appeared for class in the fall, he was surprised to learn that it suddenly had become the University of Minnesota at Duluth. It wasn't fancy, but it was close to home and it was cheap. Since neither of his parents had attended high school, he already was ahead of the game.

Jack majored in history because he "enjoyed reading about the goofs other people made in the last ten thousand years and how we did or didn't get out of it."[11] A Boy Scout leader who took Jack under his wing formed a choir. That's how Jack found out he liked to sing. While in college, Jack made some extra money performing at a nightclub in town called the Flame. Jack still likes to sing. While I was writing this book, he sent my wife and me a CD of twenty-three songs he recorded with piano accompaniment. The selection of tunes begins with "How Long Has This Been Going On?" and ends with "Every Time We Say Goodbye." At dinnertime, we call the CD "Cabaret with Jack"—and sometimes we bring Jack along for a ride in the car.

While in college, Jack also did odd jobs for the school's History Department. A good student, he thought he might get a job selling insurance after graduation and possibly attend law school at night. A history professor by the name of Ellis Livingston encouraged Jack to apply for scholarships and see what happens. That's how teachers save lives. The professor and his wife took such an interest in young Jack that she typed fifty-two recommendation letters for him sent to law schools all over the country. Jack won a full fellowship to Northwestern and off he went. It wasn't fancy, but it was very good and the price was right.

Drafted into military service in 1953 right after law school, Jack cultivated his lawyering skills as an attorney in the US Army, trying cases across the country for the Pentagon. After being discharged early when the Korean War ended, he received a surprise call from the dean of the law school at Northwestern offering him a job as assistant dean with a professorial appointment. Jack had not contemplated a career in legal academia. As he tells the story in his oral history, the "real guy" they wanted for the post turned it down. You could say that this accidental Catholic, by some odd turn, also became an accidental law professor—but with no less devotion on either count. Perhaps it was fate. His life would go on that way. One might say he has been blessed.

* * *

In 1961, the US Civil Rights Commission contacted Professor Willard Pedrick of Northwestern University to ask if he would do a study of racial segregation in the Chicago public schools. Pedrick was too busy to take it on, so he suggested that they offer the assignment to his younger colleague Jack Coons, who was on his way to raising a family of five children and could use the money. It wasn't exactly unfamiliar territory to Coons. He was hosting his own radio show in Chicago called *Problems of the City*, where he had covered issues like racial segregation, failing schools, and police abuses in the

Black community. As a member of the Catholic Interracial Council, he had worked with church leaders to integrate Black parishioners into the activities of the church and the larger Chicago community, and marched with the group at Selma. He even had a brief encounter with the Reverend Martin Luther King Jr. After being introduced by Jack Greenberg of the NAACP, Jack spent a day with the civil rights leader when he visited Chicago and sought Jack's legal counsel on a boycott he was planning there.

Jack was immediately interested in the US Civil Rights Commission inquiry, but he was about to leave for Africa on another mission. As a member of the law faculty at Northwestern, Jack had a nagging concern with how isolated and narrow legal academia could be. He was instrumental in creating a law and social science program at the university that allowed him to collaborate with anthropologists, sociologists, psychologists, and political scientists. He got to know Paul Bohannan, an anthropologist who had started the African studies program at Northwestern—which, according to Jack, was the first of its kind in the country. Jack and Bohannan developed a common interest in African tribal law and were planning to teach an interdisciplinary course together. As the Chicago project was about to commence in the spring of 1962, Jack flew off for a two-month expedition in the jungles of East Africa to learn more about tribal justice firsthand. After returning, Jack cotaught the Africa course with his Northwestern colleague and wrote two articles on the subject.

Jack did not want to let go of the civil rights project in Chicago, even though he would not be able to attend the first few meetings. His wife, Marylyn, who had been a public school teacher in the Highland Park suburb of Chicago, offered to attend in his stead and turn the project over when he returned. As Jack explains, this politically savvy woman knew more about education than he. Prior to this time, most studies of school segregation focused on the South. Now the federal government was turning its attention to northern cities. The Chicago project cast a new light on the subject, and local politicians were not happy. In his oral history, Jack recounts the intimidating hostility he felt from Superintendent of Schools Benjamin Willis, "a tyrant and a bully" whose cooperation he needed and who questioned Jack's credentials to do the work.

Jack collected enough data to complete the investigation. It was no surprise to find the Chicago schools segregated. Like most northern cities, racial separation in schools was a reflection of neighborhood residential patterns. When Martin Meeker asked during the oral history interview whether such de facto segregation was intentional, Coons responded, "I would call it deliberate at an almost unconscious level." He further explained that at one time property deeds would not allow a white owner to transfer title to a buyer who was not white. When such deeds were outlawed, an informal arrangement emerged among sales agents, buyers, and sellers that preserved existing patterns.

Nor was it surprising to Jack and his associates to discover that schools in Black neighborhoods were not performing as well as those that were white. As he investigated further, he began to suspect that the uneven performance might have something to do with resource allocations in Chicago. Black communities were indeed being shortchanged. Jack's report attracted sufficient attention in the local press to infuriate Chicago mayor Richard J. Daley, who had ruled the city with an iron fist. Despite the critical attention, things remained pretty much the same in the Windy City when it came to race. I think I know why.

In the brief time I taught at Harvard, from 1981 to 1983, the late Francis Keppel resided on the faculty as a senior lecturer. Frank was a swell guy. He was a classic example of what it meant to have an Ivy League pedigree: His father had been a dean at Columbia University who became president of the Carnegie Corporation; Frank attended Groton and Harvard College. With no graduate degree, he was recruited as an assistant dean and then assistant provost at Harvard. Subsequently, at the age of thirty-two, he became the youngest dean in the history of Harvard's Graduate School of Education. Frank had left Harvard in 1962 when President John F. Kennedy appointed him US commissioner of education, where he was a champion of racial integration. It was he who had commissioned the Coleman Report that infuriated Ron Edmonds. When federal education programs were merged into the newly created Department of Health, Education and Welfare under President Lyndon Johnson in 1965, Frank was appointed assistant secretary of education. He did not last there very long.

Frank loved to tell the story about how he got fired from his post by President Johnson. As the top education official in Washington, Keppel threatened local school districts with the loss of federal funding if they did not agree to desegregate their facilities. He specifically told Mayor Daley that if Chicago did not comply with his instructions, the city would lose $32 million. That was a lot of money in those days. After receiving the threat, Daley called the White House. He told the president that if Keppel were not fired immediately, Johnson could have a difficult time winning Cook County, and all of Illinois' rich bounty of electoral votes for that matter, when he ran for reelection in 1968. Johnson eventually decided not to seek reelection, but Keppel was fired.

The African American community did not have as strong an ally in the White House as Lyndon Johnson since Abraham Lincoln, but politics is politics. If you have difficulty understanding the cynicism felt by Black scholars like Derrick Bell and Howard Fuller regarding the perpetuity of racism, this is one story that can be instructive.

* * *

Jack Coons had his next major foray into education research when the US Civil Rights Commission invited him to participate in a second, more elaborate study of elementary and secondary schools. Law professors across the country were recruited to scrutinize urban districts from San Francisco to Boston. Jack was asked to reevaluate Chicago and compare it to neighboring Evanston. This was the survey of all surveys orchestrated by James Coleman. Jack had been recruited to collect local data for the famous Coleman Report, which found that schools are segregated by race, Black and white schools have similar resources, and Black schools could be improved through racial integration. This was the report that, with considerable fanfare, popularized the claim that the family background of students has a greater impact on academic performance than what happens in schools themselves.

Although Jack Coons's research would take him in different directions from Coleman, the two men liked each other, respected each other, and became friends. In fact, the relationship between the two grew so strong that Coleman wrote the foreword to each of Jack's two landmark books on school finance and school choice. These were the same two works that Derrick Bell referenced in his foundational legal text on race and education. It must still be puzzling to wonder how these two men—Ron Edmonds and Jack Coons—could have had such divergent opinions about James Coleman. The prospect becomes more reasonable once you appreciate how Coleman himself evolved as a scholar. His capacity to change his position in response to new evidence was admirable, especially since his reversals provoked such controversy.

Like him or not, James Coleman is arguably the most significant social scientist ever to apply himself to education policy. In 1975, Coleman participated in an Urban Institute study that would throw the academic and policy communities into a tailspin. (Let's call this *Coleman II*.) Examining desegregation patterns in nineteen cities from 1968 through 1973, Coleman, the man whose 1966 report (*Coleman I*) fueled school integration across the county, found that forced busing was a major cause of white flight.[12] In a lengthy interview with the *New York Times* published under the title "Integration, Yes; Busing No," he further explained that white flight to the suburbs would undermine attempts to eliminate racial isolation and eventually lead to resegregation.[13]

The new Coleman study findings were immediately denounced by Roy Wilkins of the NAACP and Kenneth Clark. Members of the American Sociological Association (ASA) called for a censuring of Coleman, and some demanded that he be cast out of the professional organization altogether. This extreme reaction by white liberal academicians had occurred after African American scholars like Ron Edmonds and Derrick Bell were themselves questioning the merits of school busing, and other Black social scientists were finding little evidence that integration had improved the academic performance of minority students.[14] Notwithstanding the behavior of his professorial colleagues and the reaction from civil rights litigators, Coleman stuck to his guns. He subsequently was elected president of ASA in 1992.

In 1982, Coleman completed a study commissioned by the National Center for Education Statistics that would generate more controversy, this time comparing academic achievement at public, private, and parochial high schools (*Coleman III*). He found that private and parochial schools produce better cognitive outcomes than public schools.[15] He also discovered a particular "Catholic School effect" in reducing the performance gap between Black and white students. In a subsequent study, Coleman attributed the success of Catholic schools to an unusual abundance of "social capital," found within a school community that coheres around particular values.[16] In these schools, the values happened to be religious. The sense of community, he claimed, also functions to enhance students' self-esteem and confidence, a quality that Black scholars and activists had found lacking in many public schools.

From a research perspective, Coleman's findings on the enhanced performance of minority students at private and parochial institutions constituted a rebuttal of the "schools don't matter" conclusion that his prior work, intentionally or not, had fostered. Coleman was also keenly aware of the policy implications of his new research. If the numerous Catholic schools that exist have a proven capability to advance educational equality between the races, he argued, then underperforming students should be awarded publicly financed vouchers or tax credits to attend them. Notwithstanding other differences they may have had intellectually (at least for a while), that proposition solidified the relationship between James Coleman and Jack Coons.

* * *

There remained, however, that general finding in the original Coleman report about comparable funding at Black and white schools that Coons could not reconcile with his Chicago study, and it left him unsettled. Coleman didn't mind having collaborators disagree with him, as long as they could support their positions with data. Coleman, a ruthless empiricist, would repeatedly change his mind with the discovery of new evidence. Everybody knew, moreover, that Daley's Chicago was unique in many respects, so further investigation was in order.

Comparing Chicago and Evanston would add a new dimension to Jack's scholarship: disparities evident not only within districts, but also between districts. Steve Sugarman and Bill Clune had already begun to collect data for the school finance book the three of them would write together, and it was drawing attention. Arthur Wise, a graduate student at the University of Chicago, was in the process of writing a dissertation that also would be an important contribution to the literature on school finance.[17] In 1968, Wise persuaded Jack and his colleagues to prepare an amicus brief in a Chicago case that he and others had brought in the federal district court. The recently minted PhD was convinced that he had identified a sure path to the US Supreme Court and fiscal equity.

Jack, like most sharp attorneys, tends to be wary when well-intentioned social scientists unfamiliar with the law or the courts try to develop legal arguments. He was especially concerned about this particular case, but went along with the lawsuit because he was sympathetic to the fairness principle behind the argument. Sometimes well-grounded legal principle is not enough, however. Experienced litigators will ask whether a litigation issue is "ripe."

Ripeness is a complicated and beguiling concept that entails strategic considerations: Is the court ready at this particular time in this particular political climate to break new ground or overturn established precedents? If there is a reasonable legal argument behind the case, why hasn't it been successfully made before? Neither of these questions necessarily turns on whether a proven instance of injustice exists. They are political in nature. The federal judiciary was already in the crosshairs of criticism from both Black and white parents over the implementation of forced busing. Notwithstanding the *Brown* decision of 1954, federal courts were reluctant to interfere in schooling issues because education is generally deemed a state prerogative. School finance cases are especially sensitive because they require the judiciary to intrude into spending decisions that are jealously guarded by legislatures.

"Hey," you might ask, "isn't this why we have courts of law?" If there is a clear demonstrable injustice in the way a state distributes resources to schoolchildren, shouldn't the judiciary step in? You might think so. Sometimes, however, the more deeply ingrained a particular injustice is within an existing government practice, the less willing courts are to intervene. Regardless of the merits, the "C'mon" argument doesn't always hold. Heard about systemic injustice? This is it, folks! As Jack feared, the federal court in Chicago rejected the claim, and on appeal the US Supreme Court refused to hear the case.

In the meantime, other school finance cases were percolating in the states. Jack had been living in Berkeley a year when in 1968 John Serrano, a Latino man from Los Angeles, filed papers in a state court claiming that the California school finance system was discriminatory toward low-income students. Jack and his colleagues had already laid out a legal argument to revamp the state system of funding schools in a 1969 article for the California Law Review.[18] Harvard University Press would publish their school finance book the next year under its prestigious Belknap imprint. When the trial court dismissed the claim, the attorneys in the case asked Jack, Bill Clune, and Steve Sugarman to help draft the appeal to the California Supreme Court. Jack and Steve also filed a separate amicus brief. Several of the sitting judges had read their book and wanted to hear from them directly. Another member of the court, finding their reasoning incredulous, walked out in the middle of their argument.

Coons and Sugarman argued that California's funding mechanism for schools violated the equal protection clause of the federal Constitution and several provisions of the state constitution because the amount of funding a child receives is dependent on the taxable property value of a school district. Since some districts were wealthier than others, the spending was inequitable. Aware that the court might be reluctant to impose a remedy on the state legislature, Coons and Sugarman offered several possible plans that the legislature might adopt in responding to the court's finding of a violation. In accord with what they had written in the book, these included (1) a statewide system of funding like that in Hawaii, (2) a district-based system of funding that would allow districts to set their own level of tax effort while the state enforced certain minimum standards of equity, and (3) a system of school vouchers that would support parents' choice of public, private, or parochial schools with provisions to assure equitable payments for low-income families. The last proposal would become a lifetime cause for Coons and Sugarman; Bill Clune was more enthusiastic about the Hawaii-type plan. In 1971, the California State Supreme Court decided in Serrano's favor by a vote of 6 to 1 on both federal and state constitutional grounds.[19] But that wasn't the end.

A Mexican American man named Demitrio Rodriguez later filed a *Serrano*-type lawsuit in Texas, but this time through the federal courts—hoping, like Arthur Wise in Chicago, that the case would elicit a grand pronouncement from the US Supreme Court and put the principles embodied in the American Constitution behind a national campaign for fiscal equity. When called for advice, Coons and Sugarman encouraged Rodriguez's lawyer to adopt the fiscal neutrality argument they had used in *Serrano*. Jack actually flew to Washington to witness the final courtroom battle, admittedly concerned about the quality of Rodriguez's representation. There was a clear logic to the litigation. As you may recall, in the landmark *Brown v. Board of Education* ruling from 1954, a unanimous US Supreme Court had declared,

> Today, education is perhaps the most important function of state and local governments. . . . In these days, it is doubtful that any child may be reasonably expected to succeed in life if he is denied the opportunity of an education. Such an opportunity, where the state has undertaken to provide it, is *a right that must be made available to all on equal terms.*[20]

Evidently, much had changed by 1973. After a three-judge federal panel in the district court in Texas unanimously sided with Rodriguez, the US Supreme Court voted 5–4 to reject the Fourteenth Amendment equal-protection claim upon which *Brown* stood, finding, "the Equal Protection Clause does not require absolute equality or precisely equal advantages" in education.[21] Writing for the court, Justice Powell confirmed the growing reluctance of his colleagues to exercise judicial power to meddle in the affairs of the states. He bolstered the court's reasoning by citing the Coleman

and Jencks research raising doubts that "there is any demonstrable correlation between educational expenditures and the quality of education."[22]
Specifically addressing the "district power equalizing" scheme that Coons
and his colleagues had put forward in *Private Wealth and Public Education*,
Justice Powell questioned whether requiring "wealthier" districts to supple-
ment subsidies for poorer districts might itself "violate the equal protection
theory underlying the appellees' case."[23]

Unfortunately, the plea for fiscal equity in schooling was not yet ripe in
1973. I doubt the high court, as presently composed, would find it ready
(or credible) either. Will it ever be? As Derrick Bell and other progressive
scholars have written, the *Rodriguez* decision was a complete betrayal of the
standard of justice that had been enshrined in *Brown*. This is now established
law. It is another bold illustration of the court's doctrine of judicial restraint,
which we saw exercised in *Brown II*, just a year after the initial landmark
ruling, to slow down efforts to desegregate.[24]

On a practical level, the 1973 ruling put school finance litigation entirely
in the hands of the state courts, requiring plaintiffs to build fifty distinct
arguments on the basis of state law rather than a single federal standard.[25]
Figuring on a new angle, public school officials in California dragged Serrano back into court trying to dismiss his case because his victory was in
part based on a federal constitutional provision. With the help of Jack, Steve,
and Bill, Serrano prevailed again on the state constitutional claim in the
1976 appeal, but this time by a margin of only 4–3. And of course, that
wasn't the end of the story either. Two years after Serrano's final exit from
the courthouse, California voters passed Proposition 13. The popularly supported constitutional provision imposed severe limits on school spending in
general. It would also undermine the potential utility of property taxes as a
vehicle for fair distribution.

* * *

Three months after voters went to the polls in 1978 to add the antitax
provision to their state constitution, Jack was invited to a meeting by Democratic congressman Leo Ryan. The representative from South San Francisco
had read the recently published Coons and Sugarman book on school choice
and was impressed. He asked Jack to draft language for a new ballot initiative that would provide vouchers for low-income residents so that they could
attend public, private, or religious schools of their choice. Ryan promised
to raise money and become the public face of the campaign. Jack then had

dinner with Milton Friedman and his wife, Rose, to ask for their support. The Nobel Prize–winning economist had moved from Chicago to California and enjoyed access to people with money whose backing could be crucial. He seemed on board. The initiative was given generous coverage by the influential *Los Angeles Times*.

After a hopeful start, the campaign soon fell apart when it lost its key sponsor.[26] Two months after his initial meeting with Jack, Congressman Ryan was assassinated on an airfield in Guyana. The legislator was visiting there to investigate reports that women and men were being held captive at the Peoples Temple in Jonestown. He was lost the same day that more than nine hundred people died in a mass suicide-assassination at the temple. Jack tried to keep the campaign alive without Ryan, but Friedman's wealthy friends never came through after the conservative economist criticized the voucher plan as left-leaning.

When the proposal went down in the 1980 referendum, the Catholic archbishop of Los Angeles contacted Jack, encouraging him to start a new campaign and assuring him of financial backing from his fellow bishops. A victory would allow parochial schools to serve more low-income students and gain enrollments—an illustration of surrogate politics if there ever was one. To make a long story short, the clerics never came through for Jack, and his second proposal died too. Jack tried in 1981 to recruit Cesar Chavez of the United Farm Workers to the cause, since it would directly benefit his mostly Latino and Filipino members—but the fabled labor organizer lamented that he could not afford to offend Albert Shanker, whose teachers' union donated two hundred thousand dollars annually to his nascent organization.

In 1992, Jack received a visit from the chairman of the state business roundtable, who thought that school vouchers were worth another try—all the while committing to put abundant corporate dollars behind the children's cause. Jack agreed to work with the group and draft language for the ballot, which he was assured would determine the policy thrust if adopted. Jack, with Steve Sugarman, attended all the planning meetings with the group except the last. When the ballot language was finalized, the business leaders, who had strong ties to Milton Friedman, amended the language to remove provisions designed to protect poor families. Jack and Steve publicly opposed the proposal, and it too went down. More skirmishes later highlighted the fissure within the choice camp led by these star academicians who came to education policy from very different perspectives.

Jack Coons and Milton Friedman had a complicated relationship. The two men had met in Chicago in the early 1960s when Jack invited Friedman on to his *Problems of the City* radio show. He became a frequent guest. When Friedman later acquired his own television show, he asked Jack on to debate teachers' union president Albert Shanker about school choice. In 2012, when Jack was asked to offer comments on the centennial anniversary of the deceased luminary's birth, he said some nice things and hoped out loud that they considered each other friends.[27] He readily admits that it was Friedman who breathed life into the idea of choice, and concedes a certain intellectual debt.

There is no denying, though, that the two were philosophical and political adversaries. That rivalry was open. They adamantly opposed each other's campaigns. Friedman and Coons personify the division between what some call the "voucher right" and "voucher left." It was in fact Milton who referred to Jack's plan as "left," while Jack associates Friedman with a libertarian, free-market approach to schooling. Both portraits are valid; neither man would contest. Jack does like to call himself a "centrist," but I would ask, Compared to what? I think he got that idea from sitting on a stage between Milton Friedman and Al Shanker. The political center really doesn't define itself. The center is defined by those who sit on the far ends of the left–right spectrum, and its locus varies by issue. When I brought this up with Jack on a recent phone call, he offered that the "center left" tag would be more fitting.[28]

Milton Friedman did not pretend to be an expert on primary and secondary education. He built his reputation as an economist writing on monetary theory. His 1955 essay that introduced choice into the lexicon of American schooling was based on sound market theory, but had no data to support it.[29] Friedman proposed a system of universal vouchers that would allow every parent to choose the school his or her child attended. He believed that such a marketplace of education services would optimize efficiency because parents, when presented with options, would select better schools and eventually force failing institutions to close. Although both public and nonpublic schools would be eligible to participate in this Darwinian struggle for survival, Friedman was fairly confident that nonpublic institutions would prevail. He envisioned a system of education with a minimal governmental role that would maximize individual freedom. Come to think of it, that does sound like something of a scheme to terminate public education. I should mention, though, that both he and Jack envisioned institutions resembling public charter schools before they ever existed.

For Friedman, the greatest flaw in the American system of education is its monopolistic nature: Because public schools do not have any competition for government funding, they have no incentive to improve. He believed that underperforming public schools located in poor minority communities would be most vulnerable to closure under a more competitive arrangement. Friedman's arguments did not fall on deaf ears in the Black community. As noted in the preceding chapter, Derrick Bell cited Friedman in his law school textbook on race and schools. Elaborating on the subject of choice in a 1980 book of his own, Friedman quotes an article on "alternative public school systems" by Kenneth Clark that originally appeared in the 1968 edition of the *Harvard Education Review*, which reads, "What is most important to understanding the ability of the educational establishment to resist change is the fact that public school systems are protected public monopolies with only minimal competition from private and parochial schools."[30]

Coons and Sugarman agreed with Friedman's critiques of the public school monopoly, but they had problems with the details of his market-based proposal. They were convinced that if school choice were to reverse generations of neglect in poor and minority communities, it had to be designed specifically to do so. Friedman's market model, as he envisioned it, could undermine that more progressive policy objective.

The two law professors disagreed with Friedman on three basic points. While Friedman supported an open system of recruitment for schools, Coons and Sugarman wanted to reserve a certain percentage of seats for low-income students. Whereas the value of Friedman's voucher would be the same for every student, Coons and Sugarman pushed for a needs-based system that would favor families with modest incomes. Finally, Friedman would allow schools to charge tuition above the voucher amount. Coons and Sugarman argued that to do so would effectively exclude poorer students from high-priced institutions (as it does now) while subsidizing the privileged, enhancing the latter's advantage.

Milton Friedman and Jack Coons were motivated by distinct democratic principles. Friedman wanted to maximize individual freedom through a market system that would operate more efficiently and effectively. For him, the state had no legitimate role in redirecting wealth, privilege, or educational achievement. Jack Coons embraced choice as an instrument for parental freedom, but that was not enough. He also wanted it to establish parental authority and in so doing to advance equality, which was the basic democratic value that brought him into education litigation from the start. As he wrote with emphasis on the first line in his volume on school finance and choice in 1970, "This is a book about equality of educational opportunity."[31]

* * *

Let's take a closer look now at Jack's two landmark books with which this chapter opened. While he was a coauthor, Jack took it upon himself—I'm sure with the assent of his two junior colleagues—to write the introductions for each in his own words. Indeed, he wrote both a preface and introduction to the first book that followed Coleman's foreword.

A close reading of the essays is useful for tracing Jack's evolving perspective on educational equality. The subtle dialogue between Coons and Coleman at the beginning of the volume is also interesting. It exemplifies what can be accomplished when two serious thinkers, aware and respectful of their own differences, engage in a common effort to unravel a major fixture within America's great racial dilemma.

Be reminded that Jack entered the schoolyard fray through a Chicago project investigating desegregation. Like Ron Edmonds, Derrick Bell, and the two critical thinkers we discuss in more details in the next chapters, Jack supported desegregation but was skeptical about forced integration and school busing. Nor did he think either was adequate to reverse years of educational inequality. Sounding very much like Edmonds and Bell, he writes on the first page of the preface for what I will call *Book I*:

> Common opinion has it that inequality of educational opportunity is primarily a problem of racial segregation. The outpouring of literature devoted to proving Negro schools inferior has become a mighty flood. . . . For inequities of education, integration has been the liberal's patent medicine.
>
> Integration is indeed a sound, long-run prescription for many of the basic ailments of education and our society—so long as we don't, in the meantime, die of something else; but to suppose that integration would itself produce equality of education is plainly naive.[32]

The quote stakes out Coons's common ground with the policy priorities of those who dared to challenge the precepts of the prevailing liberal orthodoxy. The mostly white surrogates for racial equality were quite capable of drowning out dissent, even when it was articulated by those who had a more direct stake in minority communities affected by segregation.

More significantly, the quote reveals Coons' insight into why the prevailing orthodoxy offended some Black intellectuals. His sagacity about their temperament becomes most apparent when Coons explains the basic principles underlying his position on parental choice—but let's not skip ahead. *Book I* was conceived as Bill Clune and Steve Sugarman began to collect data on school spending at the direction of their law school mentor.

The detective work of these budding attorneys began at just about the time the celebrated first Coleman Report appeared (1966), finding that resources at Black and white public schools were more or less equal and in the final analysis did not matter much in determining academic outcomes. If you are wondering how Jack finessed this point of difference in a book on fiscal inequity published a few years later and managed to nudge Coleman himself to write a foreword, you can find the answer right there in Jack's introduction. I actually rediscovered this nugget when I read the original edition of Derrick Bell's law textbook on race and education. The direct quote from Jack's essay supplies Bell with the five concluding lines of his chapter on alternatives to integrated schools that we reviewed earlier:

> Whatever it is that money may be thought to contribute to the education of children, that commodity is something highly prized by those who enjoy the greatest measure of it. If money is inadequate to improve education, the residents of poor districts should at least have an equal opportunity to be disappointed by its failure.[33]

The lines are classic Coons: understated, ironic, amusing, and provocative.

The major conclusion of *Book I* is that school funding depends on the differential wealth of school districts—and we ought to do something to correct it.

Jack did not pretend that equity in school funding could reverse decades of systemic social, economic, and political stratification, especially when it is abetted by substandard housing, nutrition, and health care. Nor did he deny that some students were more talented than others or the beneficiaries of cultural advantages in such an artificially stratified world. He is sympathetic to Black demands for community control like what we saw in Ocean Hill–Brownsville, Brooklyn, but skeptical about the capacity of these communities to fund their schools adequately.

According to the factual evidence, the funding disparities that Coons, Clune, and Sugarman uncovered were not only sorted by race. Income was a key factor. There are more poor white people than poor Black people in this country, yet poverty disproportionately falls on people of color. It is through no fault of their own in either case. Thus, Coons remarks, "The Negro's continuing poverty might be more tolerable if we could be persuaded that he deserved it."[34]

Coons deems the district arrangement of wealth-based funding "outrageous," and challenges the very notion of "public school district" as a fiction of bureaucratic imagination. He reminds us that our existing school districts are public only for those who can afford the taxes to live in them. If a poor child from another district sought to attend one of the better-financed schools attended by the children of privileged parents, she would not be permitted. Elsewhere and much later, Coons recounted the story of a seven-year-old Latina who in 2014 was tossed out of the high-priced Orinda, California, school district when it was revealed that she was not a legal resident.[35] Did you say public? What we have now, according to Coons, is an educational "aristocracy padded by the state" that has no legitimate place in a democracy. "It should certainly be within the purview of a people who fashion education as a gateway to opportunity to develop a system that favors rather than impedes the disadvantaged," Coons declares.[36]

Instead of disputing the data-based finding on funding inequality in *Book I*, Coleman composed an essay for the foreword that explained it. And he did it in a novel way that advanced the central thesis. He described what we have as a "continual struggle between two forces."[37] On one side are those members of society who want to offer educational opportunity for all children. On the other are individual parents who indulge a basic motivation to provide their own children with the best education they can afford.

Coleman's observation is astute in analyzing the situation as conflictual. The self-interest of discordantly endowed families drives the competition here, much as Friedman might have expected if he were analyzing the then-existing education marketplace. Whenever there is a long-standing battle between the rich and the poor, we can usually predict who wins. The economist would protest that so much money was wasted in the process. Even if that uneven outcome were not systemically preordained, the best education they can afford would be insufficient for low-income parents with high aspirations for their children. Coleman agrees that the system in place is "wholly destructive of the goal of educational opportunity for all children" and is hopeful that the book will speed needed change.[38]

* * *

In search of more equitable arrangements that could be enacted as a result of successful school finance litigation, Coons, Clune, and Sugarman had mapped out proposals that would either locate distributive decisions entirely at the state level or retain them primarily in local districts with new state protections for families of modest means. It was their third proposal in *Book I*, however—empowering parents to spend education dollars as they saw fit through a system of school choice—that energized Coons's and Sugarman's productive careers going forward. They would compose two more monographs on the topic, not to mention the several ballot proposals we saw earlier.[39] Their plan encompassed public schools resembling today's charters along with private and parochial options.

Coleman had already expressed his support for vouchers in the foreword of the earlier book from 1970. By the time *Book II* arrived, the Chicago sociologist also had spoken out about the self-defeating effects of busing and was fully supportive of the choice alternative. I can only speculate regarding how much Coleman's intimate exchanges with Coons led him down the choice path. Their potent professional relationship surely was a factor.

Coleman's foreword in *Book II* is shorter. He briefly mentions the first book as "probably the single most influential element in the court decisions . . . that have led state legislatures to revise their school aid formulas to bring about financial equity."[40] He takes the opportunity to highlight the collection of strange bedfellows aligned behind choice, including Milton Friedman, Christopher Jencks, community control activist Mario Fantini (supporting public school choice), Black Muslims, the Catholic Church, and advocates of urban free schools.[41] Coleman also enumerated the key adversaries, which at the time included the American Federation of Teachers (AFT), the American Civil Liberties Union (ACLU), New Deal Democrats, and many Reagan Republicans. Derrick Bell probably would have portrayed the pro alliance as a stunning illustration of "interest convergence" that would crumble once the differing priorities of the members became apparent.[42] What do you think Bell might have said about the opposing group? How many of the opponents would have counted themselves as surrogates for the downtrodden?

Coons's introduction once more calls to mind his differences with Friedman, distinguishing the economist's emphasis on freedom and referring to his own approach as one that would guarantee "equality of freedom."[43] Again, the two agreed that under the then-existing system, choice is only available to those families that have the monetary means to either live in property-rich communities with good public schools or afford tuition at nonpublic institutions. For Coons, however, it was not only imperative to offer the "non-rich" seats at schools that were academically sound, but also an opportunity for them to choose schools that reflect their own values, which may or may not be religious in nature. Political theorists commonly discern a tension between the democratic values of freedom and equality; Coons believes that in this case they are complementary.

In the second book, Coons and Sugarman envision an education system that prizes diversity and allows individuals to challenge the prevailing views of the ruling majority. They have not given up on desegregation. Rather than force students to attend schools where they are not wanted or may not want to be, Coons and Sugarman prescribe choice as a tool to build voluntary solidly integrated communities. They properly recognize that Black students bore the burden of being bused beyond the bounds of their own communities. Coons and Sugarman are sanguine about the inevitability of majority-Black schools, as long as the students in them are there as a matter of parental choice and not discrimination.

In a separate essay that he wrote much later, Jack tells a story of his involvement in a Kansas City, Missouri, desegregation case from 1990.[44] A federal court had ordered the district to desegregate, but there were an insufficient number of white students to realize a meaningful plan of racial balance. Adjoining public school districts that might have helped the city achieve some level of racial integration refused to participate. A St. Louis businessman stepped up to the plate and agreed to pay the costs for a group of Black residents to intervene in the case. The parents had received guarantees from more than one hundred private schools in the area to take the students at a per-pupil cost significantly below that of the public schools. The parent plan promised to reduce racial isolation and improve academic achievement. The public school district rejected it.

When Jack tried to enlist the ACLU to take the side of the parents, he was turned down. The teachers' union weighed in against the proposal. Admittedly, there were First Amendment issues at the time that would have blocked any plan involving religious institutions, but some nondenominational schools were very willing to participate. When the First Amendment issues became ripe for review by the Supreme Court in later years, many organizations that had historically identified themselves with pleas for racial equality either silently stood by or lined up against changes that would have allowed Black and Brown children access to more desirable schools. The politics of surrogacy is alive and well in America.

* * *

Coons subsequently undertook a deep philosophical inquiry on the concept of equality that animated his commitment to choice. In a book on the topic co-authored with Patrick Brennan, a former student and legal scholar at Arizona State University, the two define equality as "the capacity of every rational person to advance in moral self-perfection through diligent intention of correct behaviors towards other persons."[45] The thick volume from 1999, not a light read, is immersed in the tradition of moral philosophy. It is premised on the fundamental equality of all people, but the authors' is not an equality that can be measured by academic achievement scores, the speed of an athlete, or the talent of a musician blowing sound through a horn. Theirs is the innate equality we share freely to live a good life capable of benefiting ourselves and those around us. It is not appropriated on the basis of race or class or cultured grooming.

What does this have to do with choice? *Everything.*

There is a lot to draw from when it comes to Jack Coons's bibliography. I turn here to an article he wrote for *First Things* in 1992, which is reprinted in the Notre Dame collection. *First Things* is a magazine on religion founded by a Lutheran cleric, Richard J. Neuhaus, who converted to become a Catholic priest. It can be a bit politically conservative for my taste, and Jack could tell you better than I how one can lose an audience of liberal intellectuals by introducing the element of religion in an ongoing conversation. But take pause before you take flight. Hear what Coons has to say, even though you may not like it. You don't even need to believe in God—although Jack would probably say it would help for many reasons in many ways.

In *Book II*, Coons and Sugarman had defined family as "a community composed of a child and one or more adults in close affective and physical relation that is expected to endure at least through childhood."[46] Having established that parental choice in American education is a privilege appropriated on the basis of income and therefore race, the *First Things* article, published under the title "School Choice and Simple Justice," explains why this is intolerable.[47] It poses some tough questions for those who continue to support the status quo: Is there anything more precious to parents than their own child? Is a parent's understanding of the child's needs dependent on race or class? Assuming all schools convey values, is there any justification for allowing only advantaged families to choose schools that reflect their own values?

In passing, Coons summarizes the legacy of the enduring system, mentioning "intolerance, racial segregation, religious bigotry, discrimination against the poor, [and] irrational fiscal distinctions among districts," branding it a "masterpiece of social hierarchy."[48] The greatest harm appropriated by the prevailing education bureaucracy, according to Coons, is that it robs unrich parents of their dignity. The most obvious chance these folks have to influence the world is rooted in the message they embody through their offspring. As Coons puts it, "Children are the books written by the poor." For that reason, "choice is the therapy for the family's sense of its own dignity."[49]

A parent's lack of discretion over the education of a child, in a larger systemic context where others can exercise it, reinforces a sense of powerlessness among the unrich. Worse yet, it underscores a societal determination, sustained by governmental policy, that some people are better prepared to adjudicate the best interests of their own children than others. This demeaning lesson is bestowed on parent and child alike, and it is destructive to the family's sense of agency. Demands for community control, as occurred in Brooklyn's Ocean Hill–Brownsville, were an angry reaction to the prevailing attitude of those who made education decisions. The next generation of activists, epitomized by the likes of Howard Fuller, would turn to school choice after desegregation and community control failed to rescue the dignity they sought. The proposals they championed were more of Jack Coons than of Milton Friedman. Coons prevailed in the policy debate—at least up until very recently.

In the forward to the Notre Dame collection of Jack's essays, the editors include a quote from Terry Moe, whose influential book with John Chubb did more than any other scholarly work to advance the Friedman model. It reads, "The modern arguments for vouchers have less to do with free markets than with . . . the commonsense notion that disadvantaged kids should never be forced to attend failing schools and that they should be given as many attractive options as possible."[50] Apparently, some of those who pushed back against Coons within the choice camp were more persuaded by the social justice argument than those defenders of the status quo who positioned themselves on the outside.

* * *

Notre Dame celebrated the publication of the Coons collection by their university press with a launch at the law school in the spring of 2023 titled "Honoring Jack." Dean Marcus Cole opened the event with an overview of Jack's impactful career, and Nicole Stelle Garnett, one of the book's editors, presided over the remainder of the proceedings. I was one of several panelists who were invited to comment on the book and Jack's important contribution to the cause of school choice.[51] Rick Garnett, another of the book's editors, closed the panel by introducing Jack.

As mentioned earlier, I had known the Garnetts, two distinguished members of the law school faculty, for years. I had spoken there several times before when my book *Choosing Equality* was published, and was later invited to write an essay for the law review on President Obama's education agenda.[52] In 2000, Rick had written a comprehensive review of my book and we began to talk, which marked the beginning of our professional relationship.[53]

As plans for the ceremony materialized and I got a sense of how it would take shape, I began to wonder whether Jack knew what to expect. All of the speakers that day were strong supporters of school choice, but unlike Jack and myself, most, including Nicole and Rick, subscribed to Milton Friedman's market-based approach that Jack had made a career of contesting. I wondered if I should alert Jack in case he wanted to clarify his position when it was his turn to speak. Jack had just taken a bad fall and was struggling with health issues, so I did not want to put a damper on his celebratory event either. A few weeks before it took place, I got a call from Jack. He told me that he had just called Nicole to explain the difference between his position and Friedman's. She told him that she was well aware of that and it was fine.

Except for Jack's difficulty with the electronic hookup that was supposed to Zoom him into the event that afternoon but kept interrupting him, the day went smoothly. Each of us laid out our positions in a respectful way. Whether they entirely agreed with him, all the panelists paid tribute to the man who had devoted his life to advancing the interests of families who were not well served by their local public schools, those whom Jack would refer to as "the unrich." At a time when many college communities greet disagreement with hostility, I left Notre Dame that day hopeful and proud to be part of such a collegial gathering convened to honor my dear friend Jack Coons.

5

Diane Ravitch

A Different Voice

I first met Diane Ravitch in 1994 at a meeting convened in New York by Edward Costikyan. Diane had just completed two years of service as assistant secretary of education under President George H. W. Bush. Rudolph Giuliani had been recently sworn in as a first-term mayor of New York. Costikyan was a partner at the powerhouse New York law firm of Paul, Weiss, Rifkin, Wharton & Garrison, and a longtime player in city and state politics. His 1962 election as chair of the New York County Democratic Committee, defeating the notorious political boss Carmine DeSapio, is marked by historians as a turning point that ended Tammany Hall's control over the party apparatus. Costikyan later served on anticorruption panels for Republican and Democratic governors, including Nelson Rockefeller and Mario Cuomo. His book on the reform of the Democratic Party, one of five that he authored, is a classic that draws on his own intimate knowledge and experience.[1]

Costikyan was one of many mainstream Democrats in New York who were persuaded by Giuliani that his election would usher in a new era of bipartisan government.[2] Running in a rematch to unseat Mayor David Dinkins, the city's first African American mayor whose popularity began to wane by the end of his first term, the Republican former prosecutor had managed to line up an impressive list of Democratic endorsements—including former mayor Edward Koch and his deputy mayor Robert F. Wagner Jr., son of the former mayor who was a champion of municipal labor and grandson of the New Deal senator who helped President Franklin Roosevelt cobble together legislative packages. Herman Badillo, a leading figure in the Puerto Rican community and lifelong Democrat, was nominated for city comptroller as part of a fusion ticket led by the Republican mayoral candidate.

It is not unreasonable to suggest that, beyond the endorsements mentioned, mainstream Democrats had a larger role to play, intentionally or not, in helping the Republican challenger unseat the incumbent mayor.

Radical Dreamers. Joseph P. Viteritti, Oxford University Press. © Oxford University Press (2025). DOI: 10.1093/oso/9780197827109.003.0005

A damaging investigation launched by Governor Mario Cuomo into Dinkins's handling (some would say mishandling) of the 1991 riots in Crown Heights, Brooklyn—that escalated tensions between Blacks and Orthodox Jews—clearly did not help. Nor did a decision by teachers' union president Sandra Feldman to remain neutral rather than endorse the Democratic candidate, as was normally the practice with her organization.

Immediately after his victory, Giuliani made good on his pledge for bipartisanship when he endorsed Mario Cuomo, a mainstream Democratic liberal, for reelection over his Republican challenger George Pataki. Giuliani also kept a safe distance from GOP firebrand and US House Speaker Newt Gingrich, whose Contract with America was moving national Republicans further to the right. Yes, this is the same Rudolph (Rudy) Giuliani who, after aligning himself with Donald Trump, was indicted in several states for conspiring to overthrow the results of the 2020 election and was disbarred in New York state and the District of Columbia.[3]

The bipartisan rapprochement in 1990s New York occurred while the national Democratic Party was making a decided move to the political center under the leadership of President Bill Clinton. Giuliani and Clinton found common ground on policies in the areas of criminal justice, welfare reform, and education. They enjoyed a mutually supportive relationship until it became apparent that Rudy and Hillary Clinton both had designs on the same US Senate seat vacated in New York by the retirement of Daniel Patrick Moynihan. Although the star federal prosecutor ran for mayor mostly on his pledge to bring down record crime rates, he drew some Democrats' attention, including mine, by his determination to do something about the failing school system. In 1999, Giuliani had asked me to serve as his chancellor of schools, after his very public falling out with his own handpicked schools chief, Rudy Crew. I gave the offer serious thought and met with the central school board to discuss my nomination, but for both personal and professional reasons decided not to pursue it.

When Giuliani first took office in 1994, he had asked Ed Costikyan to bring together a group of education experts who could help the new administration fashion an agenda on school reform. I had worked on Giuliani's mayoral transition, as I had on Mayors Dinkins's and Koch's before that. Costikyan had also solicited my thoughts on whom else to invite to his gathering. I immediately mentioned Diane Ravitch, whose history of the city schools was definitive, and who had just spent the past two years advising the president of the United States and his secretary of education, Lamar Alexander.

I did not know Diane yet, but when the paperback edition of *The Great School Wars* was published in 1988, she had made some kind remarks about my book on the New York City schools in a new introduction.[4] I already had read most of her major work. Costikyan needed no explanation about who Diane Ravitch was, nor convincing that she belonged at the meeting. She would be the most respected educator in the room.

The Costikyan meeting was held at the plush Manhattan offices of Paul, Weiss. The seasoned political operative had summoned about a half-dozen of us. Upon arrival, Costikyan's assistant escorted us into a beautiful wood-paneled conference room with a long mahogany table. Not yet seated, we were chatting it up with small talk to warm the conversation when in walked Diane Ravitch. I can still picture her entering the room. She was wearing blue jeans, a red-and-white checkered shirt, and a pair of white sneakers. You can't imagine anything more incongruous than the sight of a woman passing through the corridors of a white-shoe law firm looking as if she was on her way to a Texas barbecue. Another person would have seemed out of place, but nobody would consider Ravitch out of place at a discussion about the future of education in New York. By her demeanor alone, she had made a statement to the rest of us before even taking a seat: "This lady plays by her own rules."

Ravitch walked directly over to me and said, "I liked your book." I don't remember anything else that happened at that meeting. The next thing I knew, after determining we both lived in Brooklyn Heights, the two of us were sitting beside each other in a subway car making our way back home. She told me that she had recently accepted a position as a research professor in the School of Education at New York University. I held a similar position at NYU's Wagner School. Given our common interest in education policy, she suggested we might consider collaborating on something. She then handed me a draft of an essay she was writing for a book of readings and said I should let her know what I thought. The title of the essay was "Somebody's Children." When Diane informed me that the topic was school choice, I alerted her that I was not inclined to be supportive. We agreed to talk further.

* * *

"Somebody's Children" was a plea for justice grounded in the values of equality, excellence, and pluralism.[5] To urge equality without excellence would be counterintuitive, she wrote—unless we were striving for mediocrity. Choice, while not a panacea, could offer a path to excellence and preserve diversity in a pluralistic society. Despite some progress over time, Ravitch conceded, the United States stands apart from other advanced democracies by its overall weak performance on international assessments and gaps in achievement measured by race and class. Our country also stands apart from others, she continued, by its reluctance to provide public support for students who may want to attend schools other than those run by state authorities, including independent and religious schools.

Ravitch begins her essay with a quote from a speech by Richard Riley, President Clinton's secretary of education at the time. In frank remarks about the condition of American education before a room of faculty and students at Georgetown University, Riley noted, "Some schools are excellent, some are improving, some have the remarkable capacity to change for the better, and some should never be called schools at all."[6] Ravitch picks up on the last line to rhetorically ask whose children it is that attend those schools not worthy to be called schools. As if speaking directly to a presumed set of educated middle-class readers, she responds to her own query by stating, "Not mine. Not yours." Then she adds to the list of those exempted from such a fate: the secretary (of education), the president, the vice president, the mayor, the school superintendent, and even the schoolteacher. The parents whose children are "assigned," "compelled," and "condemned" to such schools not deserving to be called schools, she observes, are most probably poor and either Black or Hispanic.

Ravitch then picks up on a quote from education philosopher John Dewey that Riley used to end his remarks, which states, "What the best and wisest parent wants for his [and may I say her] child, that must be what the community wants for all of its children. Any other ideal for our schools is narrow and unlovely; it destroys our democracy."[7] The quote elicits another question from Ravitch, asking who these "best and wisest" parents might be and what they would do if their children were assigned to schools that are not fit to be called schools. Responding to her own question again, she replies that if these parents were well-to-do or middle class they either would move to a better school district or send their kids to private schools. If they were less fortunate, they would be forced to stay put.

Getting through the first few pages of this essay evoked some familiar sentiment in me. I remembered Ron Edmonds's insistence that educational equality must be defined in terms of effective teaching and learning. I recalled community activists in Ocean Hill–Brownsville demanding influence and voice in their children's schooling. I reconsidered Jack Coons's discourses on agency and dignity that I had absorbed as compelling academic treatises, but was reluctant to embrace out of allegiance to the narrowly defined idea of public education that had never quite materialized. "Somebody's Children" put a human face on it all once again and, after considerable discussion with its author, gave me license to consider taking the next step in the long journey of my own education about education.

The remainder of Ravitch's essay maps out a proposal for school choice and addresses a host of arguments commonly launched by its opponents. Citing Jack Coons and other choice proponents, it is clear her plan was crafted to help parents whose children have been stuck in those places that ought not to be called schools. Ravitch calls for means-tested scholarships that would provide access to public, independent, and religious schools with priority given to children who attend underperforming institutions. Like Jack Coons, she argues that a scholarship program would enable disempowered parents to choose schools that are not only stronger academically but also more reflective of their own values. Ravitch would set minimum academic standards for all public and nonpublic schools accepting scholarship students.

Ravitch assails the large, cafeteria-style comprehensive high schools popular in America that try to be all things to all pupils, but meet the individual needs of very few. Reaching back into her own history of the New York City public schools, she recounts how the common school model adopted in the nineteenth century was very much an anti-Catholic project designed to assimilate the immigrant population into the culture of mainstream American Protantism, all the while pretending to be religiously neutral. More choice could reduce conflict within public schools, she claims, by no longer forcing parents to accept a single model of education.

Acknowledging that she once in 1983 wrote an article for the *New Republic* denouncing tax credits for private school tuition because they would compromise the independence of nonpublic schools, Ravitch recounts a visit she made to England in 1992 that began to change her mind. Originally there to learn more about their national curriculum and competency standards, she had been curious about "grant-maintained" schools she had heard about. Under that program, parents could vote to select institutions outside their local school districts and receive tuition support from the national government. When Ravitch requested a visit to one, she was surprised to be taken to a Catholic girls' school. While there, she was impressed with the quality of instruction, the racial diversity of the students, the condition of the facilities, the food in the cafeteria, and most significantly the strong sense of community similar to that heralded by Coleman and others who had studied Catholic schools in the United States. The experience motivated her to learn more about practices in other democratic countries.

Convinced that too many schools in America are "educationally bankrupt," Ravitch engaged head on those who might object to her proposal. In response to concerns that scholarships to religious schools might violate the First Amendment, she mentions Pell Grants that students can use at any accredited college, and cites Harvard constitutional law professor Lawrence Tribe opining that such a program would pass judicial scrutiny.[8] Responding to concerns that choice might deplete enrollments at public schools, she declares it would be better to close failing institutions. To those concerned that school choice might skim stronger students off the rosters of public schools, she underscores the requirement that seats be reserved for students in underperforming schools.

Writing in 1997, Diane Ravitch does not want to end public education; she wants to improve it. Aware that reform takes time, she recognizes our collective responsibility to provide an exit for students left in failing institutions so that they have an opportunity to learn. Underperforming students don't need good schools tomorrow; they need them today, she proclaims. That is what Dewey's "best and wisest" parent wants. That is what every parent deserves. Sounding much like Ron Edmonds, Ravitch implores her readers, "Public policy must relentlessly seek to replicate schools that demonstrate the ability to educate children from impoverished backgrounds instead of perpetuating and rewarding those that use the pupil's circumstances as a rationale for failure."[9]

Three years would pass from the day we met in Ed Costikyan's office before Diane Ravitch and I published the first of four books we edited together. The last chapter in that volume was a revised and updated version of "Somebody's Children" that she insisted we include.

* * *

Diane Silvers Ravitch was born in Houston, Texas, in 1938. She was one of eight children of Jewish parents who worked hard and struggled to remain in the middle class. Her mother was an immigrant, her father a high school dropout. Young Diane excelled in school. After graduating from Wellesley College, she went on to Columbia University, earning a PhD in history under the mentorship of Professor Lawrence Cremin. Ravitch had taught as an adjunct professor at Teachers College before departing for the Bush administration, and I had assumed she would return there. When I asked her about it, she reported that the faculty did not want her back because she was deemed too "conservative." It says a lot about a university when it rejects an accomplished scholar, an alumna no less, with a record of public service at the highest level—but Teachers College was not unusual then and it wouldn't be now for following the same narrow-minded course.

Before saying more about that, I need to pause to consider the matter of political labeling because it is central to this book project. Although I have made insinuations along the way, I already have probably delayed the point too long. Ordinarily the term "conservative" is used to identify someone who wants to preserve the status quo, who holds on to traditions. Not so with regard to education policy, especially in academia. In university settings, those people who seek to overhaul elementary and secondary education, who call for reform, are commonly labeled conservatives, especially when their agenda conflicts with prevailing political views of the tenured faculty. It is a clever and insidious form of branding. "Conservative" is not a neutral term in academia. Being identified as such in a university setting can result in isolation or rejection in a climate that proudly claims to be liberal. Hard to believe? Well, here we have Exhibit A: One of Columbia University's most distinguished alumnae being shunned by her own institution in the name of liberalism because she has a different point of view that her former colleagues describe as "conservative." I have known some very capable scholars who have been frozen out of university careers for carrying the brand.

More outrageous in this particular case of punitive labeling is that the position Ravitch took on school reform was very much intended to improve the education of students whose instructional needs have been neglected, most of whom are poor and minority. As explained in the previous chapter, there are advocates for school choice who ascribe to the free-market philosophy of Milton Friedman and proudly consider themselves political conservatives. Their model of choice, as we have seen, is concerned with protecting individual liberty and maximizing market efficiency rather than marshaling government resources to redistribute opportunity; yet these same people would hold that a free-market system could serve disadvantaged students better than we do now. Who can say? We are starting at a low bar of comparison with the existing system. The key point here, nevertheless, is that the scholarship proposal put forward by Diane Ravitch in "Somebody's Children" is very much in the tradition of Coons and Sugarman and those choice advocates identified as the "voucher left."

At the same time, many opponents of school vouchers and scholarships like to pretend that the voucher left doesn't exist. Their use of terminology is a rhetorical political maneuver. Rather than deal with the issue on the merits, they would prefer to do battle with a conservative model of education that had rarely been translated into public policy, at least as far as the choice issue was concerned at the time. Since many of them present themselves as advocates—let's say *surrogates*—for people of color and poor folks, it is more difficult for them to justify why they have problems with policies designed to improve the lives of those who struggle within our schools.

Diane Ravitch went to New York University with the encouragement of Naomi Levine, a potent figure who led the university's fundraising campaign and was instrumental in developing it into a top-tier university. Levine, trained as a lawyer, had a long history of political activism with liberal organizations, including the American Jewish Congress and the NAACP Legal Defense Fund. She knew Ravitch well, understood her politics, and had no doubts that the controversial education historian could enrich the intellectual life and reputation of the university.

Diane was given an appointment as a research professor without tenure. I had been recruited to a similar position at NYU in 1987 by Alan Altshuler, dean of the Graduate School of Public Administration (renamed the Wagner School). With such an appointment I was expected to raise money for my own research and also assumed other duties at the school with some teaching. Alan had developed a working relationship with Koch's deputy mayor Robert Wagner Jr., whom I knew well from his role as city hall's liaison to the schools chancellor, and the three of us would meet at Alan's apartment for breakfast regularly to discuss projects. I lost my principal supporter at the school when Altshuler left NYU to head up the Taubman Center for State and Local Government at Harvard.

Diane was familiar with people at the John M. Olin Foundation, a conservative institution dedicated to free-market principles, and thought we might interest them in providing a grant to establish a research program. Working on the Giuliani transition, I had made the acquaintance of Peter Flanigan, who chaired the mayor's education committee and, unbeknownst to me, was an influential trustee at Olin. I expressed doubts to Diane that a conservative foundation would support the kind of school choice we professed. She thought they were worth a try and proved to be right. After an initial inquiry, we were encouraged to apply for a multiyear grant to establish a research program at NYU. Flanigan and Jim Piereson, the executive director at Olin, assured us independence in our thinking and writing if funding materialized, and they kept their word.

My collaboration with Diane Ravitch was not received well by the new leadership of the Wagner School. Despite the fact that I had written a well-reviewed book on the city's schools and had served as an advisor to urban superintendents in New York, Boston and San Francisco, I was never asked to teach a course on education policy. One member of the faculty had actually cautioned me against working with Diane Ravitch because of her "dangerous ideas" about education. It was risky for me, as a nontenued faculty member to take up with her.

Diane and I went ahead with the Olin proposal. I was honest with Flanigan and Piereson about the problems I was having at my home institution and the possibility that our project could be thwarted. They were concerned, but encouraged us to proceed. The funding was approved and, after some haggling, was accepted by the university. We used it to establish the Program on Education and Civil Society as a joint venture between the School of Education and the Wagner School, with the two of us serving as cochairs and myself as director.

* * *

Aside from school choice, there were two policy realms where Diane Ravitch's scholarship had caught my attention even before I met her: school desegregation and competency standards. Her thoughts on the latter were at one with the kind of initiatives that Ron Edmonds had cultivated as a senior advisor to the chancellor of schools in New York. I had always admired her independence and the unusual way she spoke her mind regardless of how it would be received. She was one of the few academicians who responded to James Coleman favorably when he released his findings on the counterproductive effects of forced busing in 1975.[10]

Just months after *Coleman II* was featured in the *New York Times*, Ravitch published an op-ed there under the title "Busing: The Solution That Has Failed to Solve."[11] Both houses of Congress had recently passed measures prohibiting the Department of Health, Education and Welfare from ordering busing to promote integration. Ravitch alluded to a young senator from Delaware with a strong civil rights record named Joseph Biden who had led the legislative effort. Signaling agreement, she noted a judicial paradox wherein the court that originally outlawed pupil assignments based on race in *Brown* was of late doing just that to enforce *Brown*. In a subsequent article in *Public Interest*, she called out those who unfairly charged Coleman with subverting the civil rights cause.[12]

Taking up Coleman II in the *Times* piece, she featured the controversy around the report and how the evidence offered to refute it was mixed at best. Ravitch was especially attentive to the debate within the African American community. Citing research questioning the impact of integration on student achievement, she quoted an NAACP lawyer saying, "The purpose of the litigation is to eradicate state-created segregation. . . . It has nothing to do with the quality of education." She then introduces Black intellectuals like Charles Hamilton and Derrick Bell who challenged the civil rights organization. Identifying Bell as "a spokesman for those who believe that the focus should be on the immediate educational needs of inner-city black children," she quotes his reference to busing as "a right without a remedy." Responding to the above comment by the NAACP attorney, Bell retorted, "That explains their insistence in balancing the public schools of Detroit, even though Detroit has a school board that is majority black, a black superintendent, and nearly 80% black pupils."

Ravitch also mentions a reaction to the busing issue by the sociologist Nathan Glazer, an ardent opponent, who describes it as "legal discrimination, state action on the basis of race."[13] Glazer goes on to argue, "The Supreme Court isn't sacrosanct. It was wrong on Dred Scott, wrong on Plessy v. Ferguson, and it's wrong on this one. Race should not be the basis of public action." Glazer's position is similar to that taken by Ravitch at the opening of the essay, where she discusses the paradoxical nature of Supreme Court jurisprudence.

Let's pause here for a moment to take up the topic of political labeling again with a particular focus on those who opposed busing: Coleman, Ravitch, Bell, and Glazer. Few would deny that the NAACP and its band of litigators are worthy of the liberal label. Should all of those who oppose busing be denied it? Does such opposition automatically entitle (or, in academia, burden) someone to the conservative imprint? There is certainly a population of individuals who resist integration out of pure racist sentiment. Most would neither seek nor deserve to don the liberal mantle. Would the conservative imprint automatically fit one who harbors such bigotry? The answer to that question probably depends on whom you ask.

As far as the four individuals just mentioned are concerned, we need to underscore the fact that Coleman, Ravitch, Bell, and Glazer all deplored state-enforced (de jure) segregation of the races and believed the federal government should act to undo it. It was forced integration through busing in instances of de facto segregation that they questioned. I do believe that each and every one of them wanted to roll back decades of educational practice that undermined the progress of minority and poor populations. They did not always agree on how to do it, even though they were all skeptical about the utility of school busing and the priority given to forced integration.

So how might we define the philosophical instincts of the four when it comes to education policy? I did not know James Coleman, but was familiar with his work. If I had to describe him, I would call him a data-driven empiricist who did not preoccupy himself with political labels. The Nathan Glazer I knew was a liberal who converted to neoconservatism and finally declared himself a "multiculturalist."[14] He was an honorable man. His position on busing and disapproval of employing race as a basis for public action can reasonably qualify him as conservative. He invoked the same argument against affirmative action.[15] A thorough reading of chapter 2 should have helped place Derrick Bell in all this. Diane Ravitch considers herself a former conservative for the views she once held. It says so right there on her webpage.[16] As discussed earlier, the model of school choice she endorsed clearly belonged in the voucher-left camp. Her 1978 book *The Revisionists Revised* was a battle cry against Marxist education historians. That alone ordinarily would not qualify her as conservative, except, I suppose, among Marxist historians.[17]

Diane Ravitch, along with anyone else, is entitled to identify herself however she chooses. It is not my objective here to award labels. My purpose is to illustrate how difficult it can be sometimes to make such assignments. The same individual might lean left on some issues and right on others. Political identification can be a fluid process. That is why political labeling is susceptible to abuse and manipulation—and why if you are trying to figure out where a person fits, you should start with how that person self-identifies and work from there. Be aware of what's at stake. Be aware of who else has labeled them and why.[18]

* * *

Let me now tell you more about Diane Ravitch's early writing on deseg-regation. She was clearly influenced by the work of Derrick Bell. In a 1976 article in the *Teachers College Record*, she chastises federal policymakers who since 1954 perpetuated the view that "all-black schools are inferior."[19] A year later she cited Bell in an *American Scholar* piece, where, in light of *Coleman II*, he criticizes civil rights lawyers for refusing to accept changing demo-graphic realities in which "the cities get blacker and the educational needs of black children are ignored."[20] In the same paragraph, she quotes Ron Edmonds, who "has complained that desegregation orders frequently deny black parents the right to make educational choices for their children."[21]

Isn't it ironic that many opponents of school choice today attack it for its potential resegregating effect, especially with regard to charter schools, even though children of parents empowered to exercise choice attend charter or nonpublic schools because their parents want them there? Is it surprising that a larger percentage of Black and Brown families take advantage of choice when it is their children who are disproportionately assigned to failing urban public schools they want to escape? Would it be better if they had no choice but to stay there? Is choice really the issue when it comes to racial isola-tion in American education? Is such resistance to the self-determination of Black and Brown people an expression of American liberal values? Is it a liberal predisposition to believe that *people other than their own par-ents* are better equipped to determine what is best for a Black or Brown child?

It was not uncommon for Ravitch to cite Bell on race.[22] When Bell's provocative book *And We Are Not Saved* was published in 1987, she pro-vided a jacket endorsement stating he was "one of the most original and brilliant thinkers in America today."[23] In fact, they developed a relation-ship around their conversations. Ravitch attests to this in a more recent 2021 opinion piece written for the *New York Daily News* responding to the uproar over critical race theory (CRT) in the public schools.[24] Referring to Bell as the "father" of CRT and a "friend," she rejects claims that he was a Marxist or antiwhite. Ravitch reminisces about exchanges they used to have about racial progress, she believing it was assured with *Brown*, Bell contending that changes it imposed were superficial and minimal "because racism was so deeply rooted in American institutions." Ravitch apparently agrees with him now.

Diane Ravitch and Ron Edmonds both contributed to *Shades of Brown*, the last volume that Derrick Bell edited. Diane composed a short history on the meaning of desegregation, affirming that social scientists have consistently resisted the possibility that "Black Culture might serve as a positive source of identity."[25] In the last chapter before Bell's conclusion, Ron discussed his research and recounted his argument that having effective schools for minority and poor pupils was the proper response to educational inequality. He did not let the occasion pass without once more taking the opportunity to castigate Coleman and Jencks for popularizing the misperception that "family background causes pupil performance," and its corollary "schools don't matter" assumption.[26]

Bell's collection appeared a year before *Coleman III*. I don't know how Ron would have responded to it. I do know how Diane did. If Ron had read her *Phi Delta Kappan* analysis of *Coleman III* that appeared immediately after its release, he might have felt better about Coleman. Diane could have assured him that Coleman's findings on how private and Catholic schools successfully educate students from different backgrounds was an affirmation of the idea that "schools do matter."[27] She recognized the reversal and respected Coleman for it.

Ravitch wrote a more complete overview of Coleman's work for a festschrift published in 1993, where she devoted nearly as much space to defending him as explaining him. She admired his character and will to take a stand when his own research findings took him in controversial directions, declaring, "Coleman is not an ordinary man."[28] Commenting on the reaction to *Coleman II*, she wrote, "Coleman discovered that there were few rewards for the person who sings out that the emperor has no clothes, but he also discovered that there is a price to be paid for refuting the conventional wisdom."[29]

As controversial as *Coleman II* was, it was *Coleman III* that brought the most vicious attacks upon the distinguished sociologist. By yoking private schools, and especially Catholic religious schools, to the American common school ideal of a decent education for all, Coleman had stepped on the third rail of white liberal orthodoxy that uncompromisingly demanded a strict constitutional separation between church and state. Ravitch points out how the *New York Times*, which had granted Coleman considerable space to discuss his consequential research on busing, published two opinion pieces condemning his proposal for tuition tax credits and his use of social science data to shape public policy.[30] As Ravitch tells us, the paper accused Coleman of being a hired gun for President Ronald Reagan to advance the choice agenda, even though Coleman had supported choice as far back as 1978 (writing the foreword to the Coons and Sugarman volume) and *Coleman III* had been commissioned during the Carter administration.

Praising Coleman's exemplary courage throughout his career, Ravitch concludes, "Having learned through experience what happens to those who are politically incorrect, he seems to have developed a taste for smashing icons and enduring obloquy."[31]

Ravitch's commentary on Coleman is utterly revealing. What she admired in him was what she expected from herself. She revels in smashing icons and exposing the naked emperor. She's comfortable making us feel uncomfortable. She did then; she does now. That is what made the prospect of working with her so alluring.

* * *

During the eighteen months she served as assistant secretary of education under President George H. W. Bush, Diane Ravitch led the federal government's effort to create voluntary state and national standards. Following her tenure in Washington, President Bill Clinton's secretary of education Richard Riley appointed her to a seven-year stint on the National Assessment Governing Board (1997–2004), the body that oversees the National Assessment of Educational Progress (NAEP) testing program, commonly referred to as the Nation's Report Card. Diane had a long-term interest in the topic of education standards and testing, as did I, and we agreed on the important role they must play in school improvement.[32]

The year after I met her (1995), Diane published a book on the topic.[33] Commissioned by the Brookings Institution for completion after her government service, the new volume was billed as a "users guide" for parents and the general public. It would introduce readers to the history, purposes, and advantages of standards and assessments. As she explained it, nothing occupied more of her time and energy while in Washington. In addition to targeting basic skills, these efforts would reach into the study of science, history, geography, civics, the arts, English, and foreign languages. Commenting on the politics, she noted that the standards campaign, while controversial, was bipartisan in nature, carried on through the administrations of Presidents Bush and Clinton with strong support among the nation's governors.

Ravitch portrayed the movement as a response to the nation's declining student performance dating back to the seventies and a more recent slide in our ranking on international comparisons. She argued that a standards-based regimen of testing could serve as an early-warning system that would allow educators to pinpoint weaknesses and address them. What most appealed to me about the new movement is how it altered the terms of the conversation about educational equality from a focus on resources and inputs to a focus on outcomes. Of course, the distribution of resources would need to be fair, even compensatory toward those disadvantaged and under-served, in order to address the learning gap defined by race and class—but now we could no longer deem the struggle a success unless there was tan-gible evidence that all students were reaching acceptable levels of academic achievement. Commenting on the evolution of the new thinking, Ravitch emphasized that "many of those concerned about educational equity con-cluded that low expectations were contributing to the poor performance of students."[34]

No responsible person was promising that standards would correct all that was wrong with public schooling in America. If the effort were not carefully designed and orchestrated, it could cause more harm than good. We had learned that lesson a decade earlier sitting in the schools chancellor's office in New York City with our implementation of promotional policy for the lower and middle grades and our response to the state's efforts to upgrade graduation standards for the high schools. Testing must be coordinated with curriculum standards that define what students are to learn by subject and grade. Curriculum materials must be developed. Teachers must be trained. Resources must be made available to provide remediation for students who fall behind. We saw that standards can be applied to hold not only stu-dents but also schools and ultimately the system as a whole accountable for decent performance. These same rules of accountability can be utilized in a system of school choice that includes public and nonpublic schools. Any public or nonpublic schools that do not meet a certain threshold of aca-demic performance might and should be deemed ineligible for funding to participate.

* * *

Between 1994 and 1996, Diane and I organized a Working Group on School Organization and Educational Quality at NYU. The purpose of the seminar series was to bring together educators, government officials, journalists, business leaders, foundation executives, and anybody who was interested in school reform to hear from innovative leaders from around the country who had launched groundbreaking projects to change the face of American education so that schools could respond to the needs of all children. City council members, state legislators, and members of the New York City Board of Education and the New York State Board of Regents came to the presentations. Some of Diane's colleagues from the School of Education attended, fewer of mine from the Wagner School did.

Our lineup of guest speakers included Ted Kolderie, the man who had crafted the nation's first charter school law in Minnesota in 1991; Yvonne Chan, who had spearheaded the growth of charter schools in California; and Deborah McGriff, by then the former superintendent of schools in Detroit who had become vice president of the Edison Project, an educational management organization that had altered its original mission to run public schools on a contractual basis to focus on curriculum development and training.

For me the most memorable session of the series occurred when Howard Fuller came to tell us about his work in Wisconsin. The former superintendent of schools had been instrumental in persuading the state legislature to pass a law in 1990 that would provide state scholarships for low-income students in Milwaukee to attend private schools, finally making a reality of the kind of programs Jack Coons and others had been advocating for more than a decade.

What most affected me the day Howard visited was the reaction to his talk I got from one of my Wagner School colleagues. It was transformative for me. I had heard Howard speak before. A former basketball star with a PhD, Howard is a compelling presence in front of a room with a passionate message about the need to alter the educational prospects for Black children living in cities. When Howard completed his presentation, the same colleague of mine who had warned me of Diane Ravitch's "dangerous" ideas came over to tell me how much she was moved by Howard. She then went on about what a shame it was that a man of his talent was devoting his energy supporting vouchers rather than improving public schools for poor kids. When I innocently asked her what public schools her children attended, she looked at me rather quizzically and told me her children attended a private school in Manhattan that she and her husband thought better fit their needs. I won't say anything more about that interaction other than that I am sure this accomplished education scholar, a white woman living a comfortable lifestyle, truly believed herself to be an advocate for underserved students.

As interest in our seminar grew, Diane and I realized that what we were hearing deserved a wider audience. That led to our first written collaboration. In 1996 we wrote an essay for *Public Interest*, a neoconservative magazine edited by Nathan Glazer and Irving Kristol. I had known Nat from Harvard and Diane knew, well, just about everybody. We boldly titled it, "A New Vision for City Schools."[35] It was the lead article for the winter edition. We opened it with a critique of what we called "the factory model" of schooling. A remnant of the nineteenth century guided by Taylorist principles of scientific management, factory-model schooling was characterized by a top-down hierarchic structure that imposed uniform rules on teachers and students alike to educate the hoards of children brought to its doors through immigration. For many years this large bureaucratic machine did an adequate job, we said, processing the raw material of newcomers in need of literacy, numeracy, basic hygiene, and eventually gainful employment and American citizenship. As the nation approached the twenty-first century, that model had become outdated.

Most problematic about the large and rickety structures that govern urban school systems, we contended, is that they function primarily to fit the needs of central bureaucrats who treat both teachers and students as interchangeable parts that must conform to a uniform agenda producing mediocre results. What we imagined instead was a system characterized by diversity, choice, quality, and accountability. "Instead of a system that regulates identical schools," we proposed "a system in which academic standards are the same for all but where schools vary widely," so that "the schools are as diverse as teachers' imagination and will; students and their families choose the school that best meets their needs and interests; and central authorities only perform a monitoring and auditing function to assure educational quality and fiscal integrity."[36] The vision Diane and I put forward was not just a fantasy, however. We were hearing firsthand about alternatives that sprouted up in various parts of the country and we wanted to tell the story.

In sections that followed, we highlighted a number of innovations being implemented in school districts throughout the country including charter schools, contracting arrangements, and a variety of choice programs. We praised charter schools, then operative in thirteen states (now in forty-six), for the semiautonomy they enjoyed within a structure of public account-ability that would allow teachers and other school personnel to innovate. We welcomed the appearance of education management organizations (EMOs) in places like Hartford, Baltimore, and Boston that would enter public schools on a contractual basis to run one or more campuses. We described all these innovations as experimental with no guarantee of success. Isn't that what experimentation involves? Aren't we already failing large num-bers of students in our cities? At no point in our indictment of the status quo did we point the finger of blame at public school teachers, for they were as much the victims of the bureaucratic pathology as anyone—although, as in any profession, there were certainly teachers who were not functioning responsibly.

We then turned to the subject of school choice. Here we recounted not only the experience with charter schools, but also other forms of public school choice that had been thriving in New York City and other locations. And there were the revolutionary programs in Milwaukee and then Cleve-land that provided government-supported scholarships for low-income stu-dents to attend independent and religious schools, which were sure to be challenged in the courts. Our hope was that the growing variety of educa-tional options available would create new opportunities for students stuck in chronically failing schools so that the latter would be closed. Our proposal to replace weak schools with strong schools was not designed to foster mar-ket competition; it was motivated by a desire to maintain high standards for all students.

If there could be any doubt about where we stood on developing a choice regime, we addressed it on the last page of the essay under the subtitle "Real Choice for the Poor." We proposed that all students who attend a school tar-geted for closure should be awarded a means-tested scholarship and that nonpublic schools participating in the choice program must not charge tuition above the value of the scholarship.

* * *

The second product to emerge from our NYU seminar was a book of essays published in 1997.[37] We wrote an introduction that updated and developed the themes from our article in *Public Interest*. We repeated the argument that the once-robust nineteenth-century model of schooling no longer worked for twenty-first-century cities. I eventually came to believe we were wrong about that. The old system may have worked for some, but it neglected many immigrant families and it isolated Black children in underperforming and underfunded institutions. In our introduction, we also devoted two sections to distinguishing between the market approach to choice and what we called the "equal opportunity" model that was being put into practice in Milwaukee and Cleveland.

We coauthored a second chapter on the city we knew best that epitomized many foibles of old-century schooling and preserved them for the new. It was called "New York: The Obsolete Factory." We were none too subtle in our treatment of the subject. The description on the first page read,

> By any reasonable measure of educational effectiveness, the system is not working well. Sprawling, rigid, machinelike, uncompromising, it is the premiere example of factory model schooling. Its centennial in 1996 passed uncelebrated and unremarked, possibly because its multitude of embarrassments made celebration unseemly. The school system has become a symbol of unresponsive bureaucracy that somehow rebuffs all efforts to change it. It is a creature of another era.[38]

After laying out the evidence of academic failure, we decided to present a unit-by-unit profile of every major bureau at Livingston Street, peppered with tales of waste, corruption, and ineptitude that had become matters of public knowledge. We even attached a detailed organization chart of the huge bureaucratic behemoth. It was familiar territory for me. As a member of the chancellor's staff, I was involved intimately in ongoing reorganizations. It was my job to periodically update the chart. Since Frank Macchiarola was constantly shaking things up, it became almost a monthly exercise throughout the first eighteen months I was there.

Unless you have been there, it is difficult to appreciate the anxiety that a reorganization can produce in a self-perpetuating dysfunctional bureaucracy for longtime residents who have attained a false sense of ownership. Such a bureaucratic reorganization is like rearranging the bones of a skeleton while a live body is having its sleepy morning coffee: it's "unsettling." One such particular individual at Livingston Street was especially disturbed even though his small office at the top of the chart was never altered. Because he was close to the members of the governing board and well-connected politically, his protests had to be taken seriously.

When the first edition of the chart was distributed throughout the school headquarters, this person—let's call him "Big Pants"—made a personal call to the chancellor to complain that the size of the box assigned to his office was not large enough to represent his actual importance in the organization and, of course, I heard about it. Being reprimanded by the chancellor for exercising poor judgment, I made sure Big Pants's box was bigger in the next iteration of the chart. As time went on, I somehow forgot how important Big Pants actually was. Sometimes in later iterations, I put him in a larger box, sometimes in a smaller one, and sometimes he slipped my mind and I left him off the chart altogether.

Each time the chancellor received a call from Big Pants, the chancellor would go on about his thick-headed young aide who had screwed up again, promising to chew me out, which he ritualistically most certainly did. I would always apologize. Occasionally I was ordered to call Big Pants directly to tell him I was sorry and how important I knew he was. For whatever reason, these mistakes were repeated endlessly and Big Pants finally stopped calling. *May he rest.* While Macchiarola never admitted it to me, I am sure he knew exactly what was going on and got as much of a laugh out it as I did. In truth, though, Big Pants personified a mentality that was all too common among high-powered bureaucrats at Livingston Street and what mattered to them. That wasn't funny.

Although we were careful in our analysis of the New York City system not to place blame for its abysmal performance on teachers and other school-level personnel, Ravitch and I did not hesitate to identify the teachers' union as a major source of obstruction. Describing it as "one of the most powerful forces in the state capitol," which spends more money on lobbying than all but one organized interest (the hospitals association), we said it was "virtually impossible" to get an education bill passed in the legislature without its support.[39] We further commented that, while union leaders like to think they are "in the vanguard of reform," they bring their full influence to bear "when confronted with proposals that threaten to reduce their power, positions, or long held prerogatives."[40]

Given the resistance that we had portrayed, we could not be hopeful that the situation would be corrected overnight. Our essay on New York ended with the following words:

> As we approach the new century, the old factory still stands. A few bricks have been loosened, but the tired old machinery continues to clank and

grind. No one believes any more that it is run by the wisest and best educators in the land. The giant factory no longer commands the respect and admiration that it once did. Its assembly line is ragged, and its products frequently fail. But it endures.[41]

The remainder of the volume turned on a more positive note. We recruited an outstanding group of leading scholars from around the country to write about the kinds of reforms we were hearing about in our seminar series. The contrast between the tired pace of change experienced in New York and the encouraging march of progress evident elsewhere was stark. John Chubb, who with Terry Moe had written the most influential book on choice and markets since Friedman, contributed a chapter about the Edison Project, of which he was a cofounder. The University of Michigan's Valerie Lee, a coauthor of the definitive book on Catholic schools, explained why they do so well with low-income students. Paul Peterson and his Harvard graduate student Chad Noyes reported on the revolutionary voucher program in Milwaukee that Howard Fuller helped create. And, of course, there were chapters on charter schools and site-based reform.

The book was reviewed in the *New York Times* by James Traub, a staff writer for the *New Yorker* with an interest in education, who had attended several of our seminar sessions. Traub had his own insight on political labeling, observing that we had challenged the old paradigms. His essay ran under the title, "What Can Public Schools Learn?"[42] The subtitle read, "For one thing, their constituencies, friends and enemies aren't what—or who—they used to be."

Traub compared education debates from ten or fifteen years earlier to a "toy version of the cold war" wherein liberals wanted to "free children from deadening routine, to draw on creative rather than merely logical faculties," whereas conservatives "wanted kids to buckle down." That dichotomy was no more. He noted that public school people tend to think that the system can take care of itself and that it gets blamed for problems beyond its control, whereas reformers want to create alternatives to public schools. He declared that the book "will confound readers who think they can tell the white hats from the black." He deemed it "both an enormously hopeful book and, at least for liberals, a very uncomfortable one."

On the school choice issue in particular, Traub deliberated, "Vouchers, for example, first appeared as the hobbyhorse of free market conservatives, but have since gained the support of many black educators and politicians, who see vouchers as a means to rescue children from the wreckage of failed inner-city schools." Since the book ended with Ravitch's "Somebody's Children," Traub ended his review with a quote from her that read, "I do not advocate choice solely on the grounds that competition is good. . . . No, what I argue is that it is unjust to compel poor children to attend bad schools." With which Traub concluded, "It may take a sentiment this simple to shatter an old paradigm."

* * *

Diane Ravitch and I published our second book of essays under the auspices of the Program on Education and Civil Society in 2000.[43] The volume concentrated exclusively on New York City. More upbeat than our original profile from three years earlier, this collection was meant to exhibit exemplary projects that could be replicated in our own city and elsewhere. The message was loud and clear: "Yes, there are good things happening in New York, but not enough." Some of the centers of excellence were in the public school system where creative teachers and administrators, against all odds, had built charterlike institutions that operated with relative autonomy before a charter law enabled their capacity to do so more widely. Many could be found in the nonpublic sector: at Catholic schools, at Jewish day schools (not to be confused with Hasidic schools that have come under review in recent years), and in private scholarship programs that were able to loosen the connection between poverty and opportunity. This is the book that included Gail Foster's revealing essay on Historically Black Independent Schools, which Derrick Bell excerpted and wrote about in his *Silent Covenants*, as we discussed in chapter 2.[44]

Let me turn your attention here to the chapter written by Paul Peterson and William Howell.[45] Howell was then an associate of Peterson's at Harvard; now he holds a named professorship at Johns Hopkins after a long tenure at the University of Chicago. They wrote about the School Choice Scholarship Foundation (SCSF). Launched by a group of wealthy New Yorkers in 1997, the new foundation raised money to provide fourteen hundred dollars in annual tuition assistance for thirteen hundred low-income elementary school students over a period of three years. The great majority attended Catholic schools. Because there were many more applicants for the program than scholarships, the awardees were chosen by a lottery administered by Mathematica Policy Research (MPR), an independent think tank.

I had worked with a core group of five SCSF philanthropists who met weekly to plan and oversee the project. It was an impressive assembly of talent and know-how with deep roots in the world of finance. They were among New York's philanthropic elite. Peter Flanigan, who had served with the Olin Foundation, had a long history of giving support to Catholic schools. Richard Gilder had collaborated with George Soros to revitalize Central Park and cofounded the Gilder-Lehrman Institute of American History. Roger Hertog has been chair of the New-York Historical Society and is a major supporter of Jewish philanthropies. Bruce Kovner, who chaired the working committee, had been chair of the Juilliard School and vice chair of Lincoln Center. Thomas Tisch, was a scion of the family that was instrumental in advancing the fortunes of New York University and would later serve as chancellor at Brown University (2007–2016).

They were all political conservatives and affiliated with the market-oriented Manhattan Institute for Policy Research, for which Hertog served as chair. The SCSF scholarship program, however, was needs-based. A family had to have an income low enough to qualify for the federal free-lunch program to be eligible to participate. Eighty-five percent of the awards were reserved for students in low-performing public schools. Families could choose from a list of 225 participating schools. Catholic schools dominated the list because of their low-priced tuition, which could be covered by most of the award.

Although Flanigan had close ties to Catholic education, the other members of the governing committee were all Jewish. Flanigan also supported charter schools that were on track to compete with and deplete hemorrhaging Catholic schools of enrollments, leading to more closures. Although every one of them shared a conviction that city public schools were irredeemable, none were naïve enough to believe that a robust system of choice would put public education out of business. While they saw the project as an important social experiment, I believe that they were motivated by a genuine desire to help families in need. The program was progressive in spirit. They were proud conservatives.

Whenever the performance of students in choice programs is compared with that of students in nearby public schools, choice opponents raise the claim that the choice students are a self-selected population with motivated parents that can not validly be compared with typical public school students. It is a reasonable research question.

Peterson and Howell dealt with the issue by comparing the test score performance of SCSF scholarship winners with those who applied but were not chosen in the lottery, using the latter as a control group. Applicants from both groups were given pre- and posttests after the first year, and parents of the winners were issued questionnaires regarding their satisfaction. Students who were not among the scholarship winners were compensated to participate in the testing. That general methodology would become the gold standard for evaluating school choice programs. Researchers refer to this method as an "intent to treat" approach. Even after only one year, Peterson and Howell's data revealed that scholarship students performed better on the Iowa Test in Basic Skills (ITBS) in math and reading than those who remained in public schools. They found that parents were generally satisfied with the program. It was encouraging news, but let's put social science aside for a moment.

The real proof to emerge from the SCSF experiment surfaced on the day we celebrated the award winners. The group decided to create a spectacle in Central Park. Former New York governor Hugh Carey came to deliver opening remarks. As a congressman, Carey had worked with President Lyndon Johnson to weave together majorities in the House of Representatives to support the Great Society agenda. As governor, he crafted a plan to rescue New York City from fiscal insolvency. His speech supporting the new opportunities being offered was a hit. The main event of the day, however, came with the arrival of more than a thousand parents and their children who had been granted the scholarships.

The occasion was both joyous and melancholy. Many mothers literally broke down and cried. As a person affiliated with the program, I wore a lapel badge that still sits on the windowsill next to my desk reading, "School Choice Scholarships." With that and my white face, I was easily identified as someone who was with the program and not in it. Many of the parents I met that day embraced me and poured their hearts out about how their children were about to be saved from unsafe and ineffective institutions—those places that are not worthy to be called schools. They spoke about the state of desperation that prevails among so many others in their communities who will remain unassisted. Research data do not reveal that kind of truth. It can only be conveyed from one soul to another.

Yes, there was that nagging methodological research question about the self-selected population of parents who entered the scholarship lottery. I believe Peterson and Howell dealt with it effectively—yet opponents keep raising it every time evidence emerges that students have gained academically from choice programs, whether they involve voucher initiatives or charter schools. This methodological quibble has a backstory you should not miss.

These choice opponents assume that Black and Brown parents who take the initiative to improve educational opportunities for their children are atypical. That says a lot about what they think of the rest. These opponents assume that most people of color lack motivation when it comes to the education of their offspring. That assumption may explain why these choice opponents believe underresourced families would be better off if they let *other people* decide what is best for their children. That's not what I heard from those mothers and fathers in Central Park that day. They did not see themselves as different. They thought they were just lucky. Like the many other children who participate in various scholarship programs or attend oversubscribed charter schools, they were the fortunate beneficiaries of a lottery. Their participation was as much a matter of chance as it was of choice.

When school reformers like Gail Foster write essays explaining how much Black families value education, it is not just a pep talk to their own community. It is a plea for dignity, a retort to negative stereotyping that continues to hold people down.

* * *

When Diane wrote "Somebody's Children," she passed over claims raised by choice opponents that charters and vouchers would lead to a loss of enrollment in public schools with a "So what?" response, declaring that failing schools ought to be closed anyway. Yet the lost enrollment argument still resonates in the opposition camp.[46] With the recent wave of postpandemic choice programs sweeping the nation, the claim has more credibility now than it did back then; yet it is still worthy of further exploration because of its underlying assumptions.

I refer to this notion as the *evacuation theory*, which can be summarized as follows: "If we let them go, they will—in overwhelming numbers." It is an odd premise upon which to build an argument for public education as we know it. It does not exude confidence in the status quo or its institutions. When you understand that many parents were exercising choice already, and that the debate then was over whether to grant it to those who don't, the evacuation premise adds depth to concerns over our existing state of educational inequality. It sounds as if the reason we leave poor children in failing schools is to maintain failing schools. That takes us beyond inequality and borders on exploitation. I doubt the arrangement does much for the teachers stuck in those schools either.

As the recipients of the SCSF awards were advancing toward their third year in the program, when scholarship aid would run out, New York financier Ted Forstmann was in the process of raising funds to launch his own effort. Teaming up with John Walton, the philanthropist who had supported Jack Coons's and Howard Fuller's activities, Forstmann offered matching funds to local entrepreneurs in cities around the country to invest in privately funded scholarship programs for poor children. By 1999, his program received 1,237,360 applications for 40,000 awards. All students from the SCSF initiative were automatically transferred into the program so that they could complete their studies in place. The original SCSF sponsors contributed to the new effort. Since its founding in 1999, the Children's Scholarship Fund has raised one billion dollars to provide 209,000 scholarships for low-income children around the nation.[47]

Forstmann was a Republican with close ties to the Clinton administration. He assembled a bipartisan board of directors—not all of whom supported government vouchers—of Erskine Bowles, Barbara Bush, Joseph Califano, Henry Cisneros, Peter Flanigan, Rev. Floyd Flake, Martin Luther King III, Trent Lott, Daniel Patrick Moynihan, Colin Powell, Charles Rangel, and Andrew Young. The poet Maya Angelou helped Forstmann promote the program. Those were the days when Democrats and Republicans could sit together and get things accomplished.

* * *

With the Olin grant furnishing a baseline of support for our Program on Education and Civil Society at NYU, Diane Ravitch and I were able to attract other funding to initiate projects both in concert and independently. Not all our research was focused on the choice issue. Building on the overall theme of our program, we assembled a collection of original essays on education and civil society that was published in 2001. For that project, we solicited contributions from an stellar interdisciplinary group of scholars who do not typically write about schools.[48] The exchange there motivated Alan Wolfe, a contributor, to organize a separate conference at Boston College where a distinguished group of academicians were asked to address the moral issues behind the school choice debate. It resulted in another scholarly collection.[49]

Diane had published *Left Back*, her critique of progressive education, a year earlier.[50] She had labored at it for a decade. The 550-page book was published in 2000. In 2003, Diane published *The Language Police*, a book about how organized censure campaigns limit what children read in school.[51] (It is no wonder that she reacted so strongly to the more recent backlash against critical race theory.) Because of Diane's interest in the boundaries adults set for children, we collaborated on a book released that same year—examining the issue from the opposite direction—on the marketing of sex and violence to young people.[52]

My own research agenda had become clear early on after I fully digested the various components of "Somebody's Children." I wanted to develop the layered elements of the piece and integrate them into a new book encompassing policy, politics, history, and law.

6

All Roads Lead to Court

As a political scientist, I studied constitutional law in graduate school and became fascinated with the connection between law and policy. While at NYU, I was invited to coteach a course on state and local law at the law school, and had written a law review article drawing from Lani Guinier's work on minority representation in elections.[1] Guinier had been the first African American woman granted tenure at Harvard Law School, after Derrick Bell and others had raised a ruckus over the disgraceful slight. This publication only whetted my appetite to explore the legal contours of the choice issue. That opportunity came when I received a grant through our program from the Alice M. and Thomas J. Tisch Foundation to write on something called the "Blaine Amendment." Tom had been trained as an attorney, and I knew him as a member of the group involved with the School Choice Scholarship Foundation.

Blaine Amendments are provisions found in state constitutions that set strict standards of separation between church and state, obstructing voucher programs that provide assistance for students at religious schools. Such provisions are enforced through the state courts and involve a separate line of litigation from that in the federal courts that concern the establishment clause of the First Amendment—although state courts also opine on federal constitutional questions.

There had been very little written on Blaine as a legal issue or linking it to its bigoted origins. In 1996, I published a long article in a Yale law journal on the topic of constitutional federalism. It traced the history of federal constitutional standards and their interaction with the case law in six jurisdictions that adopted differing approaches to religious accommodation, including Blaine Amendments. Sounding a theme that would define my work on school choice, I called it "choosing equality" three years before I would use the title for my book with a different subtitle.[2] Two years later (1998), I wrote an article for a Harvard law journal that took more direct aim at Blaine and focused on developments in Ohio, Wisconsin, and Vermont, where voucher programs existed and legal challenges were imminent.[3] I

Radical Dreamers. Joseph P. Viteritti, Oxford University Press. © Oxford University Press (2025).
DOI: 10.1093/oso/9780197827109.003.0006

became fixated on the fine points of the law and would eventually write a half-dozen more essays for law reviews—all preparing me for the book assignment I had given myself.

Blaine Amendments inscribed in many state constitutions had a dark history that dated back more than a century. In 1875, Congressman James Blaine of Maine, with the support of President Ulysses S. Grant, proposed a constitutional amendment that would prohibit government aid to religious schools. For Grant, the controversy was a convenient distraction from the scandals that plagued his administration. Blaine, an anti-Catholic zealot, hoped to ride his proposal and its unvarnished bigotry to the Republican nomination for the White House with a plank nailed into the party's platform against "Rum, Romanism, and Rebellion." Blaine's amendment gained strong support in both houses of Congress, but fell four votes short of the required two-thirds majority to pass in the Senate. After that, many states took it upon themselves to incorporate Blaine Amendments into their own constitutions. By 1890, they were the law in more than two-thirds of these jurisdictions.[4] The US Supreme Court finally addressed this question in the *Espinosa* (2020) case when it ruled that the state could not exclude students at religious schools from a publicly supported scholarship if they provided such assistance to students at secular private schools.[5]

* * *

When my book on school choice finally appeared in 1999, the Ohio Scholarship Program—providing assistance for low-income students in Cleveland to attend independent and religious schools—was in the midst of an intense legal battle launched by the Ohio Federation of Teachers and the American Civil Liberties Union. Following four years of contests in the state courts, the Ohio Supreme Court ruled that the program did not violate the establishment clause of the First Amendment and let the program go forward. At that point, opponents challenged the program in federal court. After both the district court in Cleveland and the Sixth Circuit Court of Appeals ruled against the program, the Ohio attorney general asked the appeals court to lift an injunction against the program while it prepared its case for review by the US Supreme Court. The program proceeded, as did the case.

On the day in late summer of 1999 that the state solicitor for Ohio, Edward Foley, contacted me to ask if I would serve as an expert witness, he was most concerned about one particular argument the other side was posing. They were about to claim that, because a majority of schools participating in the scholarship program were religious, the program provided a state incentive for parents to choose a religious education, thus violating past judicial precedents. Some argued that the program was coercive toward that end.

Perhaps one needs to spend three years in law school to follow such reasoning, but Solicitor Foley's concerns were well founded. The claim had to be treated as a serious legal argument even though it obfuscated the fact that participating parents were most incentivized by the horrible schools they wanted their children to flee. We could actually be expected to pretend that these parents and their children were better off with no choice than with some choice in a program where no family would be forced to accept a scholarship. We could actually be expected to pretend that if the program were struck down, it would be a victory for liberty and equality. Perhaps what the argument proved most is how little value choice opponents place on the preferences of mothers and fathers who have the greatest stake in their children's education. Do you suppose these *other people* saw themselves as surrogates for social justice?

What made the opposing argument even weaker is that it was factually wrong. Ned Foley is one of the nation's leading experts on election law. At the time of his service as state solicitor, he was on leave from his faculty post at Ohio State University, just beginning to acquaint himself with the landscape of primary and secondary education in Cleveland. When he shared his concerns with me, I explained to him that Cleveland offers other choices beyond regular public schools and religious schools participating in the scholarship program. To begin with, ten of the forty-six nonpublic schools serving the 3,852 scholarship students were nonsectarian. Moreover, Cleveland also had charter schools that served 1,600 students and magnet schools serving 13,000 students that function on the basis of parental choice. These facts defined the range-of-choice argument that I outlined in my eighteen-page affidavit for the Ohio attorney general to eventually present to the US Supreme Court.[6]

There was nothing especially creative about the argument. Anyone familiar with the landscape of education in Cleveland would have been familiar with these facts. Other experts who testified on behalf of the parents with children in the program offered similar testimony. It was the opposing side whose arguments won the prize for novelty verging on absurdity in this case. Yet, given the state of First Amendment jurisprudence at that juncture in time, the opposing arguments needed to be taken seriously.

Opponents tried to bolster their claims by showing that Catholic schools were the only ones in Cleveland where tuition was low enough to be covered by the meager $2,200 value of the scholarship award. They didn't mention that it was because of their effective lobbying that the scholarship amount was so low. If greater opportunity were to be offered to low-income children in Ohio, these folks were doing their best to make sure it was being done on their terms. The court rejected their arguments. With per-capita spending at $4,500 in charter schools and $7,746 in magnet and regular public schools, spending differentials could function as a disincentive for families to enroll in the scholarship program.

* * *

During the course of litigation in 1997, I got to know Clint Bolick, the cofounder and lead attorney for the libertarian-oriented Institute for Justice (IJ). Bolick had an impressive record representing disadvantaged parents whose children were enrolled in various state scholarship programs in danger of being closed down by the courts. He and his cofounder, the late William "Chip" Mellor, had hosted a meeting in Washington where they invited constitutional scholars from around the country to discuss litigation strategy, anticipating an eventual appearance before the Supreme Court.[7] I was the only nonlawyer in the group, listened attentively, and did not sign their "lawyers' brief" when the Cleveland case was heard. Held at the Jefferson Hotel, across from the headquarters of the National Education Association, Bolick dubbed the meeting the "Shadow of the Beast" conclave.

Understanding that the Cleveland case would be decided by a closely divided Supreme Court, Bolick identified Associate Justice Sandra Day O'Connor as the swing vote. He believed that Justice O'Connor would be more sympathetic to the choice cause if we focused on education rather than religion. That suited me fine. IJ submitted its own amicus brief on behalf of the parents. The testimony I prepared at the request of the Ohio attorney general defending the state program emphasized how and why the program under attack was designed to enhance the educational opportunities of underserved and underresourced students, which was the theme of my new book. That was the reason Foley engaged me to begin with, and my being an education scholar rather than an attorney strengthened my credibility. I also laid out the "range of choice argument" with supporting data outlining per capita funding disparities between scholarship recipients and their peers in public and charter schools.

Zelman v. Simmons-Harris was decided in June 2002 in favor of the parents and the program by a 5–4 majority of the court, with Justice O'Connor casting the deciding vote.[8] In a concurring opinion, she focused on the range of choice issue, as she had during oral arguments. Writing for the majority, Chief Justice William Rehnquist explained that the Ohio law passed constitutional scrutiny with regard to the establishment clause of the First Amendment because the scholarship money had been awarded to the students, not the schools. Any funding landing in the coffers of religious institutions in the form of tuition payments was there because of the free choices made by parents, who were not legally barred from making such choices.[9]

Commenting on the case for the *New York Times*, Linda Greenhouse presented it in a larger political context. Greenhouse was then the first lady of high-court journalism before she left her assignment at the paper to teach at Yale Law School. Over her nearly three-decade career with the *Times*, she had earned a reputation for objectivity by not allowing her personal proclivities to interfere with her analysis. As with anyone, sometimes she managed that better than others. Her article about *Zelman* appeared under the title "Win the Debate, Not Just the Case."[10] She began with a quote from President George W. Bush, stating that *Zelman* was "just as historic as *Brown*," noting that the linkage between the two cases "appeared in newspapers and talk shows across the nation." She also quoted the "conservative columnist" George Will, who wrote, "Happily, yesterday, socially disadvantaged children had their best day in court since *Brown v. Board of Education* in 1954."

Greenhouse remarked on how "equating the voucher ruling with the watershed constitutional moment in the struggle for racial equality was political rhetoric at its most powerful." She elaborated, "Such strategic use of language rarely occurs by chance," but is "the result of careful preparation." She then divulged that the public campaign was organized by Clint Bolick and the "free-marketeers" at IJ who wanted the case to be framed primarily in terms of equality and only secondarily pertaining to church and state. Bolick was pleased to take credit for the campaign, as he was so entitled.

Greenhouse further explained that the idea of linking *Brown* and *Zelman* did not originate with Bolick. Instead, she observed, "The theme was central to the work" of "Joseph P. Viteritti, whose book *Choosing Equality* is often cited by voucher supporters," and who "declared in the book's opening that the 'awesome mandate' of *Brown* was his starting point for a discussion of how to increase equal opportunity in education."[11]

For the record, I never equated *Zelman* with *Brown*. *Brown* has no equivalent. I began my book years before *Zelman* with a paragraph recognizing that nearly a half-century after *Brown* and many attempts at school reform, "race and class remain the most reliable predictors of educational achievement in the United States."[12] (Unfortunately that is still true.) I proceeded to discuss those various failed efforts throughout the book and expressed hope that implementation of school choice would move us closer to the evasive goal of educational equality enunciated by the court in 1954. I insisted then, as I do now, that such equality must involve effective teaching and learning.

Greenhouse went on in her piece to ask several African American leaders how they felt about comparing *Zelman* to *Brown*. Thomas M. Shaw of the NAACP Legal Defense Fund is quoted as responding, "The notion that this is comparable to *Brown* is extraordinary." Howard Fuller, who was chairing the Black Alliance for Educational Options that he had founded, was quoted saying, "I'm not criticizing anyone, but I tend to be very careful about equating anything we do to the historic civil rights movement."

It is unfortunate that Greenhouse did not ask Howard Fuller what he thought the true significance of *Zelman* was. I wish she would have asked the same question of the parents who were the clients of the scholarship program in Cleveland, whose opinions, in my mind, are the ones that matter the most. I think she may have benefited from a dose of instruction similar to what I derived from parents five years earlier in Central Park when we celebrated the winners of our privately funded scholarship program.

I wondered at the time if Greenhouse had ever contemplated the notion that, perhaps, the strict church-state separation preferences of white middle-class secularists should not be prioritized over the desperate educational needs of less fortunate people of color. Viewed through the lens of race and class, wasn't that the real question before us with regard to school choice jurisprudence? Would the students in this program have been better off if these *other people* had won the case?

Then again, as time passed, Greenhouse's unease with the direction the Supreme Court was moving on the First Amendment proved to have merit. The jurisprudence that continues to evolve under the John Roberts court has lowered the wall of separation between church and state to a level that increasingly puts individual rights at risk. The point was to find a reasonable balance that neither side in the debate seemed to value. More on that later.

Zelman is a landmark case, and I understand it as a part of *Brown*'s legacy. There was nothing original or tactical about that. Long ago, through my association with Ron Edmonds, I became convinced that we cannot separate the dream of educational equality for all children from a sincere commitment to expand access to more effective schools. My eight-year collaboration with Diane Ravitch between 1994 and 2002 enabled me to act on that conviction.

* * *

Our project had a short lifeline at NYU. When John M. Olin created his foundation in 1953, he set in stone his expectation that the philanthropy would last no longer than the first generation of surviving Olins after his death. In practical terms, that meant the foundation would award its final grant in the summer of 2005 and cease to exist at the end of that year. Despite my scholarly productivity, probably because of it, there was no chance in heaven nor hell that I would be offered a tenure track position at NYU's Wagner School, where I had been for sixteen years.

For the academic year that began in 2003, I accepted an offer as a James Madison Visiting Fellow and Visiting Professor in the Department of Politics at Princeton, where I taught a course on education policy and began a book on the religion clauses of the First Amendment.[13] The following year I accepted a tenured position at Hunter College. Diane Ravitch remained at New York University, ending our professional collaboration. She departed from there in 2020.

7

Howard Fuller

Making of an Activist

Howard Fuller shares Derrick Bell's conviction that American society is incurably racist, as well as Bell's agonizing determination to keep fighting anyway.[1] He will tell you that his career is the personification of Bell's theory of the "interest convergence dilemma," which holds that white people will support the causes of Black people so long as it converges with their own interests and only so long.[2] The two men knew each other well, and Bell traveled to Milwaukee to help Fuller in his effort to give poor people more control over the education of their children. Fuller's career is a living exhibit of critical theory, full of political contradictions, temporary alliances, conflict, anger, pain, hope, disappointment, resignation, and occasional despair.

Unlike the other critical thinkers whom you've met in the preceding pages, Howard's historical legacy will be defined more by what he did than by what he wrote. You are more likely to find his name on the pages of a book than on its cover. As you will see, much has been written about him. I have spotted his name in more than twenty volumes documenting his role in our nation's struggle for equality. He is an unrelenting activist who defies political conventions. That said, Howard Fuller is also an intellectual who holds a doctorate and Distinguished University Professorship (Emeritus), can discuss the literature on race and education like a scholar, and has written an autobiography with the title *No Struggle, No Progress*, summoning the words of Frederick Douglass.[3]

Since Howard accepts temporary alliances as a fact of political life, I value my friendship with him that dates back at least to 1995, when he visited the NYU seminar I hosted with Diane Ravitch. Howard was also helpful to me when I wrote *Choosing Equality* at the end of that decade. I recall a New Year's Eve when he spent a good hour faxing me materials regarding developments in Milwaukee and my remarking with gratitude that most people were not sharing the evening that way. While Howard is always prepared

Radical Dreamers. Joseph P. Viteritti, Oxford University Press. © Oxford University Press (2025).
DOI: 10.1093/oso/9780197827109.003.0007

to engage with you on an intellectual level, he is ever more animated by the energy of practical politics. He once stopped me in the middle of a conversation about his activism on behalf of school choice to remind me, "Joe, Black folk in Milwaukee aren't sitting in their basements reading Milton Friedman. They just want good schools for their kids."

By literally taking to the streets, Howard adds a dimension to the discussion on racial equality that moves us beyond the significant cultural, legal, and moral realms so ably represented by the other key figures in our story, and situates us more consciously in that which is political. For Howard, the journey from desegregation to community control to school choice is about the acquisition and exercise of raw political power. Choice is both an end and a means through which Black and Brown people with modest incomes can acquire decent educations for their children. The fractured alliances he takes for granted are the occupational hazards of a political life filled with surrogates of many persuasions who claim to have the best interests of children at heart. Talk about strange bedfellows? Ask Howard about that and the criticism he has taken for it. So far as political labeling goes, though, I don't remember ever hearing Howard being called a conservative. You will see why in a moment.

Howard and I had been out of touch for years when I contacted him in early 2020 to share my thoughts about writing this book. He responded immediately, and we picked right up as though we had never lost touch. Howard was his usual self: frank, warm, supportive, thoughtful, and resigned to what was possible and what not.[4] He told me that after seventeen years in operation, he had disbanded the Black Alliance for Educational Options (BAEO), the "unapologetic Black organization" he founded in 2000 to promote forms of school choice dedicated to "social justice, not markets." As he explained, he could "never get the kind of funding white organizations got," so rather than just let BAEO run out of steam, he decided to distribute the half million dollars he had left in the bank to other groups that were doing constructive things. He was devoting a lot of his time to the charter school in Milwaukee that had been named after him. Health problems had slowed him down a bit, but he had no intention of stopping.

Howard spoke of how discouraged he was by what was happening on the national political scene as we faced another presidential election in 2020, describing Trump as "dangerous" and Biden as a politician whose "time had passed." He was most disturbed by the Democratic candidates for president who identified themselves as progressives. After our call, he sent me a sixteen-minute video of a conversation he had with Elizabeth Warren that past November (2019). The Massachusetts senator had been on the campaign trail in Atlanta seeking the Democratic nomination for president and wanted to meet with a group of Black parents to discuss education. Howard, reaching into his broad network, helped put the event together with local leaders he knew.

The video captured an intimate discussion between Warren and a half-dozen local attendees, including Howard, that took place in a brightly lit hallway after the main event around her visit. Most of the local women were dressed in black sweatshirts that read "Powerful Parent Network." Howard was wearing jeans and a gray hoodie from Malcolm X Liberation University (which he had founded, but is now defunct) with black lettering and a sketch of Malcolm across his chest. Warren's signature bright-red blazer and shiny golden mane stood out under the glaring lights as if the contrasted coloring in the screenshot was representative of people from two different worlds. The exchange remained civil and respectful throughout, with no raised voices, but their differences were striking.

Warren had just posted her education plan. It included more resources for public schools and a cut in federal funding for charter schools. They wanted to know why. One activist grandmother of sixteen told Warren that she needs to hear stories from "real people who live and breathe this everyday" and who have to organize politically to get decent schools for their kids. She spoke about a charter school that "saved my grandbaby's life," a young woman who after four generations was the only person in her family to attend college. Warren denied that she opposed charter schools. She claimed she was concerned that charter schools were not held to the same academic standards as traditional public schools.

At that point, Howard introduced himself and joined the discussion. He said that Warren had used the same buzzwords as the teachers' union and other charter opponents, who throw around terms like "privatization" and "corporate takeover." He respectfully acknowledged her expertise and said he would much rather be organizing with her to oppose Donald Trump, but that her platform gives "air cover for those who are systematically attacking charter schools." He reminded her that charter schools are public schools and how her proposal to eliminate federal funding for them would roll back the kinds of policy that Obama and presidents dating back to Bill Clinton had sponsored. Still in a hushed tone, he cautioned her, "When you attack charter schools, you attack the self-determination of Black and Brown families." He cited national test scores that are declining and showing that "our country's Black and Brown children are not being educated." He insisted, "We are not the enemy," and "What you need to do is back off from us."

After rolling through a stream of "uh-huh, uh-huh" expressions as she looked toward the ceiling to engage Howard, Warren returned to the accountability issue, noting how charter schools in Michigan had no standards. Howard agreed with her concerns and said all schools should be held to the same standards—at which point the grandmother of sixteen chimed in to note that her group had demanded accountability from both charter schools and district schools. Howard pointed out that the senator could have called for accountability without attacking charters. When Warren repeated that her plan would increase funding for public education, Howard advised her that if we put eight hundred million dollars into the system and didn't radically change its practices, it would be like "pouring money down a drain." Recalling that he had been the superintendent of schools in Milwaukee for four years, he described what he had there as a "delivery system" and "not a public school system." What we need, he insisted, is an array of different delivery systems to fulfill the promise of public education. He concluded, "If you are Black or Brown, you want no option off the table."

Democrats never got the message. Joe Biden, like Warren, had declared war on charter schools while Republicans advanced the choice agenda to new levels and another generation of Black and Brown children squandered their precious years in schools that did not equip them for productive lives. Might this obstinance concerning the opportunities that choice could provide have had something to do with the shift toward Republicans and Donald Trump in 2024 among people of color?

* * *

When Howard told me about the Warren video during our phone call, he tossed out a rhetorical question that repeats a now-familiar theme for us in this text: "What makes someone a progressive?"—which he followed with, "When did bureaucracy taking precedent over democracy become progressive?"[5] The reference to bureaucracy reminded me of my days at 110 Livingston Street. He then pointed out that Elizabeth Warren and Bernie Sanders, the Democratic Party's most left-of-center presidential candidates, had no support in the Black community. That is unfortunate, since their respective programs have had so much to say on the issue of economic equality.

As our conversation continued, Howard turned philosophical. Looking back on his own experience, he lamented how he had been called a "sellout" and an "Uncle Tom" by liberals for his cooperation with Republican president George W. Bush, who supported standards and choice, declaring, "If you do social justice, you must deal with contradictions. . . . I am willing to live with contradictions, making decisions based on the greater good. . . . . There is a difference between principle and tactics."

More than a year and a half passed before Howard and I spoke again and I finally had moved ahead with this project. It was like we just continued the same conversation we began when we first talked—one might say, in 2020 and some twenty-five years before that. It was then that he mentioned his intellectual debt to Derrick Bell, referring to interest convergence theory, perpetual racism, and his belief that educational equality will never be achieved.[6] His overall understanding of the race issue sheds light on Howard's acceptance of conflict, compromise, and political partnerships, and how difficult this political terrain is to navigate for a serious actor with a social conscience. How does one know where to draw the line between conviction and convenience without compromising too much?

Let me tell you Howard Fuller's story now, and you can see for yourself.

* * *

Howard Fuller begins his autobiography from 2014 with an episode involving George W. Bush.[7] In 1999, the then–Texas governor invited Howard to the state capitol to solicit his thoughts on education. What was scheduled as a half-hour meeting went on for ninety minutes as Howard explained why charters and vouchers were needed for poor Black and Brown children. Anticipating his election as the next president of the United States, Bush invited Howard to come to Washington to work for him. Howard immediately turned him down and offered two reasons for it: "Number one, I'm not a Republican, and number two, I'm not a loyalist. I'm not the kind of person who can just go along with the party line for the sake of politics when I disagree on matters of importance."[8] Howard would later visit with Bush at the White House and did end up helping him write his first two speeches on education policy because the president was willing to say what Howard wanted him to say.

Howard Fuller had come a long way from his roots in rural Shreveport, Louisiana, where men who looked like him were once hung from trees for no offense other than looking like him. As a child he would hide under his grandmother's front porch at the sight of a police car, suspecting that the officers inside were the same men who terrorized his neighbors with their torch-lit evening rituals as hooded members of the Ku Klux Klan. Pearl Weaver, Howard's grandmother, would suffer none of this sort of indignity. One day when she caught the young boy making a dash to hide from the police after doing absolutely nothing wrong, she forbade him to ever run at the sight of a white man again.

Howard's father disappeared right after he was born, so the boy never knew him, other than from a photo that his mother kept. In 1946, when Howard was five years old, he and his mother moved to Milwaukee, joining the Great Migration that took many African Americans fleeing the South to new homes in midwestern, northeastern, and West Coast cities. Howard's mother, now Juanita Smith, had remarried. Leaving Pearl, the family matriarch, behind in Louisiana was difficult and destabilizing for both of them, made no easier by excessive drinking and abusive behavior on the part of Howard's stepfather. Howard visited with his grandmother, whom he also called "Mama," every summer. Each trip back home became a cruel lesson about life in the Jim Crow South, with its segregated water fountains, lunch counters, movie theaters, and public transportation, not to mention the public schools.

When Howard lived in Shreveport as a child, Pearl and Juanita, neither of whom made much, managed to scrape together enough money to send him to a Catholic preschool. After arriving in Milwaukee, his mother put him in St. Boniface's Catholic School, where, because of the family's low income, he was given free tuition. They were not Catholic, nor did they convert; but Juanita preferred Catholic education and its discipline to the city's public elementary schools, even though her son would be the only Black boy in his class. You might say that she practiced choice before it was even called that. Howard remains grateful for the opportunity.

When Howard began his studies at North Division High School, the public school on the border of the Black community was 65 percent white. By the time he reached his senior year, white flight had taken its toll and the school was majority Black. It was at North Division where a young Howard began to demonstrate his potential as a leader. It was at North Division years later, an adult Howard Fuller would make his mark as a charismatic proponent of racial justice. He was both a strong student and an exceptional athlete. He played tennis and ran cross-country, but it was on the basketball court where the six-feet-four athlete became a star, playing on Milwaukee's All City Team. In his senior year, Howard was chosen as both captain of the basketball team and president of the student body. While in school, he also came under the mentorship of Wesley Scott, the president of the Urban League of Milwaukee, who would become a major influence on him.

Juanita Smith worked in a factory on weekdays and made extra money on weekends applying the skills she had acquired in cosmetology school. Her husband shoveled manure in the Armour Meat Packing plant. They lived with their son in Hillside, a public housing project, until they were able to afford a small duplex. There was no way Howard would attend college without generous financial aid. Fortunately, Carroll College, which was eighteen miles outside of Milwaukee, awarded a Trailblazer Scholarship that covered tuition and living expenses for exceptional athletes who could maintain a B average. He had been offered athletic scholarships from two other universities with stellar national teams, but Carroll was the only one that would continue his support if he became injured and unable to play.

In his freshman year at Carroll, Howard was the only Black student on campus. He was chosen MVP of its basketball team four years in a row, made the All State Wisconsin College team, and maintained excellent grades. He was treated well by the more privileged white students at the school, and his teammates refused to patronize any establishment where Howard was not welcome. Howard appreciated the friendship and support, but realized that he needed to learn more about himself and the ongoing struggle of his own people. As Wesley Scott had taught him, he also wanted to do something about it.

A Whitney Young scholarship from the Urban League allowed Howard to pursue a master's degree in social administration from Western Reserve University (renamed Case Western). His graduate program was one of the first in the nation to offer a specialization in community organizing. It was right up his alley—and it was there in Cleveland where Howard Fuller began his public life as an activist. As president of the student senate, he took the lead in organizing peaceful student protests on local issues that cropped up from time to time.

After attending a meeting of the Congress of Racial Equality (CORE) in 1964, Fuller became involved in the Cleveland school desegregation battle that had long been simmering. In order to deal with overcrowding fed by southern migration, school officials bused Black students to underenrolled white schools, where they were isolated in their own classrooms and not permitted to eat in the school cafeteria. At that time, having experienced life in the Jim Crow South, Howard believed in integration and the peaceful tactics of Martin Luther King Jr., but his views would begin to change. The NAACP had hoped to negotiate a settlement to the problem; CORE took a more militant stand. When Howard and others launched a demonstration outside the school superintendent's office, they were brutally beaten and thrown into jail.

The next month, on April 3, 1964, Howard attended a discussion at Cory Methodist Church on the future of the civil rights struggle, where Malcolm X delivered his fiery "The Ballot or the Bullet" speech. The Muslim minister told the mostly Christian congregation that they are "all in the same boat" and rather than "turn the other cheek" Black people needed to awaken to their political power and fight white oppression.[9] According to Howard, he was "transfixed" by the "raw honesty and bravery about Malcolm."[10] A few days later, Howard attended a demonstration on the site of where a school was being constructed that would have further segregated Black students. During the course of that protest, Howard witnessed a terrible tragedy in which Bruce Klunder, a young minister, fellow demonstrator, and founder of Cleveland CORE, was accidently crushed to death by a bulldozer working at the site. The experience had a powerful impact on Howard's attitude toward peaceful protests and the price to be paid to advance racial justice.

After graduation from Case Western, in fulfillment of his obligation to the Urban League, Howard spent a year in Chicago as an employment specialist helping to integrate Black jobseekers into the larger workforce. But it was not enough to satisfy his own ambitious sense of duty as a politically astute professional, so he returned to the South.

* * *

For another person, the sum total of Howard's experience in North Carolina between 1965 and 1976 could fill an entire career; for Howard Fuller, it was preparation for all he would eventually accomplish in Milwaukee and beyond.[11] He first took a position coordinating Operation Breakthrough, an antipoverty program in Durham supported by federal funding under President Lyndon Johnson's Great Society initiative. The "maximum feasible participation" edict in the legislation was meant to encourage poor people to have a role in shaping the program. When Howard read it, he took it as an opportunity to transform his role from administrator to community organizer. Using Durham as a base, he thrust himself into the life of the larger community and became a familiar face at church meetings, barbershops, and pool halls. The more he learned about local problems, the more militant he grew. As he adopted the language of Black Power activism being chanted in other parts of the country, his notoriety clashed more harshly with the political culture that reigned below the Mason-Dixon line.

Aware that a lack of local leadership would hobble any efforts to achieve effective community and economic development in North Carolina, Howard convinced state authorities to establish the Foundation for Community Development (FDC), which allowed him to create a ten-week summer internship program for recent college graduates.[12] In 1968, thirty-nine participants were selected from more than five hundred applicants at fifteen campuses to learn the basics of community organizing and how existing political, social, and economic institutions perpetuated poverty. According to historian Charles McKinney,"By the time he helped create FDC, Fuller had become the most prominent advocate of Black Power in the state."[13]

Over the next several years, Howard organized voter registration drives and launched protests against negligent exploitive landlords. He represented maids, janitors, and cafeteria workers for Local 77 at Duke University. He demonstrated against an urban renewal plan that would displace Black residents from their homes. During one angry march against police brutality, he was beaten, jailed, and prosecuted for resisting arrest. Although convicted as charged, he did not serve any time. As he gained a reputation as a troublemaker, Howard set himself up as a target for powerful politicians. After the governor publicly criticized him for his radicalism, he resigned his post at the state university in Chapel Hill, where he taught a course on community organizing. He eventually stepped down from his position at Operation Breakthrough, after a Republican congressman threatened to interfere with the program's funding.

At the request of Black students at Duke, Howard played a role in making Duke the first university in the South to house a Black studies department. As he thought further about his own identity and the political significance of race, Fuller became convinced that situating a Black studies program at a white institution might not be sufficient to properly address the needs of minority students. That led to the creation of Malcolm X Liberation University (MXLU), which Howard founded with the help of Black educators from around the country.

MXLU drew its students from a network of "Pan African" primary and secondary feeder schools located throughout the Northeast and Midwest. Its revolutionary pan-African curriculum was dedicated to the liberation of African people in America and around the world. The spirit of its student body was aptly summarized in the words of Malcolm X inscribed at the entrance, calling to a "new generation of black people who have become disenchanted with the entire system and who are ready now and willing to do something about it."[14]

MXLU immediately became another source of controversy. Even the director of the North Carolina NAACP condemned its separatist appeal. MXLU's focus on Black history and culture, along with its emphasis on developing positive self-images among the student body, shared much in common with the mission that Gail Foster—discussed in chapter 2— had charted when she led a movement for Historically Black Independent Schools in New York. It would continue to guide Howard's approach to schooling throughout his career.

There were three thousand guests in attendance when Betty Shabazz, the widow of the institution's namesake, gave the keynote address at the school's opening ceremony on October 25, 1969. An abandoned warehouse in Durham would serve as its campus for the first class of fifty students until the school moved to better quarters in Greensboro on October 5, 1970. As part of his own continuing education on liberation, Howard traveled to Africa in 1971 and spent a month with guerilla fighters in Mozambique who were rebelling against Portuguese colonialism. He assumed the African name Owusu Sadaukai. As he traveled across Mozambique, Guinea-Bissau, and Angola, many of the rebels he met urged Fuller and his party to build solidarity for their anticolonial struggles beyond Africa.

After his return the following year, Fuller worked with his contacts across the United States, Canada, and the Caribbean to organize a march in Washington, DC, to recognize the anniversary of African Liberation Day, the day when representatives from thirty-one African countries met in May 1963 to form the Organization of African Unity (OAU).[15] Gathering at Malcolm X / Meridian Hill Park, more than thirty thousand revelers from all over came together to celebrate the theme of the festivities: "Black Unity: Breaking the Chains of Oppression." The event attracted prominent Black leaders across the ideological spectrum, from mainstream progressives (Rep. John Conyers, San Francisco mayor Willie Brown, and Julian Bond) to those with more radical leanings (Stokely Carmichael, Angela Davis, and Huey Newton). Roy Wilkins of the NAACP gave the event the cold shoulder, reflecting continuing tensions between his organization's integrationist agenda and the separatist inclinations of more militant activists behind the celebration.

* * *

MXLU remained open for only three more years. Bedeviled by financial problems and philosophical debates among its leaders about whether to prioritize Black nationalism or Marxism, it closed its doors at the end of the 1975–1976 academic year. Those philosophical tensions spilled over into what Fuller referred to as the larger "movement." Exhausted, broke, and dispirited, Howard returned to Milwaukee. Milwaukee was home, and it had a long history of civil rights agitation.[16]

For a short time, Howard took a job selling insurance to make ends meet. Within a year, Howard stood out as Equitable Life's top sales representative in the region. When asked to speak to his fellow workers at a company retreat where he was celebrated for his outstanding record, Fuller jolted the audience with a talk about why American corporations should divest from South Africa. That was it for Howard's career as an insurance salesman.

* * *

In 1977, Howard was offered a job at Marquette University as associate director of the Equal Opportunity Program. He provided counseling and support services to students on financial aid who had been admitted to the Jesuit institution on a provisional basis because of their weak academic preparation. Howard would eventually complete his doctorate in education there, writing a dissertation on school desegregation in Milwaukee.[17] The city had been issued a federal court order to desegregate in 1976 by Judge John Reynolds, after eleven years of litigation. All hell broke loose in 1978 when the local school board put forward a proposal to diversify North Division High School. The school that a young Howard Fuller saw transition from a majority-white to a majority-Black student body before graduating in 1958 had become a segregated minority institution, as had the Near Northside part of town where it sat.

As the demographics of the community changed, North Division's performance declined and the school facility deteriorated so badly that the community demanded a new building. The school board finally caved to the pressure and replaced the old structure in 1978, but soon thereafter released a plan to convert the facility to a specialized citywide school with concentrations in health and science so that it could attract white students. Black students from the community would be forcibly bused elsewhere so they could attend integrated schools in whiter neighborhoods. The proposal created divisions within the Black community. Some viewed it as a welcome opportunity to realize the promise of desegregation. Others were angered about losing the new state-of-the-art neighborhood school and the simultaneous displacement of their children so that white students could reap its benefits.

The campaign launched by the Coalition to Save North Division that Howard led exposed nagging philosophical tensions about the meaning of *Brown v. Board of Education* as an instrument for achieving educational equality similar to what we saw in Boston in 1974 when Ron Edmonds met with local residents at Freedom House to discuss Judge Garrity's desegregation plan. That meeting in Roxbury, you may recall, resulted in Edmonds's drafting of the Freedom House Statement later discussed by Derrick Bell in his seminal *Yale Law Review* article, "Serving Two Masters," questioning the merits of forced integration.

It was not that the Roxbury-based group was against efforts to desegregate the Boston public schools. The point, as Edmonds argued, was to establish that improved academic performance is an essential feature of educational equity. Edmonds, like Stokely Carmichael and other activists with more radical dispositions, also challenged the assumption that a predominantly Black institution could not hope to excel without the infusion of white students. Referring to Edmonds's research at the time, Fuller remarked, "Fortunately . . . the school effectiveness literature . . . makes it very clear that irrespective of race or class, *All Children Can Learn*"[18] (emphasis and capitalization added). By the late 1970s a Blacks for Two-Way Integration movement had erupted in Milwaukee, urging that more white students be compelled to attend majority-Black schools.[19]

North Division's prominent graduate and star athlete was naturally invested in the issues that had emerged at the institution—and with his experiences in North Carolina and Cleveland behind him, he was well equipped to take them on. Howard's own research had informed him that the burden of busing in Milwaukee, as in other cities, had fallen disproportionately on Black families. It was their children who would be sent to inhospitable environments where they would remain the official permanent minority with no political agency. Meanwhile, the better schools in their own communities, actually called "magnets," were charged with the task of wooing white students.[20] Fuller wondered whether the school board's proposal was a scheme to "cleanse" the sparkling new facility of black people.[21] Regarding North Division, Black students who once automatically attended it as a function of their residence now had to file an application and hope for the best. It was the latter feature of the plan that most irked Howard Fuller.

Howard spoke at a school board meeting where the public was invited to offer comments. His "Enough Is Enough" speech became the rallying cry of the Coalition to Save North Division. When I asked Howard where I could get a copy of the speech, he shot me over an audio recording.[22] Listening to the forty-plus-year-old recording of this younger man's talk (at age thirty-seven), I could sense the passion in his voice that placed him at the head of the campaign as the audience encouraged him on like a minister leading them in prayer. Introducing himself as an alumnus and referring to North Division as "our school," he denounced the school board's proposal as "blatantly racist." He excoriated the plan in which "Black people are once again being forced to make all the sacrifices" with their children being "shuffled around, relocated and reassigned," while the only sacrifice white folks need to make is "to come into that community." "If the school is going to be so good," he asked, "why can't we stay there?"[23]

The group that Howard led held its meetings at the Urban League office across from the school, and was still overseen by Howard's mentor, Wesley Scott. They organized marches, appeared on Black radio and television, and engaged local congregations to get the word out that their hard-won school facility was about to be taken away. They also stirred up national attention. In 1980, Rev. Joseph O'Neill hosted a conference at his church titled "Desegregation: A New Form of Discrimination." Derrick Bell, who had first visited Milwaukee in 1963 as an NAACP attorney to promote school integration, was invited to give the keynote address. This time Bell criticized civil rights activists who, as he once did, rigidly supported desegregation policies that closed Black schools regardless of whether it improved the quality of instruction for Black students.[24] During the course of his remarks, he mentioned the publication of his new book, *Shades of Brown*, which included essays by Ron Edmonds and Diane Ravitch.[25]

The impasse among the various players in the two-year-long drama was resolved when Howard Fuller negotiated an out-of-court settlement accepted by Judge Reynolds that kept North Division as a neighborhood school and created a medical specialty program that was open to students from outside the community. In so doing, Fuller redefined and reclaimed *Brown* rather than rejected it—as African American scholars like Bell and Edmonds and eventually James Forman Jr. would do, linking equity to quality education. Although Fuller did not accept the notion that all Black schools are inherently unequal, he continued to support a program that was designed to encourage racial diversity and improve learning. In so doing he maintained the support of Wesley Scott's Urban League, which was concerned with strengthening the Black community, and of the Milwaukee NAACP, which had not given up on integration. Both groups were essential to maintain comity.

In finally crafting a compromise, Fuller remained sensitive to how various stakeholders in the debate viewed resolution of the race issue. As historian Jack Dougherty concluded in his excellent analysis of the episode, "Fuller supported advocates of strong black identity, but did not abandon integration in the traditional sense. . . . His genius was to craft a new language that appealed to supporters of both black self-determination and fair integration."[26]

* * *

For Howard Fuller, resolving the North Division struggle was an act of political moderation. Before long, it would become evident that the times did not call for moderation. In two months' time, the Ernest Lacy incident occurred. Lacy, a twenty-two-year-old Black man, had been on his way to the store when three white police officers, looking for someone who had raped a woman, approached and wrestled him to the ground. In order to subdue him, one officer leaned his knee against the young man's throat, cutting off his windpipe. The actual rapist was eventually apprehended. Innocent Ernest Lacy died in the back of a police van, the victim of a George Floyd–type of murder that precipitated the Black Lives Matter movement years later. The Milwaukee Police Department had a history of brutality toward Black men; the community was enraged.

Howard Fuller became a leader of the Coalition for Justice for Ernest Lacy. His group organized four major demonstrations, including one in which four thousand people marched at the sight where Lacy was arrested. After a grand jury had recommended that the officers involved be charged with homicide, the district attorney dropped the charges, claiming that the officers' civil rights had been violated because race was a consideration for jury selection. Howard was one of the demonstrators physically dragged out of the district attorney's office after that decision was announced.

Three years passed—1983—before the Milwaukee Fire and Police Commission, prompted by a complaint brought by Lacy's mother, rendered a decision that in any way resembled an attempt at justice. The officer who had applied his knee to Lacy's neck was found guilty of excessive force and fired from his post. Four other officers involved were found guilty of failing to render assistance. Two were suspended for sixty days and the other two for twenty-five days before returning to duty. Nobody was sent to prison.

* * *

If the Lacy episode underscored how fundamentally racist the political system is, it did not discourage Howard Fuller from working from within it to achieve his objectives. Although he never hesitated to call it as it was and heap criticism from the outside, Howard also emphasized, "There's got to be some of us inside the system."[27] In defiance of criticism he got from both system operatives and sworn rabble-rousers, that insider/outsider role worked for him. In 1988, Fuller startled local politicians when, after much fanfare about the designation, he returned the Martin Luther King Jr. Humanitarian Award he had received from the City of Milwaukee after hearing that outgoing mayor Henry Maier would be honored at the same ceremony. Claiming that the popular official's twenty-eight-year legacy "stood in direct contradiction" to King's and that the honor was a "slap in the face" to Black people, Fuller issued a statement reading, "There may very well be good reasons for Henry Maier to be honored . . . but being a positive force for empowerment of black people is clearly not one of them."[28]

When Democratic state legislator Anthony Earl announced his run for governor in 1982, Fuller took the lead in lining up support for the white Democrat by forming the Black Political Network. After winning a close primary and roundly defeating his Republican opponent, Earl appointed Fuller secretary of the Wisconsin Employment Relations Department, where he negotiated collective bargaining contracts and oversaw affirmative action. Being a member of the governor's cabinet enabled Howard to expand his ties with government and business leaders beyond the Black community. The connections would prove to be vital when he turned his attention back to education.

At that point, racial integration, and especially forced busing, was losing favor among Black parents in Milwaukee, as elsewhere, giving way to concerns about quality schools and accountability. With more white families moving from the city to the suburbs, the prospect of racial balance within Milwaukee would ultimately be defeated by the mathematics of migration. In 1985, 70 percent of the student body in the city would be Black.[29] A voluntary city-suburban transfer program that had been established in 1976 when Judge Reynolds ordered Milwaukee to desegregate bore modest results. A metropolitan plan put forward by the local school board and Superintendent Lee McMurrin drew little support from the suburbs. As Jack Coons observed in his story about the Latina child expelled from the Orinda, California, school district in 2014 over a residency dispute, suburban public schools are public only for those families who can afford their high-priced real estate and property taxes. Milwaukee's metropolitan plan was also denounced by Black nationalists, including Fuller, as another round of "body shuffling" and school closings.

McMurrin had been in denial about how badly the Milwaukee schools were doing. When the superintendent began to tout improvements in test scores and a narrowing of the racial achievement gap during the 1983–1984 school year, Fuller publicly attacked his report as a "sham" and an "insult," noting that three times as many Blacks than whites had scored in the lowest category.[30] If anything, McMurrin's crowing was a manifestation of the low expectations he had of the children in his charge. Think about this the next time someone tells you that things are going well in urban schools. The moment of truth would finally come when Fuller persuaded Governor Earl to appoint an independent commission to study the performance of the Milwaukee school district and its surrounding suburbs.

The Governor's Commission on the Quality of Education in Metropolitan Milwaukee not only made the public less reliant on school district leadership for information about its own performance; it engendered a new political climate—a psychological staging ground, if you will—for school reformers of different stripes to come together for the purpose of actualizing change. Three figures in particular came to the forefront.

The first was George Mitchell, a Republican conservative with strong ties to the business sector. A numbers-crunching management consultant with keen analytical skills, he was acutely aware of how ill-prepared public school graduates were to fill jobs that came available in Milwaukee and the unease it caused among business leaders. Earl installed Mitchell as chair of the commission.

Howard, then a member of the governor's cabinet, was also added to the panel. Given their differing political orientations, one had to wonder how Howard and George would get along. Having adopted a Black child of their own, George and his wife, Susan, had seen the city schools from a parent's perspective. Susan was already active on education issues. The couple became strong political allies of Howard's, at least for a while.

Then there was Annette "Polly" Williams. Like Howard, Polly Williams was a graduate of North Division High School. A single mother of four who worked hard at a variety of jobs until unemployment forced her onto public assistance, Williams eventually got her life together and finished college. Having lost faith in the public schools of Milwaukee and refusing to allow her children to be bused out of her neighborhood, she was an active parent at Urban Day School, one of a small number of independent schools in the city that managed to raise private funds to educate underresourced Black families looking for alternatives.

After two unsuccessful tries to win a seat in the Wisconsin state assembly, Williams was elected in 1980 to represent the Near North District and would remain there for thirty years. Her ascendance to the post would change the politics of the city and the state for years to come. In 1984, she led the state's effort in support of Jesse Jackson's presidential campaign and began to gain national attention. Years later, she was honored in a Rose Garden ceremony hosted by President George W. Bush for her contributions as an education advocate. Polly knew how to stir things up and never missed an opportunity to do so. She occasionally tossed out ideas like establishing a residency requirement for Milwaukee teachers or forcing them to send their children to public schools, knowing all the while that the union would never let the legislature do either.

Like Howard, Polly was very tough minded. Even though they were the strongest of allies, Howard and Polly would come to have serious differences over tactics. Those differences, however animated they could be, were usually overcome by the friendship and trust that existed between them.

When I recently mentioned Polly's name to Howard, he snapped back with the word, "Love." As he put it, "Even when Polly and I were angry, it was based on love. We would call each other the next day and say, 'How are you?' I gave her an award from BAEO."[31] In 2013, the year before she died, Williams was the first person to be inducted into BAEO's Hall of Fame. When she appeared to receive the award, she blurted out, "And now all the parents are in the BAEO Hall of Fame."[32] Like Howard, Polly knew her clients, and they were the same folks for both of them. Her collaboration with Howard Fuller would change the course of history for schooling in America.

8

Howard Fuller

"Black Power"

By the early 1980s, Howard Fuller and Polly Williams were already making common cause to promote neighborhood schools, the hiring of more African American educators, a multicultural curriculum, and better teacher training. Their demands eventually led to experimentation with site-based management, but it was insufficient to make a real difference. The Mitchell Commission began to release its findings in 1985 while discussions were proceeding about implementing a metropolitan desegregation plan. The gathered data documented consistent learning deficits on the part of Black students in the city and the suburbs, correlations between poverty and achievement, and a dropout rate in the city that was five times that of the suburbs. On the whole, suburban schools, having lower poverty rates, were doing better—and the gap between Black and white test scores was widening.[1] The commission's negative findings helped put an end to the McMurrin regime in 1985, which one school board member at the time dubbed "a white boys club."[2] His tenure was briefly followed by the selection of an interim superintendent, Hawthorne Faison, who was the first Black person in Milwaukee's history to assume the role.

Under pressure from the federal court, and sanctioned by the NAACP, Milwaukee finally reached a settlement in 1987 with twenty-four suburban districts for a compromise metropolitan desegregation plan. The city's schools that were not shuttered nonetheless remained segregated and underperforming. In 1989, George Mitchell dropped another bombshell when he published a report showing that, since 1976, the suburbs had received $76.9 million to educate students from the city—an amount far in excess of the actual cost.[3] The revelation provoked one state senator to denounce how the suburbs "made out like bandits."[4] A local newspaper editorial referred to the funding as "bounty money."[5]

If the final metropolitan plan went forward without much resistance, it did not quiet more outspoken members of the Black community led by

Radical Dreamers. Joseph P. Viteritti, Oxford University Press. © Oxford University Press (2025). DOI: 10.1093/oso/9780197827109.003.0008

Williams and Fuller. They had seen it all coming. The disparities evident on the basis of race and income would not allow anyone to avoid the perennial question of where to find cause: Was it a result of the social deficits Black children brought to school with them from home? Or was it the schools themselves? Fuller and Williams had answers to these questions too. Like Ron Edmonds, Derrick Bell, Stokely Carmichael, and other outspoken Black leaders, Williams and Fuller associated low expectations for the children they represented with attitudes of white racism.

Commenting on the school battles playing out in Milwaukee at the time, historian Bill Dahlk made a curious observation about new research that was appearing when he wrote,

> The economic and social crisis the community experienced during the 1980s played a part in shaping new directions. . . . Studies completed by analysts such as James Coleman, Michael Rutter, and Ron Edmonds, and published in the 1980s began to point to factors that might produce effective schools.[6]

Rutter was a British scholar who had contributed to the effective schools literature.[7] Dahlk goes on to enumerate the observable factors associated with effective schools. They were similar to those identified in our previous discussion of Edmonds's research. What's most striking about the Dahlk excerpt is his pairing of the Edmonds and Coleman findings as though the two men were of a single mind. By this time, Coleman had completed his surveys of Catholic schools (*Coleman III*), which Dahlk cited, and had concluded—contrary to what he had said in *Coleman I*—that schools can make a difference in boosting the academic achievement of children hampered by the effects of poverty. Having been coaxed along by Jack Coons, Coleman also had come to believe that offering choices to these students beyond underperforming public schools could advance the country toward the elusive goal of educational equality. In *Coleman II*, the distinguished sociologist had already cast doubt on the efficacy of forced busing for the purposes of racial integration.

* * *

Publication of the Mitchell Commission data was a catalyst for more intense political mobilization in Milwaukee. Once again, the scene of the action was the North Division School community. This time both of North Division High School's most celebrated graduates were at the center of it.

They were unforgiving of the public schools and their leaders. Their position could be summarized: If the white political establishment is incapable of providing a good education for our children, let us do it ourselves! Fuller and Williams led a campaign to establish North Division as a separate Black-run school district. As Williams explained, "We must develop our own plan to educate our children, since no one else seems interested in doing it."[8]

Fuller prepared a document outlining their agenda that became known as the "Milwaukee Manifesto."[9] Registering "outrage," Fuller accused school officials of resorting to a "blaming the victim" mentality whereby educators assumed that the "poor performance" of Black children was a "logical and predictable extension of their race or family income." This thinking, argued Fuller, is what fed demands for forced integration, or a "divide them up and disperse them" strategy, which "accepts as an axiom the notion that the Black community is so pathological that only a dispersal methodology offers any possibility of hope for our children."

Fuller called for the implementation of "effective educational strategies for our children in the schools" that would "not only ground them in the basic skills of reading, writing and arithmetic, but also help them develop the thinking and analytical abilities necessary for them to influence, control, and, where necessary, change their world." Like dissatisfied parents in Brooklyn's Ocean Hill–Brownsville neighborhood from a generation earlier, Milwaukee parents wanted more accountability and control over an education delivery system that had lost their confidence. Fuller and Williams also believed that parental involvement in their children's education was an essential feature of effective learning. Fuller concluded his manifesto with a quote from the then-late Ron Edmonds,

> Demographic desegregation must take a backseat to instructional reform or we will remain frustrated by the continuing and widening gap between black and white pupil performance in desegregated schools. . . . We must abandon the legal perspective that treats desegregation litigation as a matter solely of racial balance and assume quality education comes with that balance.

By this time, Governor Earl had been succeeded by Republican Tommy Thompson. Howard knew Thompson from his time in state government when Thompson was serving in the US Congress representing Milwaukee. The two shared a common dissatisfaction with the school system.

Thompson initially threw his support behind the North Division proposal, encouraged along those lines by George Mitchell and business leaders. Then the governor changed his mind. The plan was endorsed by twenty-seven locally prominent Black leaders, including Wesley Scott, who had retired from his post as director of the Urban League. But it ran into steep opposition, starting with school superintendent Hawthorne Faison and school board president David Cullin. Many more moderate Black politicians were like-minded in their skepticism. Grover Hankins, general counsel to the NAACP, referred to the plan's authors as "apostles of urban apartheid."[10] A poll taken by the *Milwaukee Journal* found that 62 percent of likely voters opposed it while 27 percent were in support.[11]

Anticipating possible litigation, Fuller reached out to Derrick Bell, who had been involved in the first North Division battle. Bell traveled to Milwaukee, and the two men discussed the issues that concerned Howard.[12] A month after the manifesto became public, Bell wrote an op ed for the *Milwaukee Journal*. A typewritten copy that Howard shared with me included legal references that did not appear in the newspaper version. It was published under the title "Control, Not Color: The Real Issue in the Milwaukee Manifesto."[13] After laying out his bona fides as a constitutional law scholar with ten years of experience as a desegregation litigator, the Harvard professor took issue with civil rights attorneys who had condemned the plan because of their "rigid" understanding of "equal educational opportunity." He declared that the "Manifesto" was "clearly legal, educationally necessary, and politically long overdue." He cited cases in Detroit and Dallas where the Supreme Court, despite opposition from the NAACP, supported community plans that maximized achievement over racial balance without entirely abandoning the long-term goals of greater integration.

Introducing the element of class as well as race as a necessary consideration for both white and Black parties in the dispute, the prominent educator chided the plan's skeptics for their hypocritical stance:

> Let us be honest. Can we whose children are not required to attend the inner city schools honestly condemn the Manifesto writers and their supporters? After all, when middle-class parents—black and white—lose faith in the administration of a public school, we move to another school district or place our children in private schools. Inner-city black parents who can't afford our options seek as a group a legislative remedy that may after a long

struggle enable them to do what we achieve independently by virtue of our higher economic status.

Bell followed this up by sending Fuller a fifty-page legal paper written by Karen J. Putnam, defending the constitutionality of the demands contained in the manifesto.[14] I assume Putnam was a former student of Bell's who wrote the paper under his supervision, but neither Howard nor I were able to confirm that. The cover letter that Bell sent with the document was on Harvard Law School stationery, and it closed with the request, "Please call me and tell me about the Milwaukee situation."[15]

Putnam began her document with a quote from Ron Edmonds, who had already left us—physically at least—five years earlier. It also included references to Diane Ravitch's essay that appeared in Bell's *Shades of Brown* collection. I will not delve into the legal arguments Putnam offered here or her poignant analysis of "desegregation" efforts that had been under way for a decade since the federal court stepped in. I do, however, want to highlight an illuminating observation she made about how the desegregation goals agreed to by civil rights attorneys ran smack up against the community's desire for more control over the education of their children.

Citing data that the Milwaukee school district was less than 35 percent white, Putnam explained that under the existing negotiated settlement, a school that was 60 percent white would be deemed "desegregated" by the court, but a school that was 55 percent Black would be considered "segregated."[16] This standard not only guaranteed Black students and their parents minority status in their schools, it was a recipe for Black political disempowerment. Be reminded that the schools included in the North Division manifesto were more than 90 percent Black, and the plan did not exclude white students.

Due to the perseverance of Assemblywoman Polly Williams and her allies in the state capitol, the Wisconsin State Assembly passed the bill on March 17, 1988, by a vote of sixty-one to thirty-six, to establish a North Division District consisting of the high school and its feeder schools.[17] But its champions could not overcome opposition in the Republican-controlled state senate, where the bill ultimately died. The defeat did not discourage institutional separationists; rather, it emboldened them to demand more. If Derrick Bell's class-based analysis of educational opportunity could justify creating a separate school district, it could do the same for a broader program of school choice. If parents could not get the kind of accountability they sought through neighborhood-based political decentralization, school choice could give them the ultimate form of control.

* * *

Hawthorne Frazier would have remained as superintendent after completing McMurrin's term in 1988, but the school board wanted change and decided to conduct a national search. All of a sudden, the world seemed to get smaller when they chose Robert Peterkin from Massachusetts as their new schools chief. Peterkin had originally made a name for himself as an innovative school principal in Boston, and then as an aid to Superintendent Robert Wood. He is the same Bob Peterkin who, through the good graces of Ron Edmonds, served as an inside resource for me in 1981 when I ran Bud Spillane's transition replacing Wood. Bob stayed on as Bud's deputy superintendent. He was awarded his own superintendency in 1984 when he was chosen to run the Cambridge schools across the Charles River from Boston.

Peterkin, on the lookout for new talent in Cambridge, brought on as his top deputy Deborah McGriff, whom he knew through a network of educators involved in the effective schools movement. This was the same Deborah McGriff who, as a young educator in New York in 1984, helped found the Ron Edmonds Learning Center in Brooklyn, right after Ron died. It was she who would put me in touch with the Edmonds family as I wrote this book.

Unlike previous public school leaders in Milwaukee, Peterkin and McGriff were not opposed to school choice. They had gained national attention in Cambridge by adopting a system of "controlled choice." Students had access to all thirteen elementary schools in Cambridge so long as space was available and their enrollment met the racial goals of the city's voluntary desegregation agreement. In an article Peterkin coauthored years later for the *Journal of Negro Education* that ends with a quote from Ron Edmonds, he remarked that he initially found Cambridge's magnet program "exclusionary."[18] His plan featured "excellence and equity" as "twin goals."[19] Under his leadership, the percentage of Cambridge students who passed all three of the state's mandated tests improved from 54 percent to 89 percent.[20]

When Peterkin and McGriff arrived in Milwaukee in 1988, public schools in Black neighborhoods were being closed and the selection process for so-called specialty schools was under criticism for being unfair. They experimented with a decentralization plan designed to bring school administrators closer to parents and a magnet program that would create new opportunities in two separate zones.[21] Neither gained much support or approval from parents and local politicians. Peterkin and McGriff also created an immersion program for at-risk Black males that focused on African culture and racial pride. It drew opposition from integrationists for "resegregating" the system that was already segregated.

In 1989, Peterkin and McGriff launched a "controlled choice" initiative modeled after their Cambridge program. By then, such plans were under criticism for not providing a sufficient number of options for students stuck in underperforming schools.[22] Peterkin and McGriff finally pushed the envelope to the edge when they came up with a proposal that would have given at-risk students access to programs at private community-based schools with proven records that met set standards for accountability.[23] The idea of utilizing nonpublic schools as a remedy for perpetual failure died a sudden death at the hands of the teachers' union. But it wouldn't end there.

The political climate was warming to demands for greater choice in education beyond the chronically failing public schools available to most Black families. Howard Fuller and Polly Williams remained relentless in their efforts to give parents more control over the education of their children. They received indispensable, if unassumed, support for their cause from Republican governor Tommy Thompson. The state executive was feeling pressure from business leaders about the rising costs and declining performance of Milwaukee's public schools. In 1988, Thompson submitted a bill in the state legislature that would have provided scholarships for low-income children to attend private and religious schools. It went nowhere—immediately opposed by state school superintendent Herbert Grover and the teachers' unions. The bill also gained little support from minority lawmakers, including the chair of the state legislature's joint finance committee, who declared it dead on arrival. Even assembly member Polly Williams sat the battle out, declining to get behind the Republican governor.

In 1989, Williams put forward her own school choice proposal, excluding the participation of religious schools. Her sponsorship, along with Howard Fuller's grassroots organizing that brought busloads of parents to the state capitol, drastically altered the stakes of the contest. Most Black lawmakers lined up behind Polly. Governor Thompson helped bring along the Republican lawmakers. Additional outside support came from Milwaukee mayor John Norquist, a white Democrat, and Michael Joyce, chair of the conservative Lynde and Harry Bradley Foundation, which had a history of providing scholarships for disadvantaged children to attend parochial schools. The NAACP and most white liberals lined up with the teachers' organization against the bill. This time, Williams prevailed, carrying the proposal through the assembly and wining senate support. Governor Thompson signed the bill into law in April 1990.[24]

If you ask Howard Fuller, he will tell you that this odd alliance among Black nationalists, public school parents, Republicans, Catholic educators, businesspeople, and conservatives was a shining example of Derrick Bell's interest convergence phenomenon, to which Fuller enthusiastically subscribes.[25] I don't think Polly Williams would disagree with that, but she definitely viewed the episode from a more cynical perspective. She did not trust the motives of religious leaders or conservatives. She thought they were self-serving and more concerned with subsidizing their tuition than the children she deemed to be her own constituents and clients. That is why she would not support the participation of religious schools in the program.

I never heard her use the term;, but if one person understood the pitfalls of surrogate politics, it was Polly Williams. She was ever aware—"suspicious" may be a more accurate descriptor—of people's motives, and would not hesitate to say so when she saw fit, no matter whose name was at stake.

Beyond Polly's suspicion of her conservative allies for choice, she also had some choice words for white liberals who feigned support for the cause of racial justice, but fought against her bill to expand opportunities for underserved children. Celebrating the moment of victory, she declared,

> We have been saved from our saviors. . . . Our friends have built their whole lives around taking care of us and they still want to feed us with pablum. . . . At some point we want to make our own decisions.
>
> You've got to go directly to the people experiencing the problem. They'll work out how to get out of this despair. . . . You should not go through the hands of these so-called saviors, who benefit from our misery. . . . They benefit from keeping our kids dumb. . . . Then you keep constantly generating funds, and they all get jobs.[26]

The opponents would exact their price in the form of a negotiated law that had a limited reach and impact. Although its benefits were targeted at low-income families (175 percent of the poverty level or twenty thousand dollars for a family of three), the number of participants was limited to 1 percent of the entire public school population. The amount of each scholarship could not exceed twenty-five hundred dollars, whereas the state appropriated approximately six thousand dollars per student to the city public schools. Imagine that: A program created to address the needs of underserved children underfunded these same children.[27] The exclusion of religious schools from the program, moreover, made most nonpublic schools in the city ineligible to participate.[28] Given the changing political landscape of the country, however, the passage of the Milwaukee School Choice Act was a monumental and historic accomplishment that further influenced the political dynamics surrounding American education.

* * *

Soon after the law was passed, Superintendent Robert Peterkin accepted a position at the Harvard Graduate School of Education. Peterkin had endorsed the choice bill, and his school board was fine with it. As the board began to search for a successor, many, including Howard Fuller, saw Peterkin's erstwhile deputy, Deborah McGriff, as the obvious candidate to carry forward his agenda. She was one of two final candidates. But as Deborah soon discovered and frankly explained to me, "Milwaukee wasn't ready for a woman superintendent."[29] Deborah was eventually selected to serve as superintendent of schools in Detroit. After Detroit, she went on to serve as a vice president at Edison Schools. She became a star in her own right.

When Howard Fuller got word that Deborah would not be chosen, he put his own name forward. The news that this man who had molded his career as a leading critic of the school system now wanted to run it caught many veteran observers off guard. It unsettled Polly, who blamed the system for shortchanging so many lives.

* * *

By the time he was sworn in as Milwaukee's superintendent of schools in 1991, Howard Fuller had all the markings of an ultimate system insider. Following his service in Governor Tony Earl's cabinet, he had added lines to his resume as dean of general education at the Milwaukee Area Technical College and director of the Milwaukee County Division of Health and Human Services. But real insiders, those who are the true careerists, don't tend to make waves. They go along to get along, and that was not Howard's style. As dean of the technical college, he had seen how unprepared Milwaukee's public school graduates were for the challenges of work and study. In overseeing social services for the county, he witnessed firsthand the toll those deficits could take on a person's life.

Coming into the city school job, Howard enjoyed strong support within the Black community and the backing of Democratic mayor John Norquist, but he also had his doubters. Integrationists, especially the local NAACP leadership, remained uncomfortable with his Black nationalist tendencies. Polly Williams supported his appointment but was unable to get beyond her deep suspicion of the system her partner in protest would now lead— and who could blame her? Howard was now in the top perch, but it would be a rocky ride. He could guarantee that all by himself by just being Howard.

Fuller followed through with many of the initiatives undertaken by his predecessor Bob Peterkin. These included reduced busing, an emphasis on early childhood education and the elementary grades, and smaller class sizes. Concerned that an entire generation of Black kids was being raised "with absolutely no connection to their history and culture," Fuller also continued to accentuate the significance of race and identity as essential elements of academic instruction and psychological development.[30]

On Saturday mornings, Howard took time out to teach in the Afro-Centric Commando project on North Avenue, which was attended largely by Muslim students from Milwaukee Area Technical College. He also introduced students to a broad cross-section of Black thinkers representing diverse attitudes and philosophies, including Marcus Garvey, W. E. B. Du Bois, Booker T. Washington, Martin Luther King Jr., and Malcolm X. As superintendent, Fuller supported the creation of two African American Immersion Schools. That idea ran into problems with the teachers' union when Fuller proposed that the schools should be staffed primarily by Black teachers who could better function as role models and mentors. The union was more concerned with protecting seniority, which happened to favor its white members with more years of service.

As Fuller's instructional agenda came into its own, the influence of Ron Edmonds's effective-schools research grew more apparent. Sounding very much like Edmonds, Fuller insisted that if we sincerely strive to do better with urban schools, "it is not a question of research; it is a question of the political will to do what has to be done and to do it now."[31] Howard was more inclined than Ron to speak about the raw stakes of politics, so he bluntly added, "There are going to be tensions. . . . There are going to be racial tensions. We are talking about changing the culture of the organization." Thinking pedagogically, he outlined the perquisites of effective schools in terms of five key variables: higher expectations, improved teacher morale, safe and orderly schools, increased parental involvement, and accountability for results.

The first and last factors especially were keystones to Fuller's approach as superintendent. With regard to the first, he cautioned that there are "some people who for a variety of reasons have given up, have decided that these kids cannot learn."[32] He went on, "We have to have people who believe in these children. . . . We cannot say, 'Well these are just *those* kids. What can you expect from *those* kids.'"[33] As superintendent, Fuller was unsparing on the accountability issue, mindful that "there are no consequences for failure; everybody was protected, everybody, that is, but the children themselves."[34]

On another occasion, Fuller was quoted lamenting, "There are people in our system who believe that the system was created for their jobs. That they own their jobs. Not that this belongs to the community, but that it belongs to them. . . . And we're going to have to root all that out."[35] The types of personalities he is referring to can be found in all large public bureaucracies. They are not representative of the larger population of dedicated public servants, but they can wield an inordinate amount of influence and set the tone for doing business. In New York, if you recall, we had Big Pants, who presided over his fiefdom at 110 Livingston Street as though he had a proprietary stake in the organization. We also had the naysayers who cautioned the chancellor in the presence of Ron Edmonds not to overpromise what we could deliver with the students in our care.

Although Fuller did not articulate it in theoretical terms, as the top official in the school system he was intimately aware of the political dilemma Ron Edmonds described as the dichotomy between constituents and clients—and he knew what he had to do about it. It shaped his behavior whether he was playing the role of insider to the system or outsider. It governed the way he defined the political alliances he formed, however lasting they might or might not be, to achieve his objectives.

Commenting on Fuller's tenure as superintendent, historian Bill Dahlk wrote, "Technically, Fuller was the school board's agent, but in reality his main allegiance was to the Milwaukee black community and especially to the community's low-income families."[36] Jonathan Coleman similarly observes, in his rendering of the Milwaukee story, Fuller's understanding that "the school system needed to view parents and their students as customers, as people who had a right to satisfaction and could take their business elsewhere, without cost, if they didn't find it."[37]

* * *

Coleman's astute observation sheds light on Fuller's broader vision of education that was very much his own. It called for replacing the centralized bureaucratic public school system with "a system of schools."[38] He had alluded to the idea in his contretemps with Elizabeth Warren during her campaign stop in Atlanta in 2019. His approach was a complete rejection of the "One Best System" common school model we inherited from the nineteenth-century Taylorists, those same reformers who had deemed the factory to be an optimal workplace.[39] Stripped of ideological branding, Fuller's philosophy could be reduced to a "try any damn thing that might work" approach. To careerists and protectors of the status quo, Fuller's vision was heretic.

Seated in the superintendent's office, Fuller advocated for charter schools that would replace failing public schools. He sought to bring in private corporations to run them on a contractual basis with the understanding that the schools would be staffed with more Black teachers and administrators and held accountable for their performance. As Bob Peterkin had tried earlier, Fuller wanted to engage private schools with strong academic records to work with public school students who needed extra help. Cautioned by school board members who were becoming increasingly uneasy with his provocations, Fuller rarely spoke of school vouchers during his tenure, though he obviously remained a supporter.

These same wary school board members also understood that to Fuller, trying anything also included giving public schools everything they needed to succeed. That fact can get lost on some of Fuller's more severe critics, who mistake his opposition to perpetual failure as opposition to public education itself. He demonstrated his commitment early in his tenure as superintendent. In 1992, his second year on the job, Fuller put forward an ambitious ten-year capital plan to address problems he identified as overcrowding, large class sizes, excessive busing, insufficient space for kindergarteners, and deferred maintenance.[40] If realized, the $474 million project would have built fifteen new schools and expanded fourteen others.

The popular new superintendent's proposal proved to be divisive, mostly along racial lines. Mayor John Norquist, usually a Fuller ally, was concerned about the costs as he faced reelection. Most white city council members shared the mayor's concern and lined up with him against the superintendent. Trusting Fuller as an advocate for their communities that had much to gain, every African American council member supported it. With the promise of more resources pouring into the public schools, Fuller and the teachers' union were for once on the same page. Surprisingly, the tax-conscious business community also got behind Fuller, hoping he could do something to turn around the ailing system. Most surprising of all was the opposition Fuller's proposal drew from Polly Williams, who could not get past her suspicion of the system that had consistently betrayed so many of her constituents.

When Howard could not get the council and the mayor to fund his plan, he persuaded the school board to present it to the voters in the form of a popular referendum. A heated televised debate between Howard and Polly that took place a week before the February vote went down as the most memorable face-off of the entire controversy. With an unusually high turnout at the polls, the ballot issue was defeated by a margin of three to one largely along racial lines. White districts voted eight to one against it; Black districts supported it by a vote of two to one.[41] The humiliating defeat prompted Fuller to press harder in exposing the shortcomings of the system and to demand more accountability. He published a rating system that ranked individual schools according to three levels of academic performance: high achieving, improving, and in need of assistance.

Fuller also knew that information was not enough to rescue students from instructionally bankrupt institutions. He began to lose support on the school board and especially infuriate the teachers' union when he endorsed a plan that would reconstitute failing schools and replace their staffs with personnel employed by privately run education providers, such as the Edison Project or EAI (Educational Alternatives Incorporated).

In 1993, the Wisconsin state legislature passed a charter school law that would have allowed Fuller to reconstitute only two schools—and he would be required to use the schools' own personnel governed by the existing labor contract. Fuller refused, objecting that he was not being granted the flexibility needed to implement a viable model for effective schools. With tensions increasing between Fuller and the education establishment throughout the 1994–1995 school year, the Milwaukee Teachers' Education Association (MTEA) decided to invest a significant amount of campaign money in the upcoming school board elections that spring. Five of nine seats were at stake. Union candidates took four of them. Fuller resigned two weeks later.

* * *

Following his resignation, Howard accepted a position as a Distinguished Professor at Marquette University, where he established the Institute for the

Transformation of Learning. From that point forward, his career would be dedicated to the implementation of school choice locally and nationally. Two perpetual questions have dominated that policy debate: What schools should be permitted to participate in publicly supported programs? Which students should be targeted as its beneficiaries? The interaction of tactical and principled considerations was now on full exhibit, populated by an ever-changing cast of allies and adversaries.

The terms of the Milwaukee Parental Choice Program (MPCP) passed by the Wisconsin legislature in 1990 were so limiting that only a total of 341 low-income students attended seven nonreligious private schools during its first year of operation.[42] The program was actually conceived as a pilot that would gradually grow in size, but by 1994 it still only had enrolled 830 students in twelve schools. MPS enrollments exceeded 100,000. That year, the business sector and the Catholic Diocese of Milwaukee got behind a campaign that would raise the enrollment cap and allow religious schools to accept scholarship students. A key player in the effort was Michael Joyce of the Bradley Foundation, whose philanthropy subsidized the education of nearly 4,500 low-income students attending private and religious schools.[43] Bradley's scholarships not only expanded educational opportunities for students who needed relief, they also created a broader political constituency for school choice. Moreover, Joyce and his foundation were a major source of funding for Howard Fuller's institute at Marquette, a Jesuit university.

Assembly member Polly Williams was not happy with how the more conservative players in the choice camp were taking over the cause. She had never entirely trusted their motives, complaining, "They [conservatives] want religious schools to be tax supported. Blacks and the poor are being used to legitimize [the conservatives] as the power group."[44] Commenting on how Republicans had replaced Democrats as the key power players in education, she drew a harsh parallel that spoke volumes on the politics of racial surrogacy, proclaiming, "The unions and the Democrats have always had it [power over education]. Now the Republicans and the businessmen want to take over.... Neither cares about the children. It's like changing slave masters."[45]

Howard Fuller was more calculating in his reasoning. He understood that students needed more options. He knew that Catholic and religious schools had a history of serving Black and poor communities. He himself was a product of Catholic schools. That said, Howard was also cautious.

Mindful that some of his own supporters—including Michael Joyce, Mayor John Norquist, and many business leaders—wanted to move toward a Milton Friedman–type universal voucher program that would be open to all students, he was adamant, "I would argue vociferously against any effort to expand choice beyond the needs of low-income people. Such a strategy would defeat the reason why we fought for choice."[46]

Polly understood all that too. She eventually embraced hopes that an expanded choice program would encourage Black pastors to open schools affiliated with their churches. After Republicans captured majorities in both houses of the legislature in November 1994, their leadership pulled an unorthodox parliamentary move by appointing Polly Williams, a Democrat, to chair the Assembly Urban Education Committee. It was she and Republican majority leader Scott Jensen who crafted a bill that allowed up to 15 percent (approximately fifteen thousand students) of the MPS population to attend private or religious schools at no charge using state funds. All scholarships remained needs-based by income. Governor Thompson signed the law in 1995.

It took no time at all for the teachers' unions, the American Civil Liberties Union (ACLU), and the NAACP to bring litigation in the state courts to stop the program, claiming that providing public assistance for students to attend religious schools violated constitutional requirements for the separation of church and state. Although the original program was allowed to proceed, religious schools were barred from participation while the case was litigated over a period of three years. The uncertainty created by the court challenge discouraged many parents from enrolling. It also brought national attention to Milwaukee. Most notable was a signed editorial that Brent Staples published in the *New York Times* on May 15, 1997.[47]

Staples was one of the few Black men or women to have ever served on the powerful editorial board of the paper at that time. His signature on the piece indicated that he spoke for himself rather than the full board. A man from modest beginnings, he eventually earned a doctorate in psychology from the University of Chicago. His compelling memoir about crossing the boundaries from an isolated Black world to one dominated by a white majority is a testimony on how far some need to travel and the obstacles in their way to a full life.[48] He was not one to hesitate in speaking his mind on racial issues, and Milwaukee drew his attention. Describing how "abysmal schools and an onerous busing program made the city an obvious candidate" for school vouchers, he was mindful to distinguish between Milton Friedman's original proposal and newer "means-based strategies aimed at the poorest of the poor." He noted how the busing program had "scattered inner-city children" to "far-flung schools" doing "little for integration," but "afford[ing] handsome subsidies for suburban schools that took children from the inner city."

Staples described how a "broad coalition" had come together to provide "poor families an escape hatch from miserable city schools." He gave due credit to Polly Williams, the representative from a "poor district in Milwaukee," for writing the law and took issue with the teachers' union, the ACLU, and the NAACP for challenging it. He identified the NAACP among the three for making the weakest argument against the law, because "it defends failing schools on the grounds that vouchers might destroy them."

In 1998, the Wisconsin Supreme Court upheld the constitutionality of the expanded choice program, and the US Supreme Court refused to hear an appeal. The First Amendment issue was resolved once and for all in 2002 when the US Supreme Court favorably reviewed the Cleveland school voucher program in the *Zelman* case.[49]

* * *

I return to the legal questions in a later chapter. For now, let's remain in the political arena. Battles over the scope of school choice in Milwaukee continued after the Expanded Choice Law was passed in 1995. The repeated conflicts underscored how deliberately Fuller proceeded as he navigated his way through tactical considerations and his basic principles. The next two legislative squabbles were especially revealing.

Polly did get her wish granted. Although most of the 100 church-affiliated schools in the program (out of 130 nonpublic in total) were either Catholic or Lutheran, one estimate by Bill Dahlk found that by 2000, there were nearly 20 Black church–affiliated schools in the program; by 2005, they totaled between 30 and 49.[50] In 2002, Wisconsin elected Jim Doyle, its first Democratic governor in sixteen years. The 15 percent (or 15,000-student) cap that appeared generous as a result of the 1995 expansion all of a sudden seemed paltry in a system of 100,000 where excellent public schools were all too rare and many more families wanted their kids to be elsewhere. When Polly Williams and Republican leader Scott Jensen led a bipartisan effort in the Republican-controlled legislature to completely eliminate the cap in 2003, Governor Doyle vetoed it. In November 2004, as choice-friendly Republicans increased their majority in the assembly,

Democrats who were determined to reduce or eliminate the choice program took control of the senate.

The new political alignment led to a disagreement within the choice camp over strategy. Susan Mitchell, who had strong ties with Republican lawmakers, wanted to work with her former allies, who had crafted together their past wins, and go to war with the Democrats. Howard Fuller, seeing that Republicans were incapable of producing the necessary votes to advance their cause, decided that the answer lied with convincing Democrats, including the governor, that they could not afford to betray Black parents—most of whom supported choice—if they wanted to maintain electoral victories. But first, Fuller had to convince Black parents and their political representatives that they could prove his point. He did that artfully.

Fuller launched a fifteen-month campaign to organize affected families, educate community leaders, and raise funds for a media campaign that petitioned Democrats to save the program and open more seats.[51] The coalition members contacted Democratic campaign contributors who were sympathetic to their "Raise the Cap" message. They brought in a national polling firm to determine which opposing legislators were most vulnerable. Pastors took to the pulpit. Signs were posted at participating schools. Ads were run on television and radio in which students related emotional stories about how the program made such a difference in their lives.

In another ad, a burly truck driver brushed back tears confessing that he didn't know how he would tell his daughters that they might need to abandon the school they loved if the program were ended. He also mentioned that Governor Doyle and his wife, who proudly had adopted two African American boys, sent their sons to expensive private schools. A story in the *New York Times* reported, "Governor Doyle, a Democrat, looks like public enemy No. 1 for African American school children."[52]

The governor was scheduled to deliver his State of the State speech in January. It provided choice advocates with a timely opportunity. Customarily delivered with much pomp and circumstance, it was especially significant in this 2006 election year, marking the unofficial launch of Doyle's bid for a second term. As Doyle made his ceremonial walk from the governor's office to the legislative chambers that day, he found the halls crowded with Black children politely holding signs reading, "Please don't destroy my dream." It rattled him. That evening, as TV news stations were about to cover his speech, another ad appeared featuring well-spoken Black children in their school uniforms discussing the challenges they had overcome and begging the governor to hear their desperate pleas. The next morning, when the governor and his staff showed up at their offices for work, they were greeted by a prayer vigil led by one of Milwaukee's most prominent Black ministers.

Howard took it upon himself to win the support of Black Democratic legislators. He began by reaching out to Lena Taylor, a key senator who chaired the Joint Finance Committee.[53] They had been through some brutal battles with each other before, but she agreed to hear him out and they managed to cooperate. Howard likes to tell the story of the "Pound Cake Meeting" where, through Taylor's good graces, he invited the Black Democratic legislators from both chambers to his home and served them his mother's famous pound cake. He also persuaded them to support lifting the cap, which left the Democratic governor no choice. (Pardon the pun.)

After meeting with Howard and other coalition leaders, including Milwaukee's Catholic archbishop Timothy Dolan (now Cardinal Dolan of New York), Governor Doyle agreed to raise the enrollment cap from 15,000 students to 22,500. The deal added some new accountability measures designed to evaluate the success of the program that Howard strongly endorsed. Still peeved over the aggressive tactics taken by his opponents, Doyle refused an invitation to hold the March 2006 signing ceremony at a participating school.

* * *

The political scene had changed significantly when the next battle over the terms of the Milwaukee choice program took place in 2011. So had the coalition that amassed on each side of the debate—especially as far as Howard Fuller was concerned. Republican Scott Walker had been elected governor, and his party dominated both houses of the legislature. Walker was a determined right-wing conservative who began his tenure by sponsoring a law that eliminated collective bargaining rights for public employees. He also wanted to amend the Expanded Choice Law by eliminating the cap on enrollments and allowing all students regardless of income to participate. Many of Howard Fuller's choice allies were on board with Walker's proposed amendments. Howard broke ranks with them on the issue of student eligibility.

In an act of protest, Fuller drafted a document, signed by thirty-four mostly Black members of his coalition, that he personally delivered to the governor and legislature. It outlined the signers' understanding of why the choice program had been instituted from the start and what had to be done to maintain its integrity of purpose.[54] The document begins by explaining that the Milwaukee Parental Choice Program (MPCP) "had its origins in the struggle to educate poor Black children in Milwaukee" and that it "came out of the relentless demand from the Black community to have more tools to seek and gain access to quality education for their children." It then listed a set of policy recommendations the signers supported "to ensure that the MPCP will continue its focus on enabling low-income families in the City of Milwaukee to have the power to choose a quality educational option for their children."

Among the key recommendations were as follows:

- Lift the cap on the number of students who can participate, but remove schools from the program that do not provide quality education.
- Assure equity in per-pupil funding between students in the program and students in the Milwaukee public schools.
- Maintain accountability measures written into the amended law of 2008, including the requirement that students in the program take a state test to establish a common source of data on performance.
- Continue income restrictions for entry, but these requirements "could be adjusted to make sure low-income and struggling working-class families are served."

A new law signed by Governor Walker in 2011 lifted the cap on the number of students who could enroll in the choice program and raised the maximum family income requirement to 300 percent of the federal poverty level ($77,000 for a family of four to allow some working-class families to participate.[55] The latter provision was a compromise signaled by the Fuller group in the fourth item above as an alternative to a Friedman-style universal voucher program that would have opened the program to all students regardless of family wealth or income. Lifting the cap was a long-awaited goal. Accountability measures were maintained. Students in the choice program had never been granted equal funding, nor would they ever. And the Republican conservative push for universal vouchers, though temporarily defeated in Wisconsin, was a sign of things to come on a national scale.

* * *

Howard Fuller had established the Institute for the Transformation of Learning at Marquette in 1996 to serve as a center for information and education on how underserved communities could secure better educations for their children. After the Wisconsin Supreme Court placed its stamp of approval on the Milwaukee Choice Program in 1998, Fuller convened a symposium at the institute to explore the topic of school choice. In 1999, he invited to the institute 150 Black leaders who were committed to redefining public education as a more diverse service delivery system. They discussed vouchers, tax credits, charters, and public-private partnerships. They agreed to continue meeting and to hold annual symposia. They also reached a consensus that if they wanted to transform learning, disseminating information would not be sufficient. They needed to take organized action and they needed to take it beyond Milwaukee.

In December 1999, fifty of those same people met again at the Mayflower Hotel in Washington, DC, to develop a planning document for forming the Black Alliance for Educational Options (BAEO).[56] They went public in July 2000 at a National Press Club event carried by C-SPAN, where Howard Fuller was named chair of a twenty-seven-person board composed entirely of Black men and women. Fuller had secured an $895,000 grant from the Walton Foundation. He subsequently received significant funding from the US Department of Education, the Bill and Melinda Gates Foundation, and the Bradley Foundation. For seventeen years, the group pursued an agenda that combined public information and political advocacy on behalf of choice. They set up regional offices at various locations to encourage grassroots action.

BAEO had a distinct purpose for Howard. Unlike other civil rights organizations that had been founded and, at least in part, run by well-intentioned white advocates, BAEO was organized, run, and populated solely by men and women of color who unambiguously supported a wide range of educational choices for Black and Brown children. Even the staunchest proponents of choice among white school reformers did not have a place in BAEO. When Fuller was asked about this strategy in 2000, he recalled how many meetings he had been invited to around the country to discuss charters, vouchers, and choice, and he reflected,

> What was really interesting to me was that most of those rooms were full of white people, and the discussion was invariably about programs that were going to impact children of color and African American children in particular. So I remember getting up and saying at one of those meetings that there was no way that this battle could be won if the room did not

change, if we did not have more African American people and, I believe, Hispanic people and other people of color involved in the movement.[57]

With that strategy, Fuller, a practitioner of critical race theory who espoused Derrick Bell's convergence dilemma, placed limits on how much his organization would rely on white surrogates to advance the cause of equal education for Black students. It was a dicey strategy to be sure, especially from a fundraising perspective. When I recently asked him about it, he attested, "There would be no BAEO without John Walton." He went on to tell me about an awkward conversation he had with Walton when he called to ask for money and informed the philanthropist, "John, there can be no white people involved in this." Walton, according to Howard, responded favorably, saying, "Okay, I will support anything you do."[58] That was that; then was then. BAEO thrived for seventeen years. I wonder, though, if that strategy had something to do with the organization finally running out of steam for a lack of funding. In case you haven't noticed, most philanthropy and wealth in America is controlled by white folks.

Howard was willing to take the chance because he had a deeper understanding of choice that went beyond the expansion of educational opportunity. It was about race and power. If you read the planning document that he and his BAEO cofounders composed in 1999, it calls for a new educational infrastructure that "truly empowers parents, allows dollars to follow students, holds adults as well as students accountable for academic achievement, and alters the power arrangements that are the foundation of the existing system."[59]

Howard Fuller sees choice as an avenue to power. That is what struck me as a political scientist the first time I heard him speak some thirty years ago. I don't remember where it was, but I clearly remember him stating, "When you give poor folks who have been ignored the power to leave the system and take funding with them, people will pay attention." For me, that was a new insight into the significance of choice beyond the opportunity argument that had brought me to the fold.

When I recently reminded Howard of his remarks from so many years back, he referred me to Albert Hirschman's book *Exit, Voice and Loyalty*.[60] Howard had developed the idea from there, even though, ironically, Hirschman once told him that he did not support school vouchers. (Hirschman eventually changed his mind and became a supporter of school choice.)[61] After sharing the story, Howard proceeded to elaborate, "If you have no power to exit, you have no power. If you have a choice to exit, it actually enables you to materially affect the entity you are exiting."[62] He then added wryly, "Unions and other people who oppose choice understand that better than we do."

When I asked him about the change in direction of the voucher movement toward universal choice, he responded,

> I have always been clear with the road this has put me on. You need to be willing to live with contradiction and carry forward. I knew I was going to be criticized. . . . I always knew some saw low-income vouchers as the nose under the tent. I told them if you change that, I am off the train.[63]

9
Black Women Center Stage

The revolution that began in Milwaukee in 1990 did not end there. Nor was Howard Fuller the only Black leader in America to understand the power dynamic behind choice. He would be the first to remind you of the leadership role Polly Williams played in securing choice in the Wisconsin legislature and fighting to maintain its orientation as a program targeted at the mostly Black children who were not being educated in public schools. Other women—like Deborah McGriff and Gail Foster, whom you met earlier—also come to mind for helping us to understand how choice dignified the parental role and challenged racial stereotypes. Whether that political consciousness would be sufficient in the long run to redirect institutions controlled by the white political class with more abundant resources is another matter. But, of course, that is all part of the larger story on how American education has failed—and we are just scratching the surface here and waiting to see what comes next.

Let me introduce you to two other women, one in Cleveland, another in New York, who appeared to be made from the same mold as Polly Williams and her reform-minded sisters. I know there are many others like them, yet still wonder whether there will ever be enough of these ladies to get us where we need to be. Drawing on an article by Patricia Hill Collins, one scholar has referred to the deeds that women like them perform as "motherwork."[1] The term, according to Professor Terri Watson, applies to motherhood of various types, whether defined by blood or other relationships, all of which describe the "efficacy of the Black mother."[2] Watson elaborates,

> Many African American women receive respect and recognition within their local communities for innovative and practical approaches to mothering not only their own biological children but also the children in their extended family networks and in the community overall. Black women's involvement in fostering African American community development forms the basis of this community-based power.

Radical Dreamers. Joseph P. Viteritti, Oxford University Press. © Oxford University Press (2025).
DOI: 10.1093/oso/9780197827109.003.0009

That brings us to Fannie Lewis, a native of Memphis, Tennessee, where she had worked in a laundry until she moved to Cleveland in 1951 at age twenty-five. For a while she was on welfare, continuing to iron shirts and take odd jobs to make ends meet. She became active in local affairs after the Hough riots of 1965 burned much of her neighborhood to the ground and brought seventeen hundred National Guard troops there to restore order. She subsequently devoted much of her adult life building the area up and resisting the demolition of public housing that was occurring on a grand scale in other cities. She held positions with the city's Neighborhood Youth Corps and the Model Cities program, and was active in efforts to register local residents to vote. After five failed attempts to obtain a seat on the city council, she was elected in 1979 where she reigned in the Hough-based district for nearly thirty years. Referring to her as "Mother Hough," one local journalist lauded her for "her ability to fire a single sentence that can simultaneously lighten the mood, quote scripture, and flatten the poor schmuck who stands in her way."[3]

Like Milwaukee and other northern cities, Cleveland had a long history of failed attempts at school integration and lingering gaps in academic achievement defined by race and class. Cleveland, you will recall, is the city where a young Howard Fuller began his career as an activist for school desegregation in 1964 while completing his studies for a master's degree. In 1995, the same year that Wisconsin passed its Expanded Choice Law, the federal judge overseeing the Cleveland desegregation case determined that the management of the local school district was so inept that he ordered the state superintendent of instruction to take it over. In that same year, the Ohio state legislature passed a bill that supplemented the tuition of students attending private and religious schools.[4]

Many of the ingredients that led to the legislative success of the choice bill in Milwaukee were also present in Cleveland, including a determined woman who had credibility in the Black community. Polly Williams had actually visited with Fannie Lewis while the Cleveland campaign was unfolding. As a local council member with grassroots support, Fannie Lewis helped organize a six-bus caravan of three hundred parents to appear at the state capitol in Columbus when the bill was being debated. Two of her grandchildren were already attending a Catholic school in Cleveland to avoid the disappointing experience her own children had endured in public schools.

As a Democrat, Fannie also worked closely with a Republican governor, George Voinovich; an African American four-term Democratic mayor,

Michael White; and a local philanthropist, David Brennan, who was passionate about school reform. Brennan also had close ties to the Catholic Church, which stood to gain enrollments from the availability of vouchers. The scholarship program was also endorsed by all three of the major newspapers in the state, and enjoyed the backing of the business community.[5] Opposition came from the usual corners, and many Black residents needed convincing to support the proposed program and do something to make it happen. When the Republican-controlled legislature passed the law, Lewis spoke out for the residents of her Hough community: "The people in this neighborhood have been without hope for years. . . . This will give them hope."[6]

Fannie was in the courtroom on that cold day in February 2002 when the US Supreme Court heard oral arguments for the case that would determine the constitutionality of the Ohio Scholarship Program and establish a landmark precedent for similar programs being challenged across the country. After the proceedings were done, the seventy-five-year-old grandmother from Hough appeared on the steps of the Supreme Court, raised both hands into the air, and, months before the decision was officially handed down, proudly declared aloud, "We won!" A photo of that image appeared with a *New York Times* article by Linda Greenhouse reporting on the case.[7]

Lewis was correct. She had listened carefully to the arguments being presented to the court and could sense whose would carry the day. Her side had won the legal battle, and her victory, like that of Howard Fuller and Polly Williams, would go down as a touchstone in the history of American schooling. Let's now take a look at what that win amounted to in policy terms.

As with the Wisconsin law, the end product of the legislative process in Ohio was a compromise. The Cleveland pilot program was a compromise to a statewide program that had been bandied about in the Ohio legislature during budget negotiations. Under the plan, scholarships were awarded by lottery and open to all students in Cleveland with priority given to low-income families. The amount of the award varied by income: Students whose families were at or below 200 percent of the federal poverty level were granted a $2,200 scholarship or an estimated 90 percent of the tuition costs at participating schools. Students with family incomes above that amount were awarded $1,875 or 75 percent of tuition costs. Of the 6,244 families who originally applied, an estimated 58 percent were below the poverty line.

Public schools in Cleveland's surrounding suburbs were also permitted to participate in the program. Students who attended those schools would receive a more generous award of $6,000 that would be given to the school. None of the suburban districts accepted the offer. Fifty-five private and religious schools signed on. In 1996, approximately 1,800 students participated in the program. The following-year's enrollment grew to 3,000. In all, this was a tiny fragment of the total 75,000-student population in Cleveland. Here again the cap was prohibitive, given the need for education alternatives in a city where the state had taken over management of the public schools.

Perhaps most egregious and revealing was the level of spending invested in the program compared to public school spending in Cleveland. Per-capita spending in the city schools was about $6,195 in 1995. At its maximum, the scholarship amount was about 35 percent of that figure. That was the price exacted by the program's opponents through the legislative process. Only in the context of student choice can a program supposedly designed to help economically disadvantaged children come with less spending on those very children than is appropriated for everyone else.

When all is said and done, the same political actors who exact such demands pat themselves on the back as the true champions of public education. We saw it in Milwaukee. We see it here in Cleveland. We witnessed this injustice in nearly every city where the early choice programs appeared. This is why we need to give marginalized parents every opportunity to speak for themselves and have as much control over the education of their own children as possible.

* * *

One more pertinent story draws on a personal encounter I had with a group of parents in Harlem at the behest of a woman named Babette Edwards. It was another one of those pivotal instructional moments—like my encounter with the mothers in Central Park whose children had been lottery winners in the privately funded Children's Scholarship Program that allowed them to exit failing public schools in their neighborhoods, or my conversation with a privileged white colleague with children in elite private schools who could not understand why a gifted Black man like Howard Fuller would devote his energies to creating educational choices for poor Black children beyond the limits of their neighborhood public school boundaries. In such precious moments, you don't just comprehend what you learn; you feel it.

A native of Harlem, Babette Edwards began her advocacy work after a neighbor in her public housing project told her about the condescending treatment she had received from a public school principal when the mother complained that her son's teachers were not using textbooks. That led to "living room meetings" with other parents and eventually to a storied career, some of which is documented and archived in a permanent collection at the Arthur A. Schomburg Center for Research in Black Culture.[8] The initial spark from that neighbor in Harlem's projects was lit shortly after the Supreme Court had handed down its *Brown* decision in 1954, and it carried Babette's unrelenting activism forward for more than a half century. She also managed to pick up a doctorate along the way.

Babette's career trajectory as a community activist resembled that of other Black women and men previously mentioned, but she arrived at her conclusions on the proper course of racial politics much earlier. In 1958, she became involved in an effort to create an integrated high-quality public school in Harlem, but it failed because of its inability to recruit white students. In 1966, having given up on racial integration as a feasible goal, Edwards was part of a group that occupied the central school headquarters at 110 Livingston Street in Brooklyn for three days, where she and members of her community symbolically swore in a People's Board of Education.[9] They were finally arrested and thrown into jail, but the takeover fueled a nascent community-control movement in New York of which the Ocean Hill–Brownsville uprising was a part.

The following year, Edwards served as cochair of the East Harlem Task Force for Quality Education, which demanded that IS 201 be allowed to elect its own independent governing board of parents and community members. Harlem was named as one of three "Demonstration Districts"—along with Ocean Hill–Brownsville and a district in Lower Manhattan—to experiment with the idea of community control. Disappointed with the scope of the Decentralization Law that the state subsequently passed in 1969, Edwards resigned from the local board and called for a boycott of the school board elections held in 1970. It was then that she established the Harlem Parents Union to help local families advocate for their children in a school system that resisted their demands for meaningful representation and reform.

Edwards explained her journey in an essay she wrote for an anthology on school choice that appeared in 1977.[10] The volume was edited by none other than University of Chicago professor James Coleman, and it included an essay and a model statute written by Jack Coons. In a chapter that appeared under the title "Why a Harlem Parents Union?" Edwards alluded to an "authoritarian school system" where "paid workers" are "aggressively represented by organizations devoted to their own interests." She stated her belief that "parents are consumers with a vital interest in their children's academic achievement and must exert a controlling presence in the public school system." Citing data indicating that 87 percent of the students in her district scored below grade level on standardized tests in reading and math, she deemed the "record of the public school system in teaching black children . . . nothing but disgraceful."

Edwards pledged that the Parents Union would "challenge the widespread notion that home conditions are responsible for poor academic achievement in isolated minority communities." She asserted that "in efforts to explain their own professional failure," school officials purport that "the majority of black and Puerto Rican children are 'unteachable' because of inadequacies in their homes." I know her claim to be true because I heard several of these officials say so at a meeting of the chancellor's senior staff just a short time after Edwards wrote her essay. Babette Edwards, who by that time had been advocating on behalf of Harlem students for more than twenty years, had the same response to that allegation as Ron Edmonds did the day of the Livingston Street meeting. She had followed his work, and the two of them later became acquainted during the time he spent in New York.

Edwards went on in her essay to highlight her own struggles over the years, first with efforts to desegregate, then with battles over meaningful community control, only to be discouraged and "made to feel unwelcome" by those in power. By this time, Edwards was already on a different path. Having lost faith in the public schools, she had begun to seek solutions on the outside. As Brittney Lewer has written in a more recent biographical essay about Edwards, "Disappointed with a community control experiment that she felt failed to live up to its name, Edwards backed tuition vouchers and later supported charter schools as ways around the city's entrenched education bureaucracy." Lewer further explains, "[Edwards] saw vouchers and charter schools as community control over schooling, not merely neoclassical economics," thereby, as Howard Fuller would later do, establishing a link between choice and power rather than Friedman's free-market allusion.[11]

Edwards had first petitioned for vouchers in 1975, when she wrote a letter to the state commissioner of education on behalf of families in Central Harlem requesting relief from schools where 90 percent of the students had performed poorly on statewide tests.[12] She claimed that she was only asking for Black and Puerto Rican parents the same opportunities that rich white folks take for granted. That fall, seven families associated with the Harlem Parents Union withdrew their children from local public schools and staged a boycott to support their demands. Their action drew national press coverage and a limp response from state school officials.[13] That was it for school vouchers in New York.

Serious discussions about charter schools did not occur in the Empire State for another twenty years. After three unsuccessful tries over two years, Republican governor George Pataki finally convinced the state legislature to pass a charter school law in December 1998 by threatening to veto a generous pay raise the members had voted to award themselves. Babette had something to do with that also.

* * *

Early on, after Governor Pataki had introduced the charter bill in January 1997, Babette Edwards had begun to invite experts to meet with local residents under the auspices of the Harlem Parents Union to discuss its terms. That is how I met her. There was a sense of urgency in her voice when she called and said, "I need you to come up here." She wasn't about to take "no" for an answer, nor was I about to refuse. The event was held on a weeknight at the Adam Clayton Powell Jr. State Office Building on 125th Street. The large meeting room was filled with local parents, mostly women, and Babette stood at the front of the room near the platform where speakers were to assemble. I would learn more from those women that evening than they could have possibly ever learned from me.

As I entered the large room, I noticed state senator David Patterson, his celebrity status established by the crowd of local constituents that surrounded him. Patterson was a member of Harlem's political royalty. His father, Basil, was one of the famous "Gang of Four" who emerged from J. Raymond Jones's legendary political club that controlled Harlem politics for generations and got white mayors and governors to pay attention. (The others were Mayor David Dinkins, Congressman Charles Rangel, and Manhattan borough president Percy Sutton.) David subsequently went on to serve as minority leader of the state senate, lieutenant governor, and then governor for three years, finishing Eliot Spitzer's term after Spitzer was forced to resign in the midst of a sex scandal.

When I walked over to pay my respects, I told Patterson that I hoped he would join the discussion and fill us in on developments in Albany. He cracked a big smile and said that he and his fellow Democrats were not on board yet with the push for charters, and that he was planning to return to his office upstairs before the session began. Patterson and his fellow legislators did eventually come around. I learned from a colleague who was close to Harlem politics and had written a doctoral dissertation on the charter school battle that Howard Fuller was one of the people who worked on Patterson to change his mind.[14] Howard later confirmed with me that he had spoken with Patterson.

There were two other speakers on the agenda that evening. Robert Bellafiore was a senior aide to Governor George Pataki and would eventually become the governor's press secretary. He was obviously there to promote the administration's bill. I don't recall who the third person was, other than that he was a skeptic on charter schools. There was a lot of chatter in the room as we started, but it hushed quickly when Babette called the meeting to order. After her introductions, we each spoke for about fifteen minutes and then started to field questions. In an audience composed primarily of mothers, there was only one white face to be seen. I immediately recognized his streaming shock of white hair. It was Herbert Kohl, the progressive educator who had founded the Open School Movement.

Kohl is a prolific and highly respected author who was affiliated with George Soros's Open Society Institute and the Fund for New York City Education, neither of which supported charters. At some point during the Q&A, he raised his hand to make a provocative point: "What would happen," he asked, "if the Ku Klux Klan or the Nazi Party decided to open a charter school in Harlem?" Before any of us on the platform could respond, a large woman stood up in the back of the room and shouted with unquestionable authority, "I'll answer that."

In a scolding tone, the public school parent assured Kohl that if the Ku Klux Klan or the Nazi Party opens a school in Harlem, "We won't go." The packed room broke out in laughter. She then explained that it wasn't the Klan or the Nazis they were concerned about in Harlem. What concerned her and other parents in Harlem, she said, was the public school down the block where less than 20 percent of the students are learning to properly read. Now the room turned serious and heads nodded in agreement. She confidently ended her remarks with, "Don't worry, we know what's good for our kids."

The charter school law that the New York state legislature passed in 1998 included serious restrictions on the number of charter schools that would be allowed to open. That limit as of 2024 stood at 460. There are over 4,400 regular public schools in New York state. In 2023, Governor Kathy Hochul made a pale effort to raise the cap, but it went nowhere because of vigorous lobbying by the teachers' unions and a coalition that describes itself as progressive. In the meantime, charter schools consistently outperform regular public schools in the city, and a waiting list composed mostly of Black and Brown students seeking better educational opportunities continues to grow. In 2024 the number exceeded 173,000.[15]

In the 2024–2025 school year, the student population at charter schools in New York City was 46 percent Black and 43 percent Latino. Eighty-two percent of those enrolled were economically disadvantaged. Black students at these charters outperformed their public school peers on state tests with 61.2 percent (vs. 34.3 percent) achieving proficiency in math and 56.6 percent (vs. 40.3 percent) achieving proficiency in English Language Arts (ELA). Latino students at charters outperformed their public school peers reaching proficiency by a 60.5 percent to 35.7 percent margin in math and by 55.2 percent to 39.4 percent in ELA.[16] Yes, those mothers in Harlem knew what was best for their children that evening nearly three decades ago. And we know why they still can't have it.

* * *

I could say more here about the politics of racial surrogacy as I conclude this chapter. This far into the book, with Howard Fuller in plain sight—not to mention Polly Williams and the other women introduced here—however, I thought you might discern its relevance on your own. I'll just make a few concluding points. Surrogacy is a function of power or, more precisely, the lack of it. Howard Fuller and these women make no bones about the clientele they represent. They are disadvantaged Black and Brown children who are denied the opportunity of a genuine education.

Because the parents of these children don't have the political wherewithal to demand what they need on their own, they rely on more influential advocates. They don't get to pick and choose those with whom they make their political bed. If you represent these families and the influence they carry, you do the same. You take what you can when you can and go with the moment. You are not surprised when surrogates flex their muscle, depending on their political disposition, to either limit choice or expand its benefits in ways that undermine the interests of those you represent. You treat the encounter as an opportunistic dalliance rather than a lasting commitment. And, as Howard

Fuller discovered, you prepare yourself for the shame you are dealt from other people who, before the convergence of their pale common interest fades, pretend to be friends. I don't think Polly Williams, Fannie Lewis, or Babette Edwards would have suffered their insolence. Nor did Howard. Surrogacy is an occupational hazard of poor people's politics that one just learns to accept.

10

Ravitch Revised

How does an author reconcile himself with a sympathetic portrait of a former colleague who has renounced just about all the ideas that originally brought them together? Well, he begins by acknowledging her honesty as the characteristic that solidified their relationship and proceeds from there. Perhaps at this point, I should remind you of that subway ride back to Brooklyn the first day I met Diane Ravitch when I told her I did not agree with her support for school choice and we agreed to keep talking. We still are.

* * *

When I informed Diane that I would not be returning to NYU in 2004 after my year at Princeton, she was very supportive. Within a couple of years she would commence work on a new book. Throughout our eight-year collaboration, Diane and I would usually share drafts of what we each of us were writing on our own and invite the other's comments. The book that she had begun work on was different. She had mentioned nothing. After my move to Hunter, we did not see each other as regularly, so I ascribed her silence to distance. Then one evening during the winter of 2010, my wife and I had dinner with Diane and her future wife, Mary Butz, in their Brooklyn Heights brownstone, and I found out more.

After dinner, Diane invited me over to the couch and said she had some news to share. She was about to publish a new book—and it would refute just about every policy position we had taken together during our eight-year partnership at NYU. She said it would make some people angry and hoped we would remain friends. I was surprised, but not annoyed. She was entitled to be honest about her thinking, and I would expect nothing less from her.

Ravitch's *The Death and Life of the Great American School System* was published in the spring of 2010.[1] It was the first volume of what might be considered a trilogy. Although the three books shared common themes and—her being unable to presume every reader had read all three—covered some similar ground, each had a definable purpose. *The Death and Life of the Great American School System* (*Book I*), which drew its title from Jane

Radical Dreamers. Joseph P. Viteritti, Oxford University Press. © Oxford University Press (2025).
DOI: 10.1093/oso/9780197827109.003.0010

Jacobs's indictment of the urban planning profession,[2] essentially explained why Ravitch changed her mind. *Book II* was an elaboration of what she, with the benefit of hindsight, would do to revamp education policy.[3] *Book III* was nothing less than a bare-knuckled thrashing of the institutions, organizations, and individuals who were behind the policies she now opposed.[4] If the first two volumes did not make former allies of hers angry enough, *Book III* did the trick.

* * *

The subtitle of *Book I, How Testing and Choice Are Undermining Education*, was a clear indication of the author's primary targets. When the book was released in March 2010, Ravitch published an opinion piece in the *Wall Street Journal* to explain: "Why I Changed My Mind About School Reform."[5] After mentioning her service as assistant secretary of education under President George H. W. Bush, she acknowledged work she had done with conservative reform groups like the Koret Task Force at the Hoover Institution and the Thomas B. Fordham Institute. I was pleased that I was one of two former collaborators whom she referred to as friends, and that she didn't call me a conservative.[6] In the book, Ravitch identified President George W. Bush's No Child Left Behind (NCLB) Law of 2001, which emphasized testing and choice, as the epitome of what was wrong with American education. Her explanation of why she changed her mind on NCLB and everything it stood for could be summarized in two words: It failed.

Ravitch cited data from tests administered under the auspices of the National Assessment of Educational Progress from 2003 through 2007 showing no improvement in student reading across the country. She then cited data from the same tests and research conducted by Stanford University economist Margaret Raymond indicating that charter schools were performing no better than neighboring public schools. These facts were difficult to argue with, especially at that point in time a decade and a half ago. Raymond's more recent work is more positive about charter school performance.

As described by Ravitch in her book,[7] NCLB included seven basic provisions:

1. All states would choose their own tests (apart from the Nation's Report Card), adopt three levels of performance (basic, proficient, and advanced), and be permitted to define proficiency how they saw fit.

2. Public schools with federal funding were required to test all students in grades three through eight annually and once in high school in both reading and math. Scores were disaggregated by race, ethnicity, income, disability status, and English proficiency.

3. All states were to establish timelines leading to proficiency in reading and math for 100 percent of their students by the 2013–2014 school year.

4. All schools and school districts were expected to make annual yearly progress (AYP) for every subgroup of students.

5. Schools failing to make AYP would be designated as Schools in Need of Improvement (SINI) subject to increasingly severe sanctions as follows: Year 1: Put on notice; Year 2: Offer students an opportunity to transfer out with transportation expenses paid for; Year 3: Offer students free tutoring; Year 4: Require schools to take corrective action, such as curriculum changes, staff changes, or a longer school day or year; Year 5: Require the school to restructure.

6. Restructuring could involve replacing the principal and/or staff or turning the school over to a private management organization. Or it could mean converting a school to a charter school or putting it under state control.

7. All states were required to participate in the nationally administered NAEP tests in reading and math.

NCLB was passed in 2001 with strong bipartisan support, bringing together the likes of Republican president Bush and Senator Ted Kennedy, the Democratic liberal icon from Massachusetts. As a result of the legislation, federal funding for elementary and secondary education increased nearly 60 percent during its first few years. According to Ravitch, NCLB, with its focus on testing and choice, was the culmination of the direction in which federal policy had begun to move during the Clinton years, and Washington's emphasis on testing and choice would continue under President Barack Obama's Race to the Top.[8] NCLB could be considered neither Democratic nor Republican, reflecting a national political consensus. Although not every Republican and few Democrats supported school vouchers, charter schools were the reform of choice among leaders in both parties.

As described in our earlier chapter on Ravitch's career, Diane has a long-standing commitment to the promulgation of curriculum-based national standards. It was her primary responsibility as assistant secretary of education during the first Bush administration. It was the topic of a book she wrote for the Brookings Institution in 1995 following her government service.[9] In 2010, she once again declared, "We must make sure that our schools have a strong, coherent, explicit curriculum that is grounded in the liberal arts and sciences for children to engage in projects and activities that make learning lively."[10]

Ravitch's problem with the post-NCLB standards campaign is that it was "hijacked" by a testing movement that prioritized basic skills to the exclusion of subjects like science, literature, history, civics, and the arts. State tests required by the law in reading and math would become the sole means for judging schools, students, teachers, and districts. For her, the consequences of failure as defined by the law were punitive rather than constructive. Ravitch was especially disturbed by the prospect of school closings on the basis of test scores that she found to be inadequate measures of performance. And if each state could establish its own benchmarks for proficiency, what should we conclude it all means in the end? With that, it was still ludicrous to believe that every school, every district, and every state could attain 100 percent proficiency by 2013–2014 or any time thereafter.

Ravitch's position on charters was somewhat more nuanced. She was regretful that charters were not designed to collaborate with traditional public schools and function as laboratories for experimentation rather than competitors for students and dollars. She acknowledged that some performed well and was particularly complimentary toward the KIPP (Knowledge Is Power Program) network of schools that have longer instructional days, Saturday sessions, and summer programs typically amounting to 60 percent more class time per year than regular public schools.[11] She compared them to American public schools of the 1940s that cultivated behaviors and attitudes that students needed to succeed.

I myself had been given a personal tour of a newly opened KIPP school in the South Bronx by KIPP cofounder David Levin, which he established in the mid-nineties as a model for the growing network. When I was a member of the chancellor's staff, I had visited many New York City public schools. I had never seen anything comparable to this school in the middle of a high-poverty area where basic skills were steadily improving, every child was taught to play a musical instrument, and the overall atmosphere appeared conducive to learning. KIPP's motto, "Work Hard, Be Nice," was plastered across the walls throughout and said much about the core values of the organization and the dedicated educators who run it.

Ravitch also expressed sympathy with the mission of Catholic schools, convinced by James Coleman that they have been especially effective with minority students, who are more likely to take advanced courses and pursue higher education than their peers in public schools.[12] I suspect that Diane's positive attitude toward Catholic schools is also influenced by the firsthand accounts she has heard from her wife, Mary Butz. Like many people of her generation, Mary is the product of an immigrant family whose life was changed by the opportunity to receive a Catholic education. Mary herself had a notable career in the city's public schools.

Notwithstanding her positive attitudes toward Catholic institutions as well as some charter and independent private schools, Ravitch decisively had changed her mind on choice. She was now making arguments that she had previously rebuffed. Not only would choice fail to produce schools that excelled on their own—be they charters, private, religious, or privately managed—it would neither improve public education nor help close the learning gap defined by race and class. It would instead skim off the better students and deplete public institutions of resources. It would exacerbate segregation. Choice, in her mind, is part of a larger institutional reconstruction that will alter the stakes of public education as we know it.

For Ravitch, choice and test-based accountability would infect American schooling with the most pernicious features of capitalism, replacing public education with a market-based system operated according to the principles of competition and deregulation beyond anything Milton Friedman could have imagined. Her analysis left no room for the possibility of a progressive choice regime that would channel opportunities to needy students and demand accountability from any institution accepting public money: the kind of system advocated by Jack Coons, Howard Fuller, and she herself when she wrote "Somebody's Children."[13]

Now Ravitch would agree with Fuller on one essential point: choice is a function of political power—but the outcome for her more resembles a hostile takeover than a process of reform. The choice regime she describes is one engineered by conservative foundations and think tanks that want to see schools run like a business: fashioning a top-down hierarchic management style and an antiunion ethos that adopts private-sector practices like merit pay.

In the final chapter of *Book I*, titled "The Billionaire Boys Club," Ravitch presents a cast of key characters behind the movement that includes Bill Gates, John Walton, Eli Broad, and Michael Bloomberg. They are all-powerful and accountable to no one. Ravitch reserves several chapters in the book to demonstrate what could happen when large urban school systems are taken over by individuals who have no background or expertise in education. These include case studies of Chancellor Joel Klein in New York and Superintendent Alan Bersin in San Diego, who were responsible for major shakeups with modest results. She also includes a chapter on Anthony Alvarado, an innovative educator from New York who had been recruited to serve as Bersin's deputy.

Ravitch was hopeful that with the culture wars fought over history standards fading into the past, fair-minded people would come together to determine what and how best to teach the essentials of an interdisciplinary curriculum that goes beyond basic skills. She was confident that school districts run by elected school boards would remain a foundation for fostering a democratic process in educational decision-making.

* * *

Diane Ravitch never has trouble drawing attention. The dramatic abnegation of her own prodigious scholarly output at such a late stage of her career would certainly be noticed, and *Book I* was generally well received. A segment on National Public Radio praised Ravitch as a "distinguished historian" who "isn't easy to categorize politically" but "calls 'em as she sees 'em" in a "passionately and persuasively" argued new book about how the Great American School System "flunks out."[14] Chester Finn, a friend and former collaborator who had not changed his mind, remarked that the book "will surely stir controversy" and—knowing its author well—added, "exactly as she intends."[15]

Of particular interest was a review written by Alan Wolfe for the *New York Times*.[16] Wolfe is one of the leading public intellectuals of our time. Trained as a political theorist, he is an independent thinker with an open mind who can take any discussion to the next level without being weighed down by the usual academic jargon and other pretensions. Alan had contributed to one of the books Diane and I coedited. He had assembled his own high-octane collection on moral issues underlying the choice debate to which I contributed.[17] Wolfe's review of *Book I* was a respectful rendering of its central arguments. Depicting Ravitch "less as an ideologue than a critic of fads," he vouched, "I have always relied on Ravitch's intellectual honesty."

Surprisingly, Wolfe did not take up the fundamental moral question behind the choice debate, which queries how we can justify a political and legal arrangement that allows parental choice as an option for those who can afford it on their own, but denies it to those who need it the most, leaving their children to fend for themselves in schools that ought not to be called schools. It is a topic he is well equipped to address and one that Diane Ravitch handled so deftly in her persuasive plea for justice, "Somebody's Children."

As did most reviewers, Wolfe agreed with Ravitch about the paramount role curriculum development must play as an instrument for meaningful reform, but he did not share her optimism that the culture wars had passed or that consensus on what to teach would be easily reached. Perhaps in 2010 these questions were debatable. Now it is apparent that if the combat had subsided over how to teach American history, it was a temporary ceasefire at best rather than the war's end.[18] Diane Ravitch, who herself joined in vigorous recent debate about the teaching of critical race theory, book banning, and other thorny issues, is well aware of that.

Michael Apple reviewed the book for the journal *Educational Policy*.[19] Apple is an educational theorist who could easily find his ideas in the line of fire when a more conservative Diane Ravitch let loose on the fuzzy-headed thinking of progressive intellectuals. Obviously pleased that the woman had finally come to her senses, and granting that "Ravitch is deeply committed to education," he couldn't help but to ask, probably with a smirk across his face, "Given the immense evidence against the positions she had originally so strenuously supported, what took her so long?" He also found her "more than a little cautious about the promise of charter schools."

Apple appreciated Ravitch's defense of neighborhood schools but faulted her for failing to deal adequately with race or racism and how they affect politics at the community level. You might recall how many of the Black activists we met in the last chapter were incensed that their children were trapped in inferior neighborhood schools. Some of these same players, in successive bids to meet their children's educational needs, had fought hard to gain community control.

Of course, the culture wars are not over, Apple insisted. Curricula and the values that ground them are anything but neutral. Apple also understood that the questions implicit in these debates necessitated a deeper inquiry into the meaning of democracy.

Overall, the accolades kept rolling in for *Book I*, especially from mainstream academics. Ravitch's great transformation was packed into fewer than three hundred pages and wrapped in a bright blue cover that pictured an old wooden schoolhouse. Joseph Featherstone called it "a masterly new book."[20] Writing for a leading policy journal, James Spillane found it "compelling" and an "engaging read."[21] Referring to the work as both a "*mea culpa* and a manifesto" by a "distinguished educational historian," Carl Anderson took note of Ravitch's conservative instincts around curriculum design, a charge to which she herself pled guilty.[22] Warning that the "technocratic narrowing of the curriculum is here to stay," he wondered, however, whether Ravitch was prepared to accept the probable consequences of a move toward the nationalized one she had encouraged.

A symposium hosted by *The New Republic* set the stage for more spirited disagreement. That is not difficult in the field of education policy, where opinions are polarized, especially when it comes to hot-button topics like choice and testing. If you tell me what questions are being posed and who is being asked, I usually can tell you what their answers will be. This exchange was a good one that included Ravitch herself.

Ben Wildavsky, an education scholar and reformer, stepped right into the ring with pointed criticism.[23] Granting that Ravitch had contributed some "useful insights" regarding the limitations of ongoing polices, he lamented, "the rhetoric is so overblown it doesn't seem in keeping with her analytic gravitas." Why shouldn't the business sector and wealthy foundations participate in education reform? he asked. He explained that many successful charter organizations like KIPP, Achievement First, and Uncommon Schools are nonprofits, but then he tossed out the proposition "Why shouldn't educational entrepreneurs get rich?" Wildavsky challenged Ravitch's basic narrative suggesting that public schools were "doing pretty well until evil corporate titans and their politician henchmen rolled into town," pointing out that test-based accountability and choice were a response to "lackluster" academic achievement in public schools. He said that Ravitch was being "uncharacteristically naïve" in dismissing the negative effects of teachers' unions.

In a second set of remarks, Wildavsky took on the skimming issue and concerns that choice would deplete public schools of their most motivated students and families.[24] He approached the topic in terms of educational equity, asking, "Isn't it preferable for some kids to have superior alternatives than for all kids to remain in underperforming schools?" He juxtaposed the question with Ravitch's support for Catholic and private schools on the condition that parents find a way to pay the costs on their own. That arrangement, currently operative in most communities, would certainly exacerbate the skimming factor, he argued.

Former Clinton aide and Democratic Party activist Andrew Rotherham addressed his remarks directly to Ravitch, stating that "your stature as arguably the most important education historian of the twentieth century gives your opinions weight," all the while expressing disappointment that she had turned education debates into a "battle of good versus evil."[25] He endorsed her demand for a standards-based curriculum. He concluded, however, that while her effort was a "powerful *cri de coeur*, it is neither granular or forward-looking enough to serve as a blueprint for policy makers." Kevin Carey, the policy director of a pro-choice think tank, echoed Rotherham's "Where's the beef?" solicitation.[26]

Richard Rothstein, the symposium's most left-of-center contributor, took the discussion in an entirely different direction. Rothstein was preoccupied with a phrase George W. Bush regularly used referring to the "soft bigotry of low expectations." It was persistently invoked by the former president as an expression of his "compassionate conservatism," which so annoyed liberals who believed they owned compassion as a birthright. Bush repeated the phrase in speeches across the country as he whipped up support for his signature No Child Left Behind legislation. Rothstein's piece gave me a start when he linked the phrase to language that is commonly associated with the late Ron Edmonds. Let me quote him at length:

> NCLB's proponents have asserted that poverty is correlated with low achievement mostly because educators confront disadvantaged children with the "soft bigotry of low expectations" and forget that "all children can learn." But, in truth, even the best curriculum, instruction, and teacher expectations of children who come to school with limited vocabularies and are unfamiliar with books and the treasures of imagination they unlock will learn less, on average, than children who come to school prepared to learn.[27]

I'll admit, I never thought I ever would see the wordsmanship of George Bush and Ron Edmonds mixed together in the same political cocktail. What's going on here?

It is difficult to say whether Rothstein understood the origin of Ron's words or the context in which they were articulated. Rothstein, nonetheless, had an important caveat to add. He was beseeching Ravitch that if America as a nation does not provide economically deprived children with the kinds of supports they need to learn, educators will not be able to do it on their own. The point is well taken and Ravitch would agree. Edmonds spoke for others, though, who knew that many white educators would observe the precarious condition of disadvantaged families and write their children off as hopeless failures. At what point does genuine sympathy cross the line into systemic racism? That's the bottom-line question.

In four separate essays, Ravitch took it upon herself to respond to just about each and every concern that her panel of reviewers raised.[28] In several she returned to her original empirical observations, which were difficult to refute: NCLB had failed to alter the achievement gap; charter schools, by and large, perform no better than regular public schools. For some reason, the topic of school vouchers never became a significant part of the exchange. In one piece, Ravitch suggested that the federal government should encourage states to send inspection teams to low-performing schools for the purposes of identifying problems and prescribing corrective action. That way educators could utilize evaluative data to improve performance rather than to punish students and teachers.

The latter suggestion probably did not satisfy those reviewers who criticized Ravitch for not furnishing a detailed agenda on how to move forward. In fairness to her, that was never the purpose of *Book I*. Its purpose was diagnostic, not prescriptive. She would take up the latter assignment in *Book II*.

* * *

Reign of Error appeared in 2013. Its subtitle—*The Hoax of the Privatization Movement and the Danger to America's Public Schools*—did little to lower the temperature around its discussion. The author restated the basic arguments from *Book I* with a few modifications. There was less focus on George Bush and more on Barack Obama, whose Race to the Top (R2T) not only extended the NCLB agenda but put more of a focus on test-based teacher evaluations and accountability. Ravitch reported that

95 percent of the one hundred billion dollars Congress authorized during the Obama years was designed to keep teachers employed in the aftermath of the Great Recession precipitated by Wall Street's self-imposed subprime mortgage crisis.[29] Eleven states and the District of Columbia had successfully competed for R2T funding. At Secretary of Education Arne Duncan's urging, most states had adopted the Common Core curriculum standards developed by a private consortium of educators, even though the standards had not been field-tested.

Ravitch added Washington, DC, as another case study of an urban district taken over by someone she deemed unqualified. Michelle Rhee, a fixture in the reform movement who went head-to-head with the teachers' union, had only taught in Baltimore for three years and had never run a school before the mayor of Washington appointed her as schools chancellor. Ravitch also devoted more space to Amazon's Jeff Bezos, Netflix's Reed Hastings, and the News Corporation's Rupert Murdoch among the billionaires who funded the ever-growing number of think tanks and lobbyists behind privatization. She was distressed to learn that even the son of civil rights leader Martin Luther King Jr. could be seen marching arm in arm with hedge fund managers who she believed undermined public education and its unions.[30]

If public schools are at risk, Ravitch continued to insist, it has more to do with the unfair criticism they withstand from people who want to replace them than inadequacies evident in the schools themselves. In her words, "Public schools are working very well."[31] Devoting an entire chapter to NAEP scores—the only standardized test in which she has real confidence— Ravitch cited "significant increases in both reading and mathematics" since 1992, with the most pronounced improvements in the years preceding NCLB.[32] She did not deny that some racially isolated school districts with high poverty rates were not doing well. In another chapter focused on the achievement gap, Ravitch observed that there has been "genuine progress," but that the gap will remain large if we do not address the underlying socioeconomic causes.[33] Other than undoing the reforms with which she disagreed, *Book II* focuses on how we might address those causes.

Ravitch continued to stress a strong multidisciplinary curriculum as the foundation for a sound education. She said more about overhauling the teaching profession, requiring that each candidate have undergraduate instruction in an academic discipline, graduate training in child psychology and development, on-the-job mentoring, and peer evaluation. Although still finding Catholic schools praiseworthy, Ravitch cited studies showing that children participating in voucher programs in Milwaukee and Washington did no better. Mindful that many charter schools were community based, her attitude seemed to be turning more sour toward them as she criticized their operators for demanding public support without accepting public accountability. Virtual schools have escaped serious scrutiny and are ripe for abuses, especially when motivated by profit, she warned. *Book II* also recommended instructional enhancements such as early childhood education, smaller class sizes in the lower grades, and quality after-school programs.

As promised, a large portion of *Book II* entered the realm of social policy. Referencing the work of Richard Rothstein, she joined him and other progressive thinkers in arguing that schools could not close the learning gap on their own. She challenged billionaire philanthropist Bill Gates in particular, who had made a speech at the National Urban League, professing, "We know you can have a good school in a poor neighborhood, so let's end the myth that we have to solve poverty before we improve education."[34] But why not eradicate poverty in the richest country on the planet? Wouldn't that alleviate the obstacles impeding urban schools—not to mention those overcome by rural poverty? In the meantime, the government could invest resources to enhance prenatal care and deliver enriched physical and mental health services directly to schools. Ravitch argued that a wraparound service model for schools would give children in poorer communities the kinds of supports that middle-class families take for granted.

Riled by the more contentious tone of *Book II*, the response by reviewers was predictably more polarized. Liberal commentator Jonathan Kozol seemed delighted to report in the *New York Times* that a figure with such "impeccable credentials as a scholar and historian" had now turned her "arrows more directly, and polemically, on the privatization movement."[35] T. Rees Shapiro, reviewing the book in the *Washington Post*, sang a different tune when he called the book "a vicious attack on reformers" even if it was "reinforced by plenty of data and 41 charts." He begged the question "If, according to Ravitch, 90% of all American students attend regular public schools and only 5% charter schools, is this movement really a takeover?"[36]

Trevor Butterworth's piece in the *Wall Street Journal* was somewhat sympathetic.[37] As he put it, "Any reform movement that trades with for-profit education puts public money on the line and needs to be scrutinized," even when it involves a "constellation of well-intentioned philanthropists." In his estimation, however, Ravitch had undermined her own arguments with her mixture of "stridency, selectivity and spin" as well as her "defense of public schools at all costs."

Perhaps the most brutal attack on *Book II* was that hurled by Jay Greene, a University of Arkansas professor with a long record of research on school choice and education policy. Printed in *Education Next*, a Harvard-based journal long associated with the reform movement, the review denigrated *Reign of Error* as "obviously not a work of scholarship nor is it intended to be."[38] Calling it a "form of therapy" that "soothes the outraged educator," he suggested that the book "speaks only to those already converted to 'the Cause.'"

Greene went on to accuse Ravitch of misinterpreting test data on voucher programs in Milwaukee and the District of Columbia, and took her to task for failing to mention that those students who won scholarship awards boasted stronger high school graduation rates. Greene also made an important methodological point that addressed the "selection bias" argument made by choice opponents. Choice critics claim that it is invalid to compare test scores of voucher recipients with students who attend public schools because the former population is composed of a highly motivated self-selected group of families that are not representative of the public school population. State-of-the-art voucher studies, like the Peterson and Howell evaluation of the private scholarship program in New York discussed in chapter 5, actually compare the performance of voucher recipients with students who entered the lotteries but lost and remained in public school.[39]

Michael Petrilli, of the pro-reform Fordham Institute, wrote a second review for *Education Next*, in case you missed the first. Referring to Ravitch as a "double agent" who switched sides, the usually even-tempered Petrilli took umbrage with her "condescending tone" and characterized the work as "neither fair minded or even-handed."[40] And (you guessed it), Petrilli read the existing research record to conclude, "the overwhelming evidence" finds that "school vouchers generally benefit a great many recipients while harming none."

Petrilli is an award-winning writer and analyst, an important voice on education reform. Unfortunately, he devoted much of his essay attempting to refute what in my mind were some of the most credible "solutions," as he called them, Ravitch had put forward in *Book II*.[41] Here is a paraphrased smattering of his thoughts: The government already provides prenatal care. There is only patchy evidence that preschool works. Well-rounded schools with content-rich curricula haven't existed for a long time (Don't blame us). In order for class-size reductions to be effective, they need to be steep and expensive. Research shows that many charter schools are as effective as schools in the Harlem Children's Zone, which has distinguished itself by implementing a costly, difficult-to-replicate network of wraparound services. There is some evidence that desegregation works, but very few people (possibly still including Diane Ravitch) want to return to busing.

We return to these questions later. Now let's move on to something more contentious.

* * *

If *Books I* and *II* served as declarations of war, *Slaying Goliath* (*Book III*) was a celebration of victory—as the war continued to wage on and the opposing sides marched toward one another armed with determination.[42] The reformers have now been branded the "The Disrupters," who, according to the author, are devoted to slashing taxes, cutting spending on public schools, and turning control of education over to private corporations and people with no relevant expertise.[43] They might also be labeled "deformers," the "financial privatization cabal," the "Destroy Public Education Movement," or just plain "privateers."[44] If their campaign of "creative destruction" were to actually succeed, they would replace teachers with computers.[45]

At this point, it is 2020, after the first Trump takeover. His secretary of education, Betsy DeVos, emerges as one of the prime villains of the story— as if Trump himself were not evil enough to make this a compelling drama. DeVos, who has sunk large chunks of her family fortune into campaigns to promote choice and charters in her home state of Michigan and elsewhere, was then positioning herself to emerge as the face of the movement. She is also a major financial backer of the American Federation for Children and the American Legislative Exchange Council, both of which have played outsized roles in state-level politics and elections.

There are numerous pages in *Book III* devoted to the "dark money" behind The Disruption, with lots of glossy mug shots of its chief purveyors, only some of whom were heard about in the earlier volumes. Facebook's Mark Zuckerberg stands out in the gallery. Religious fundamentalists and mainstream churches also play a big part. Yet Ravitch sticks by her admiration for Catholic schools and what they do to improve the lives of those who are not so privileged.

This band of billionaires may have won the sympathies of formerly left-of-center Democratic politicians and had their messages carried in influential liberal media outlets like the *New York Times* and *Washington Post*—but the point of *Book III* is to assure us that this David-and-Goliath matchup is about to conclude with a just ending and the salvation of public education. As the story goes, Goliath's fall comes at the hands of a less potent adversary, or in the case of school reform, a loose coalition of adversaries, if teachers' unions can be persuasively portrayed that way. Ravitch illustrates this resistance with episodes of parent revolts, teacher strikes, and dissent by established rights groups.

Ravitch witnessed one such outburst in her own backyard when public school parents in New York decided to have their children opt out of standardized tests the state had aligned with the Common Core. A similar protest occurred in Providence, Rhode Island. Teachers themselves boycotted high-stakes exams in Seattle. Ravitch applauds teacher walkouts against budget cuts and low wages in Chicago, West Virginia, Oklahoma, Colorado, Kentucky, and Arizona. There's momentum here!

Ravitch was especially pleased to observe that mainstream civil rights organizations like the Education Law Center and the Southern Poverty Law Center had joined the anticharter resistance. In 2016, the NAACP passed a resolution at its national convention calling for a moratorium on charter school expansion. According to Ravitch's account, the document demanded that the moratorium remain in place until charter providers agreed to accept transparency and accountability, stopped excluding students they did not want, and ceased diverting money from public schools.

The NAACP's national board of directors also appointed a task force that held public hearings in seven major cities across the country. In its own report the task force acknowledged, "Many traditional inner-city public schools are failing the children who attend them, thus causing parents with limited resources to search for a funded, quality educational alternative for their children." The more important punch line read, "While high-quality, accessible, and accountable charters can contribute to educational opportunity, by themselves, even the best charters are not a substitute for more stable, adequate and equitable investments in public education in communities that serve our children."[46]

It's a good bet that the most gratifying parts of *Book III* for Diane Ravitch to write were those that elaborated on the tangible victories that the resistance she herself was a part of had chalked up. They are substantial. For example, when test scores tied to the Common Core standards began to be released in 2013, opposition to them began to build and politicians walked away from them. As Ravitch put it, "The Core Curriculum is now an orphan."[47] This all transpired after the Obama administration appropriated sixty million dollars toward the development of the Common Core, and forty-five states and the District of Columbia had signed on to adopt the standards.

Extending previous broadsides against choice, *Book III* walks us through negative evaluations of voucher programs in Wisconsin, Ohio, Indiana, Louisiana, and the District of Columbia. It lauds victories in the state courts engineered by groups like Americans United for the Separation of Church and State that brought down voucher programs in Florida and Colorado. And it recounts a successful grassroots effort in Massachusetts defeating a ballot measure in 2016 that would have increased funding for charter schools.

As Ravitch reports, the ACLU set its critical sights on charter schools designed to accentuate racial identity—institutions similar to those embraced by Black intellectuals and activists like Howard Fuller, Polly Williams, Derrick Bell, Stokely Carmichael, Gail Foster, Babette Edwards, and the people of Ocean Hill–Brownsville in Brooklyn and the North Division of Milwaukee who saw such schools as expressions of community and racial pride rather than instruments for exclusion.

Although the narrative in *Book III* was hardly dispassionate, neither was it devoid of evidence that, indeed, Goliath was beginning to stumble, especially on the charter front.[48] Ravitch cited competing data from organizations on either side of the debate showing that, since 1991, between 15 percent and 40 percent of the charters that had opened closed, no doubt precipitated at least in part by stories of fraud and waste appearing in the popular media. Ravitch draws on information compiled by the National Association of Charter School Authorizers (a pro-choice group), indicating that charter growth began to decline in 2012–2013.[49] In that year 640 new charters opened; three years later only 329 opened. About 7 percent of all charters close every year.

In her final analysis, charters haven't taken over public education after all. *Slaying Goliath* attests that charter schools tend to cluster in several states where they educate significant portions of the student population— and modest minorities even in those jurisdictions as of 2018: Arizona (17 percent), Colorado (13 percent), Louisiana (11 percent), California (10 percent), and Florida (10 percent). Even in states where charter advocacy has been strong, growth has been meager as a percentage of enrollments because of political opposition usually led by teachers' unions—as, for example, in New York (5 percent), Massachusetts (4 percent), and Indiana (4 percent).

* * *

For sure, not everyone was cheered by Diane Ravitch's joyous obituary to school reform. The acrid language she employed intensified the polarized response to the trilogy along predictable political lines. The editors at the *New York Times* must have thought it necessary to reach beyond the battle-fields of choice and reform to find a reviewer who could give *Book III* a fair hearing. Diane had already hinted in *Book III* that the Gray Lady had a horse in the race to reform anyway. Annie Murphy Paul is an acclaimed science writer with a thin profile in the field of education policy. Apparently familiar with Ravitch's previous work, Paul devoted much of her *Times* review to the elements of tone and style.

On those dimensions, Paul takes her subject to task, commenting, "Missing from these pages are the subtle insight and informed judgment for which [Ravitch] was once known." "Ravitch takes a defiant leap over the line separating reasoned case building from empty sloganeering and *ad hominem* attacks. . . . She is more interested in settling scores." And finally, "Ravitch has let go of some admirable intellectual practices and well-founded convictions. She would be wise to recover them."[50] By her own admission, Ravitch hadn't set out to tell both sides of the story.[51] She proceeds through the book like a prosecuting attorney bent on an indictment. Although Paul's last sentence indicates agreement with some of Ravitch's lost convictions, nothing in the review suggests why these convictions are worth recovering.

Paul agrees with Ravitch that to close failing neighborhood schools is more harmful to families and communities than working to improve them, but does not explain why or how. Paul does register one particular critical comment on Ravitch's treatment of the most recent school wars that is worthy of attention. Labeling Ravitch's portrait of the combatants as "curiously selective," Paul remarks, "Not included among them are the mothers and fathers, many of them people of color, who engage in activism in favor of bringing charter schools to their neighborhoods, seeing these institutions—though new and untried—as a better alternative to the public schools they already know." In Ravitch's "cynical calculus," Paul alleges, those who disagree with her "have either been bought or duped."

The *Washington Post* gave the review over to a public school English teacher in Arlington, Virginia, by the name of Melanie McCabe, who found the book "inspiring" and called it "a thought-provoking, painstakingly researched account of those who have sought to privatize and monetize America's public schools." McCabe's ample summary captured both the mood and the message of the book when she referred to it as a "rallying cry" against a "foe with the intimidating strength of Goliath."[52]

Writing for the scholarly journal *Church & State*, Rob Boston declared, "Diane Ravitch writes with anger—but it is righteous anger, it's justified and it's what we need right now." And he is clearly persuaded that with the "impressive collection of fact and figures" presented in its pages, "Ravitch's book has outlined the threats and shown that the Disrupters can be turned back."[53]

The team at the pro-choice *Education Next* was certainly not going to let this final installment of the trilogy produced by a former ally pass without weighing in. This time they awarded the assignment to Frederick Hess, a director at the conservative American Enterprise Institute (AEI). Rick Hess is a well-respected education researcher who can usually be relied upon to be cool-headed and deliberate. This occasion brought out another side of him. Branding the collection an "I was such a fool trilogy," Hess describes the work as "long form pamphleteering" that is lacking in proportion and "heavy on conspiratorial dogma."[54]

Hess's essay poses a variety of weighty rhetorical questions: Do reformers just want to break things? Doesn't Ravitch know that some of the villains demanding change are parents, grandparents, or graduates of public schools? Are teachers' unions mere frail collectives?

* * *

I laid my cards on the table in the preceding chapters, so by now you the reader should know where I stand on the school choice question. Having shared the chapters on our four critical thinkers at the heart of this project, I now can begin to explain my position in a broader context, also taking into consideration the revised thinking of Diane Ravitch.

A good place to start is where Diane Ravitch does in explaining her reaction to George W. Bush's No Child Left Behind (NCLB) initiative. What made the law appealing to me was the overall philosophy behind it. The very title of the legislation recognized that our nation had tolerated educational inequality in the form of an achievement gap long before *Brown v. Board of Education* forced us to admit it some seventy years ago. The 60 percent increase in federal funding Congress put behind it wasn't a bad start either.

The mandate requiring all fifty states to achieve 100 percent proficiency within a dozen years may have seemed unrealistic, but it was in fact aspirational. To target anything less ambitious would have wedded the nation to a goal that accepted failure and inequality already apparent for too long. If the gap in learning had been random, then perhaps the statisticians could have consoled us by dismissing it as a normal distribution of the bell curve. In the past, analysts have been known to draw conclusions about the disparities with pernicious racial implications—a position not to be confused with Ravitch's, either before or after her recanting.[55] We do know, nonetheless, that the pattern of educational inequality in America vividly falls along the lines of race and class. So long as that condition persists, the drive to hold educators and schools accountable is admirable.

Whether we like it or not, whatever its shortcomings, testing remains the most valid and reliable instrument for measuring academic achievement on a large scale, but it must be done carefully and responsibly. Permitting states to develop their own tests and standards was a political bow to federalism and demands that Washington refrain from taking over a historical state function. Requiring the states to participate in the nationally administered NAEP tests would allow federal officials to pour NAEP results over politically motivated claims of excellence by state officials utilizing flawed assessment instruments. But NAEP tests are not intended for measuring achievement at the school or individual level. As Ravitch asserts, tests must be used for the purposes they were designed. Tests need to be designed for specific levels of assessment and they need to be administered properly. They weren't in the past.

As Ravitch explained, the process needs to begin with curriculum standards that define what students should learn at each grade level. I would add that once standards are established, training must be provided for education administrators and teachers so that standards can be translated into curriculum materials for the classroom. Tests need to be developed that align with the curriculum standards. I believe this was faithfully intended by the innovators who got behind the Common Core. Unfortunately they never fully accomplished what they set out to do.

This is a long, costly, and laborious process. It is reasonable to begin such a process with a focus on basic skills, as NCLB did. A child who can't read cannot appreciate literature. A child who can't calculate cannot perform science experiments. Basic skills are a prerequisite to broader interdisciplinary learning—but, as Ravitch insisted, they are not sufficient on their own. As ambitious and as costly as the Bush and Obama agendas were, they did not do enough. Later on, Trump had no interest in supporting a serious education agenda during his first term in office. President Biden wasn't much better for that matter.

As Ravitch argued, the absence of a sound comprehensive curriculum aligned with teaching materials and tests undermined the goal of meaningful accountability. Bush's and Obama's inclination to pursue such accountability was well founded, however. The disaggregation of test scores by race, ethnicity, income, disability status, and English-language proficiency would have allowed public authorities at the federal, state, and local levels to pinpoint where our efforts to educate all children at an acceptable level were coming up short. These efforts must ultimately be evaluated at the school level.

It is well known that not all students start out at the same level of proficiency. Because of this, the most reasonable way to assess instructional quality at a school is by measuring progress, as NCLB mandated. The law not only required school districts to measure Annual Yearly Progress (AYP) for every subgroup of students, it provided that educators identify schools that could not demonstrate such progress.

It is a given that some, far too many, schools are not doing a decent job of educating students. Unfortunately these schools tend to be concentrated in places resided in by people of color who often lack personal resources. If you are responsible for running a school district, or even a school, it is your job to know where it fails and to do something about it. To do less would constitute a dereliction of duty. You cannot ignore failure. You owe it to the parents and children who have put their faith in the system, the people whom Ron Edmonds would call your clients.

You may recall from an earlier chapter that the New York City schools, several decades ago, guided by Edmonds, first experimented with a transitional class program that delivered remedial services in the early grades where class sizes were kept small (between fifteen and twenty students). That program was soon defunded by the city council to address budget shortfalls. The centerpiece promotional program utilized state standardized tests to evaluate performance at the school level. Before that, Edmonds, working with teachers and other professionals in the system, had developed a standardized curriculum aligned with the tests. With limited time and resources, the process may have been too rushed, but the administration did its best to follow the principles of sound pedagogy, working cooperatively with teachers and their union.

Promotional gates were established in grades 4 and 7, where students would be retained if they did not demonstrate proficiency. Retention was not a punitive measure; it was remedial. Retained students were placed in small remedial classes that were available in the summer so that a student could advance a grade by the fall. Smaller class sizes were maintained in first grade throughout the system to give all students a decent start, since preschool programs were not available then on a large scale. The chancellor had to threaten to resign his position during an election year in order to prevent the mayor and city council from cutting the remedial part of our promotional policy. You may recall also that the chancellor had early on opposed the state regents' decision to impose harsher graduation standards in the high schools before preparation and remediation programs were in place. So, while the overall philosophy of NCLB had merit, so did some of Ravitch's concerns about it.

As Ravitch explained and many serious educators agreed, the entire project was compromised by the absence of a basic curriculum. The instinct of NCLB's architects to monitor performance and hold educators accountable, however, was well founded, beginning with the provision of identifying failing schools and putting them on notice. Once a school was so identified, a step-by-step process became operative that was both gradualist and supportive of students, as follows: offering students an opportunity to transfer out, offering students tutoring, requiring a school to take corrective action, restructuring. The wonkier among us might differ with the order of action or merge some steps. The most drastic of these, after all efforts to effectively improve the school or the performance of students failed, was the last: restructuring, reconstitution, or choice.

Closing down a school in New York City during the 1980s was never on the table. It just wasn't a viable political option in those days. Nor did we deny that some schools were failing. State test scores might be a crude and unfair measure for evaluating teachers, but they can be used to compare the performance of schools functioning in similar communities under similar circumstances. The chancellor did remove principals, even if it meant sidelining them at the Livingston Street bureaucracy so that new leadership could be installed. He would occasionally do the same with teachers who had egregious records. Until a serious process is put in place to construct a testing regime around a quality curriculum, along the lines that Ravitch has outlined, we should not use them as a primary instrument for evaluating teachers or determining retention or tenure. That was one feature of Obama's Race to the Top that I opposed when I wrote my review of it in 2012.[56]

By the time NCLB was passed with bipartisan support in 2001, there was a consensus that sometimes more aggressive action is needed to relieve disadvantaged populations from decades of inferior instruction. That impulse was progressive in spirit. In those cases where it is deemed necessary, a radical restructuring of a school by completely replacing the staff and transferring them elsewhere is warranted. So is offering choices to underserved families and communities outside the jurisdiction of a student's public school district.

Ravitch's impassioned trilogy, the last volume of which appeared in 2020, was harsh on the choice regime and it enraged many well-intentioned reformers. Yet, within a few years it would prove to be prophetic as Milton Friedman–type universal choice programs came into favor across the country, undermining progressive objectives targeted at underperforming populations and allowing public accountability for results to slide. If Goliath seemed to be stumbling a bit while Ravitch was hammering out the last volume of her trilogy, it is now on surer footing than ever. With Trump's return to the White House, Republicans in control of both houses of Congress, and the US Supreme Court sliding further and further to the right, Goliath is back with a thunderous roar.

PART III
CONCLUSION

11

America's Failed Journey

This project has been both descriptive and normative in scope. I set out to explain how our nation has failed to achieve educational equality for all and support a policy that would help us inch further toward that goal. Because inequality is deep seated in our political and economic structure, I don't pretend that my proposal is sufficient or that it will get us there anytime soon. Because people of color have had to endure centuries of discrimination that burdens them beyond the deficits of class, this story of American failure is very much about race. Even when choice programs are available, underresourced parents can have difficulty reaping their benefits because of inadequate information, lack of proximity to where they live, or the usual frustrations of navigating bureaucratic requirements.[1]

I have focused on the choice issue as a window into a larger pattern of politics that has shortchanged generations of children since the landmark *Brown v. Board of Education* decision (1954). Our schools remain segregated, and academic achievement continues to reflect the contours of race and class. The federal courts have refused to recognize equitable school funding as an American constitutional right. Despite forty years of litigation at the state level since Jack Coons first stepped into a courtroom, we are only beginning to see signs of progress with the way funding is distributed among rich and poor school districts.[2] In the previous pages, we witnessed how Black parents who lost confidence in public school leadership have sought to take matters into their own hands, first under the banner of community control and later with demands for school choice.

That plea for control has a long history. Whether it takes you back as far as the Reconstruction era when former slaves founded their own schools, or mid-twentieth-century demands heard in Brooklyn's Ocean Hill–Brownsville and the North Division of Milwaukee, the pattern of injustice that defines America's experience with public education has been characterized by racial isolation, a calcified bureaucracy out of touch with minority cultures, and a finance system that has shortchanged people who

Radical Dreamers. Joseph P. Viteritti, Oxford University Press. © Oxford University Press (2025).
DOI: 10.1093/oso/9780197827109.003.0011

are most in need. Who knows what the future holds as we proceed into a second Trump presidency? It is not hopeful.

The choice proposition itself is continually under siege: on the left, by activists who do their best to either prevent it or deplete it of the resources needed to succeed; on the right by those who have restructured programs in ways that blunt the salutary benefits it promised for targeted students in earlier programs. Heard about systemic racism? It is not always imposed intentionally. It doesn't need to be for it to continue. Often its wounds are inflicted casually, when powerful actors pursue their own priorities unmindful of how their plans will affect others. Some manage to persuade themselves that what they do for their own good eventually will benefit others. Some have even taken stances that do in fact benefit people of color before forsaking them. In the long run, it doesn't work. As Derrick Bell astutely explained, alliances among those with conflicting stakes in politics are temporary at best. And as Howard Fuller discovered the hard way, surrogacy is a risky favor for the weaker among us.

I describe my plan for choice as progressive because it is redistributive in purpose. It is specifically designed to benefit those children who remain at the bottom of the performance scale. Simply stated, it supports charter schools as well as needs-based private school choice with public accountability expected of all participating schools. I emphasize academic achievement because it is essential for any individual who hopes to have a productive adult life. I focus on choice because it is a fitting place to start if we are to enable every parent with the opportunity each deserves and most others enjoy. The opportunity to choose goes beyond academics. Choice also is about dignity, agency, and power.

I am, by no means, suggesting that we abandon the public schools that a majority of American children attend, but we need to do better. We must proceed with wise investment in both instructional and support services for all schools. That means clear curriculum standards, proper preparation of teachers, and effective remediation for struggling students. We can't do it on the cheap. Low-performing schools that do not improve after repeated interventions should lose their eligibility for government funding whether they are public or private.

I don't claim any originality regarding my diagnosis or prescriptions. My extensive debts have been duly acknowledged in the previous pages, although I accept full responsibility for my conclusions or recommendations. I was fortunate to receive such instruction out-side the classroom from people who understood inequality on a human level, not as an academic exercise. It prepared them to translate what they knew into lifelong commitments to promote a more just system of schooling.

The Hard Facts

Failure is a bold assertion, but difficult to deny in the face of substantial evi-dence. The COVID-19 pandemic was a watershed moment with regard to the widespread reaction that swept the nation in response to evidence that American students are not doing well. There was the usual head-scratching, finger-pointing, and more than enough partisan bickering. No need to argue. The failure of American education has been a bipartisan project for as long as we can remember. Consider it gross neglect. Ours is a failure defined most conspicuously as one of inequality between the races.

Tests administered by the National Center for Education Statistics under the auspices of the National Assessment for Education Progress (NAEP) have served as the "Nation's Report Card" for K–12 schools since 1969. Long-term assessments from the 1970s through 2020 had shown that scores in math and reading were on the upswing.[3] The overall pattern of improve-ment, however, began to change with the release of scores in 2022, showing serious across-the-board losses since 2019 in both grades tested (4 and 8).[4] Results from more recent 2024 tests released earlier this year were even more discouraging. Except for fourth-grade math, scores on the other three tests had plunged to record lows. Even the improvement in fourth-grade math was insufficient to make up for its losses since 2019, and the gains were primarily driven by higher-performing students. Gaps between low-performing and high-performing students have widened across the board.

The most tragic evidence to emerge throughout the sixty-five-year history of the national testing program is one defined by race. At no time since 1970 has the performance of Black and Latino students ever approximated that of their white and Asian peers.

Let's look at the facts in terms of average scores for each racial group by grade for 2024 (but for HS only 2019 was available):[5]

	4 Reading	8 Reading	HS Reading	4 Math	8 Math	HS Math
Asian	235	280	299	257	305	175
White	225	267	295	247	286	159
Hispanic	203	245	274	227	258	138
Black	199	243	263	220	252	128

There is nothing subtle about these numbers. The learning gap that separates Black and Hispanic students from their white and Asian counterparts is as wide as an ocean. Further analysis shows how Black and Hispanic students cluster toward the bottom. In fourth-grade math, 70 percent of Black students and 60 percent of Hispanic students scored below average compared to 34 percent of the white students and 22 percent of Asian students. In eighth-grade math, the gap was larger: 74 percent Black, 67 percent Hispanic, 37 percent white, and 23 percent Asian.[6] The reading scores were no less distressing when profiling those students who performed below average. In fourth-grade reading, it was 63 percent for Blacks, 59 percent for Hispanics, 35 percent for whites, 25 percent Asian. For eighth-grade reading, it was 64 percent Black, 59 percent Hispanic, 36 percent white, 23 percent Asian.[7]

So long as racial differences in academic achievement persist, we need to admit that America's commitment to education equality for all has been a failure—unless we as a nation are prepared to claim that we can expect only so much from certain people, that they might even be "uneducable." It would not be the first time in the life of our nation that such a claim has been made. Anyone familiar with the writing of Ron Edmonds can tell you that.

This attitude has deep historical roots going back at least to Thomas Jefferson. The author of the Declaration of Independence did not see any merit in educating Black men and women at all because he believed they were incapable of benefiting from formal study. He accepted the "scientific" evidence of his time, which held that Black people belonged to a distinct race with limited capacities.[8] He held similar views about Native Americans.

For too long, our nation, either explicitly or implicitly, has pretended that the ultimate source of academic failure lies with those who have been left behind. It is with good reason, therefore, that in the summer of 2024, over one thousand NAACP delegates who attended a national meeting in Las Vegas passed two resolutions declaring basic literacy a civil right.[9] Shortly thereafter, a local unit of the organization filed a complaint with the US

Office for Civil Rights against thirty-four districts in the City and County of St. Louis highlighting steep racial disparities in the NAEP reading scores.[10]

We cannot deny that systemic social and economic disparities imposed on those at the bottom have hindered their academic progress, but we should not employ the same injustices as an excuse to tolerate or impose more injustice.

The Socioeconomic Quandary

Soon after I wrote the section of the previous chapter on the exchange between Richard Rothstein and Diane Ravitch about the relationship between education and poverty, I had occasion to observe a public conversation that took place at the University of Wisconsin between Howard Fuller and Donald Trump's former secretary of education Betsy DeVos. Rothstein and Ravitch are in agreement that we can never expect to erase the performance gap if we don't first address the social and economic factors that inhibit learning. The conversation in Wisconsin was more wide-ranging, with a third person serving as moderator. Despite the obvious differences of opinion between the two main speakers, the exchange was polite and respectful. Toward the end of the evening, the moderator asked Howard to identify what he thought the major obstacle was to effective schooling in his community. Howard quickly responded, "Poverty."[11]

As might be expected, there is a strong correlation between NAEP scores and family income, as the table indicates.[12]

	4 Reading	8 Reading	4 Math	8 Math
Low SES	197	239	221	250
Middle SES	212	255	235	270
High SES	236	279	257	300

As of 2021, the poverty rate in the United States was 11.6 percent.[13] Variations among distinct racial groups are sharp: Asians (8.1 percent), Whites (8.2 percent), Hispanics (17.1 percent), Blacks (19.5 percent). The relationship between academic performance and poverty is well established.[14] Are people of color poor because their schools do not generate high academic performance? Or are their schools underperforming because their students are poor? People are poor because they have modest incomes and no accumulated wealth. Their schools underperform because relatively few schools are strong enough to overcome the effects of poverty, but some manage to do it better than others.

Is it fair to expect educators to overcome the effects of poverty in schools populated by students who have been raised in a culture of poverty? No, but it is fair to expect a school to add some value to children's lives by improving their capacity to learn. This is not to suggest that we ignore the effects of poverty or understate them. Poverty, however, should never serve as an excuse for long-term unabated failure in an institution of learning. We have seen too many effective schools of all types in poorer communities to dismiss these more favorable outcomes as not being possible. We should never abandon Ron Edmond's admonition "All children can learn" as a basic assumption behind pleas for social justice.

This returns us to what I referred to in the last chapter as the bottom-line question: When does an appreciation for the effects of poverty on learning cross the line into becoming a recipe for the perpetuation of systemic racism? That happens when we allow poverty to justify generations of systemic failure. That happens when parents are denied the prerogative to decide whether the fault for failure lies with the school or the child. That happens when we allow other people to determine when a parent should be empowered to change their child's school.

Disparate Outcomes by Sector

The results of the NAEP tests were not consistent across education sectors. Because of their relatively large number (5,458 schools serving 1,693,327 students),[15] Catholic schools are the only private institutions for which NAEP data are regularly collected. As indicated here, Catholic schools outperformed both regular public schools and charter schools in 2024, and the differences were notable.[16]

	Mathematics Score		
	Public school	Charter school	Catholic school
Grade 4 (2024) *(out of 500)*	237	236	247
Grade 8 (2024) *(out of 500)*	272	272	293
Grade 12 (2019) *(out of 300)*	149	138	Not reported

	Reading Score		
	Public school	Charter school	Catholic school
Grade 4 (2024) *(out of 500)*	214	214	230
Grade 8 (2024) *(out of 500)*	257	257	277
Grade 12 (2019) *(out of 500)*	284	275	Not reported

If all the Catholic schools in the nation were treated like a state, they would rank first above the other fifty.[17]

The differences between the sectors are more sharply delineated when results are broken down by race.[18] Compare, for example, the average point difference for Black students who attend Catholic versus public schools: Grade 4 Reading (17 points), Grade 8 Reading (15 points), Grade 4 Math (9 points), Grade 8 Math (16 points). The depressed performance for Hispanics is even steeper: Grade 4 Reading (18 points), Grade 8 Reading (24 points), Grade 4 Math (8 points), Grade 8 Math (29 points). Black and Hispanic students who attend Catholic schools outperformed their public school peers on all four NAEP tests. They do so with a fraction of the spending that public schools have.

In 1982, James Coleman, surveying high schools, referred to these learning advantages as the "Catholic school effect," confirming what Ron Edmonds knew all along—that schools do indeed matter.[19] Is it any wonder why generations of Black and Brown families from American cities have fled to these institutions when they were not satisfied with the education available to them in local public schools?[20]

Charter Schools

As of 2024, there were 8,150 charter schools in forty-six states and the District of Columbia that enrolled 3.8 million students.[21] (See research addendum, Q1 through Q5, for more detailed information pertaining to this section.) While charter schools are public schools open to all, they tend to attract a disproportionate number of students of color with modest family incomes. An estimated 60 percent identify as Black or Hispanic compared to 44 percent in regular public schools.[22] An estimated 59 percent of charter school students are eligible for free or reduced-price lunch, compared to 50.3 percent in regular public schools.[23] (See research addendum, Q2.)

The Center for Research on Education Options (CREDO) at Stanford University has been conducting studies on student performance at charter schools for more than twenty-five years. Its most recent study, released in 2023, involved 1,853,000 students at charter schools and their traditional public school (TPS) peers in twenty-nine states.[24] It found that between 2014 and 2019, charter school students gained on average the equivalent of sixteen days of learning in reading and six days in math over their TPS peers. Eighty-three percent of charter school students performed the same or better than their TPS peers in reading, and 75 percent performed the same or better in math. Charter school students who live in poverty gained twenty-three days in reading and seventeen days in math. English-language learners gained six days in reading and eight days in math. Overall, Black and Hispanic students in charters gained more than their TPS peers. (See research addendum, Q5.)

Compared to district-run public schools, charter schools have more precise standards of accountability. A basic principle behind the idea of charters is that they would be granted more flexibility in exchange for such higher expectations.[25] As the table in Q3 of the research addendum indicates, grounds for termination are written into the charter laws in each of the forty-six states (except for Maryland), plus the District of Columbia, that has a charter school. A majority of states require satisfactory academic progress to remain open.

The findings on charter school performance are especially impressive when one acknowledges that per-capita spending at charters is not on par with spending at local public schools. Estimates of differentials vary from $2,145 per pupil[26] to $,2730 per pupil[27] to 30 percent.[28] Although these studies vary in their conclusions, depending on their distinct approaches, they all reach the same bewildering conclusion: Students who attend charter schools—a disproportionate number of whom are Black or Brown and from families with lower incomes—do not receive a fair share of funding.

These disparities are the result of effective lobbying by charter school opponents, most of whom are Democrats. Recall the tense conversation between Howard Fuller and Elizabeth Warren in an earlier chapter as the liberal senator from Massachusetts tried to explain away her hostility to charters. Be reminded of President Joe Biden's proposed regulations in 2022 that would have made it more difficult to create new charter schools and his constant threat to cut their federal funding.[29]

Because the demand for seats outpaces the supply, many charters have long waiting lists, as we saw in New York. The lists exist because the same charter opponents who pressure state legislators to underfund the schools persuade them to limit the supply so that it does not meet the real demand. The only justification behind those policies is to protect enrollments in district-run public schools that parents have found undesirable. Opponents of choice know that if parents were allowed to flee, they would. Most schools that need this kind of protection to stay in business are found in Black, Brown, and economically challenged communities. It is a form of human warehousing.

Failure by Design

By the end of 2024, there were seventy-five choice programs operating in thirty-three states, Puerto Rico, and the District of Columbia that subsidize tuition and other educational costs for 1,038,487 students.[30] As explained in detail in the addendum section prior to Q6, these programs come in a variety of forms. Except for a federal program that provides low-income families in the District of Columbia with scholarships for private schools and other privately supported initiatives, these programs are funded by the states.

As the tables in Q9 in the research addendum indicate, among the various types of offerings, voucher/scholarship programs are the most redistributive in orientation and more likely to target students who either are from low-income families, have special needs, or are attending low-performing public schools. A majority of tax credit programs target low-income students. Education Savings Accounts (ESAs) are the least redistributive. Recent efforts to expand such programs are focused on making them universal in nature so that they are available to all students.

Research on the effectiveness of these programs in raising student achievement is quite varied in terms of both the quality of the assessments and the outcomes derived. Much of it has focused over the years either on voucher/scholarship initiatives or scholarship programs financed by private philanthropy, which were also among the earliest, like the ones we saw in Milwaukee and Cleveland. There are evaluations of individual programs, and more sweeping studies attempt to integrate the findings of multiple studies to draw more general conclusions about their effectiveness. A brief overview of some of this scholarship appears in Q13 of the research addendum.

One needs to be extremely cautious in drawing major conclusions about the overall success of these programs. Early research on public and private programs operating in New York, Dayton, and Washington, DC, revealed encouraging gains on standardized tests. Early findings on the academic impact of the Milwaukee program were mixed.[31] With the accumulation of time, later studies in Washington, DC, saw little evidence of such gains. Some programs (Indiana, Louisiana, and Ohio) were found to have negative effects. The most positive discoveries to emerge from these evaluations seem to have appeared in the form of higher graduation and college attendance rates, as found in Florida, Milwaukee, and Washington, DC.[32] Programs with clearly defined standards of accountability seemed to perform better. Private and religious schools that are part of larger operating networks also exceled. The latter two observations are similar to those that CREDO made with regard to charter schools, although accountability standards for private school programs are generally not as rigorous as those written into charter laws.

The one finding from voucher, ESA, and tax credit surveys (Q10, Q11, and Q12 in the addendum) that puts the varied academic outcomes in bold relief involves per-student spending levels. Across the board, they are not on par with what is spent on students in district-run public schools. We saw such terms negotiated between proponents and opponents of the early scholarship programs in Milwaukee and Cleveland. We saw disparities that exist with regard to charter schools. Both offer tangible evidence of inequity. What makes the inequities about the voucher and scholarship initiatives so egregious is that these programs were specifically created to help under-performing students from families that did not have the resources to attain better opportunities for their children.

One might say that it is miraculous that these voucher and scholarship students perform even as well as they do under such circumstances. We should not, however, need to rely on miracles to address the needs of our most challenged students. These discriminatory effects in spending may be undergoing a reversal with the creation of ESAs and more recently enacted choice programs. The new programs, however, are capable of imposing their own regressive effects on underresourced families, which we discuss shortly.

It's Not Just Schools

We cannot understate the important role that Diane Ravitch and Howard Fuller have attributed to socioeconomic factors as inhibitors of academic progress. Hard evidence on multiple correlations between race, income, and academic achievement have already been cited. It is undeniable. I want to offer here a few paragraphs to explain how that works. Simply stated: It's politics! And it is systemic, in a uniquely American way.

Our nation, despite rhetoric to the contrary, maintains one of the highest rates of economic inequality in the world. According to Gini score data used to calculate economic inequality collected by the Organisation of Economic Co-operation and Development, the United States has the highest level of economic inequality of any G6 nation.[33] This inequality has grown precipitously over the past thirty years and continues to get worse. Between 1990 and 2021, our Gini score increased from 0.43 to 0.49 (a score of 0 represents perfect equality). According to the Economic Policy Institute, the average annual salary for the top 1 percent of earners in the United States is $1,316,985, which is 26.3 times what the average person earns ($50,107).[34] Sliced another way, the top 1 percent take home 21 percent of all income. We have entered a new Gilded Age.

Americans more than tolerate inequality. We foster it, promote it, and maintain it with policies enforced through the political process. Sociologist Matthew Desmond describes poverty as an American addiction rooted in the exploitation of the poor by the affluent that many of the latter assume as an entitlement.[35] The present century has been a high point of corporate power, and its exercise in the fields of finance, insurance, and real estate (the FIRE industries) has led to the passage of business-friendly legislation in the areas of taxation and regulation. Repeal of the Glass-Steagall Act in 1999, which had separated investment banking from commercial banking, was a pivotal moment in the erosion of consumer protection, conflict of interest, and transparency rules.

The Supreme Court's *Citizens United* ruling in 2010 that invalidated controls on corporate donations for election campaigns has opened the floodgates for spending and lobbying efforts like none seen in any Western democracy.[36] According to Open Secret, a nonprofit that monitors campaigns, by election day in 2024 total spending was on course to exceed $15.9 billion, a new record.[37] Americans for Tax Fairness has reported that 150 billionaire families spent nearly $2 billion.[38]

A robust body of literature has emerged documenting the corrupting process in which corporate money has been invested into election and lobbying campaigns to influence tax policies and business deregulation in ways that restructure the economy in favor of the wealthy.[39] The proceeds from those investments are reinvested in a politics that rewards corporate greed at the expense of those at the bottom of the economic ladder. It is a wicked cycle that coincided with the loss of union membership and power. Even philanthropy that passes for generosity is a form of influence peddling subsidized by tax relief.[40] Democrats and Republicans have both been complicit in this nefarious process.

These inequities and their reinforcement through political spending will only grow worse under a second Trump administration, with his promises to lower the tax liability of the richest among us. On the day after his inauguration, the *Wall Street Journal* reported that five of the world's richest men, whose market value added up to $12 trillion, sat nearby on the dais when Trump took the oath of office.[41] As plutocrats from the finance and tech industries genuflect before Donald Trump upon his return to power and both houses of Congress appear to be in lockstep with his agenda, more deregulation of the banking, business, and communication sectors is just on the horizon.

Revisiting the First Amendment

When demands for wider school choice entered the mainstream of politics in the late 1980s, American jurisprudence on church-state separation was full of confused and confusing contradictions.[42] Compulsory education laws that required all children to receive an education were an assumed feature of American life. States permitted parents to fulfill these expectations by sending their children to public, private, or religious schools. It was a system of unsubsidized choice. While public schools were free, government support for a private or religious education was limited to specific expenses, such as transportation and textbooks.

The legal rationale for the latter payments—as defined by the US Supreme Court's interpretation of the Establishment Clause, referred to as the "child benefit theory"—was that such aid was granted directly to students rather than the religious institutions they attended. Direct government aid to religious institutions was prohibited as violating the Establishment Clause's required separation of church and state. Federal jurisprudence and many state constitutions continued to outlaw tuition aid for students at religious schools. Jack Coons, better than anyone, has explained the basic inequity of the latter arrangement as a matter of parental prerogative. Stated simply, it ensures that only parents of certain means, sufficient to pay tuition, enjoy the opportunity to have their children educated in the tradition of their faith if they so desire.[43]

The movement that eventually led to the enactment of voucher programs in Milwaukee, Cleveland, and elsewhere in the 1990s was energized by a more inclusive argument for equity defined in terms of effective schools for the underserved.[44] The Supreme Court's 2002 decision on the constitutionality of the Cleveland voucher program had a profound impact on the legal landscape, but it was still limited in scope. Although the *Zelman* ruling deemed that Ohio's law providing educational assistance to poor children fulfills a "valid secular purpose," it did not establish an absolute right to such assistance.[45] In that sense, it still left the same economically disadvantaged children in a more vulnerable position than those better-off children whose parents, for religious or educational reasons, preferred faith-based schools.

Writing for a 4–3 majority, Chief Justice William Rehnquist conditioned judicial approval of the Cleveland program on (1) its providing aid to students and only indirectly to schools, (2) attendance at religious schools being purely a function of parental choice, and (3) the program offering students alternatives to religious schools.[46] The distinction between direct and indirect aid followed previous judicial reasoning involving transportation and textbooks resting on the child benefit concept. Significantly, the court also underscored parental choice as a factor that neutralized claims of coercion or compelled attendance at religious schools. If Ohio had not provided secular choices for students fleeing public schools, the program might have been shut down in response to plaintiffs' claims of "coercion."

Even as the First Amendment wall that confined many children to failing public schools began to fall, a more impenetrable boundary to educational opportunity continued to stand at the state level with the inclusion of Blaine Amendments in state constitutions.[47] A year after *Zelman* was handed down, the Supreme Court again signaled a gradualist approach to the First Amendment when it reversed a circuit court ruling to affirm the State of Washington's action withdrawing Joshua Davey's state-sponsored college scholarship because the young man intended to use the award to study for the ministry.[48] Notably, Washington's action was premised on a nineteenth-century state constitutional provision that had been adopted in the wake of Congressman James Blaine's effort to ban aid to religious schools nationally. Republican delegates to the 1889 constitutional convention in the Washington territory (then seeking statehood) were allied with Blaine, and their speeches supporting the proposal reflected his same anti-Catholic bigotry.[49]

The court signaled a changing direction in 2017 when it ruled that Missouri unconstitutionally excluded a religious preschool from a government-supported playground resurfacing program.[50] It addressed state Blaine provisions directly in 2020 when Kendra Espinoza, assisted by attorneys from the libertarian Institute for Justice, challenged a Montana law that would not allow her to use a state-supported private school voucher to send her children to a religious school. These cases marked a new focus in First Amendment jurisprudence. For nearly ninety years, most federal litigation had focused on the Establishment Clause and determining the limits on government action that might cross the permissible boundary separating church and state, as did *Zelman. Espinoza,* especially, turned the court's attention to the free exercise clause and the safeguards it provided to protect individuals from government action that unfairly burdens the practice of religion.

The court's ruling in *Espinoza* favoring the plaintiff's claim of religious discrimination was another landmark in the history of American law.[51] Here too, though, the court's reasoning was conditional. What made this mother's argument of discrimination persuasive was the fact that the program under review allowed participation of nonsectarian private schools and singled out religious institutions for exclusion. It did not establish a basic right to a state-supported religious education, nor was that question under consideration.

The court ruled similarly in a 2022 First Amendment case in Maine involving a program that appropriates funding for students to attend non-public schools in local districts that do not have public high schools.[52] Together, the two cases will serve as strong precedents for challenges to Blaine-like provisions in state law that subject religious institutions and their members to unfair treatment. They will open more doors of opportunity for families who need alternatives to public schools that do not adequately address their children's educational needs. These cases have also added momentum to a wider movement to redefine the meaning of the First Amendment.

A More Dangerous Branch

Eventually, the deliberate gradualism of the Court presided over by Chief Justice William Rehnquist (1986–2005) that coaxed constitutional interpretation to the political center gave way to a jurisprudence with a right-leaning bend less anchored by precedent.[53] This shift to the right was accelerated once Donald Trump added to the court three conservative justices who became part of a governing majority under Chief Justice John Roberts. The first shock was felt in 2022 when a five-person majority handed down *Dobbs v. Johnson*,[54] overturning *Roe v. Wade*[55] and a forty-nine-year precedent that protected a woman's right to make her own decision on whether to carry a pregnancy to term.

Increasingly relying on an originalist interpretation wedded to a supposed fidelity to the intentions of the Founders, the majority's reasoning at times has seemed more aligned with the customs of the eighteenth century than the needs of the twenty-first, except when it chose not to. Its most dramatic break with the original thinking of the Founders came in 2024 when the Roberts court handed down *Trump v. U.S.*[56] granting the president of the United States broad immunity from criminal prosecution. If there was one thing the founding generation prioritized after fighting a war of liberation from the British monarchy, it was protection from a chief executive who was above the law. To upend such a cherished democratic doctrine at a time when Donald Trump—a convicted felon who refused to accept the results of a democratic election that removed him from office—was seeking a second term in the White House violated an American tradition that was a fundamental feature of the original constitutional compact.

Such is the larger legal context in which the US Supreme Court is operating as our school system advances into the second quarter of the present century, which takes us back to the First Amendment. In the same term that the court handed down the *Espinoza* decision (2020), the court delivered a ruling in a California case with different and far-reaching implications that did not attract the same attention.

Espinoza invalidated a state law that discriminated against faith-based institutions and the families who preferred them. *Our Lady of Guadalupe School v. Morrissey-Berru* concerned an employee dispute at a Roman Catholic elementary school.[57] In 2014, after years of service, the school demoted Agnes Morrissey-Berru and then refused to renew her contract the following year. School authorities alleged that her teaching was not up to par. She claimed that she had been let go because of her age and sued under the federal Age Discrimination in Employment Act of 1967. The case had been joined with a similar one in which Kristen Biel had been dismissed for unsatisfactory performance from a Catholic school in California in 2014 after she had been diagnosed with breast cancer. Biel filed suit under the American with Disabilities Act claiming discrimination on the basis of her medical condition. In neither case did the school claim that the employee was dismissed for any act or behavior that undermined its religious mission.

I am not in a position to judge the validity of the claims on either side of the two cases. What is concerning about *Guadalupe* is the basis upon which the court denied relief to the two plaintiffs. The ruling turned on precedent set in a 2012 case that established something called a "ministerial exception."[58] Based on a presumption that the First Amendment prohibits public authorities from interfering with church governance related to matters of "faith and doctrine," *Hosanna-Tabor* grants faith-based institutions wide discretion in dealing with members of their ministry to the point that courts are excluded from many employment disputes. This forecloses employees from bringing many discrimination claims against religious institutions.

From a human rights perspective, the legal protections lost under the 2012 *Hosanna-Tabor* decision are substantial for those who voluntarily choose to join a religious order. At stake in *Guadalupe* was the determination of which employees might be considered ministerial members of a faith-based institution. The *Hosanna-Tabor* court had expressly declined to adopt a rigid standard to determine whether an employee could be considered a minister. Neither Morrissey-Berru nor Biel had ever been members of a religious order. Their employers argued that the two women performed ministerial duties because they were expected to participate in faculty prayer services, teach religion classes, lead students in prayer, accompany students to Mass, and, in short, model Catholic faith and morals. The court accepted these arguments in a 7–2 decision written by Justice Alito that granted faith-based institutions wide discretion in determining which employees perform ministerial duties and remain unprotected by laws or regulations designed to guarantee basic rights to employees.

These precedents are troubling and part of a larger pattern in which the court is applying the Free Exercise Clause to diminish other basic

rights. Given the overall disposition of the Court's conservative majority, women and members of the LGBTQ+ community are especially
vulnerable under this emerging jurisprudence. The repercussions these
recent rulings have on future employment cases must be monitored and
exposed.[59]

With the present direction that state legislation is moving and the proclivities of a more conservative Republican Congress, a potpourri of education-
related issues are working their way through the courts involving issues like
religious charter schools, school prayer, Bible reading, and posting of the Ten
Commandments on school grounds. The religious charter school question
is most immediate.

In June 2024, the Supreme Court of Oklahoma voted in a 6–2 ruling
that a virtual charter school opened by the Catholic Church violated federal and state laws. The suit to close the school was brought by the state
attorney general and was supported by the National Alliance of Public
Charter Schools (NAPCS) and the National Association of Charter School
Authorizers (NACSA), the nation's leading coalitions of charter schools.
Issuing a statement that applauded the decision, the NAPCS"s leadership
insisted,

> All charter schools are public schools. The Alliance firmly believes char-
> ter schools, like all public schools, may not be religious institutions.
> We insist that every charter school must be given the same federal and
> state civil rights and constitutional protections as their district school
> peers.[60]

When the US Supreme Court reviewed the state ruling in April of this year, it
handed down a split 4–4 decision with Justice Amy Coney Barrett recusing
herself from the case.[61] This left the state ruling in place with advocates for
religious charter schools promisng another go of it with the hope that Justice
Barrett will support their cause. That outcome would push the boundary of
church- state separation beyond the standard set by the court in *Zelman*
(2002), which approved the Cleveland voucher program because, among
other reasons, the funding was provided to students and not directly to the
school. Such a decision would change the character of the charter school
movement and jeopardize the most promising experiment in public school
choice the nation has ever seen.[62]

The Death of Public School?

In the summer of 2022, Arizona passed a new law that a *Wall Street Journal* editorial heralded as "a bellwether of things to come."[63] The Empowerment Scholarship Act of Arizona creates an ESA valued at 90 percent of the state per-pupil funding amount for every student in the state regardless of income.[64] It may be used for private (including religious) school tuition or a broad range of education-related expenses. Prior to its passage, the state scholarship program was limited to students who attended failing schools or were defined by other categories of vulnerability.

In 2023, state legislators across the country took up a total of 111 pieces of choice legislation. Seven states enacted new laws, and ten expanded programs already in existence. Advocates declared 2023 the "Year of School Choice." By the start of the 2024–2025 school year, ten states had universal programs in place.[65] In all, by the end of 2024, there were 81 choice programs across 33 states, the District of Columbia, and Puerto Rico. Over one million students were enrolled; with the new programs in place, twenty-two million or 40 percent of all students in the nation were eligible for at least one program.[66] Florida led the nation with 455,000 students qualifying for one program or another.[67] Within the first four months of 2025, new programs were enacted in Idaho, Tennessee and Wyoming; the governor of Texas also was poised to sign a law he had ushered through the state legislature and New Hampshire was not far behind. In many places, the demand for private school choice has outpaced the growth of charter schools.

There have been exceptions to the pro-choice momentum that has built since the pandemic. At the end of 2023, Illinois discontinued its Invest in Kids tax credit program that had been in operation since 2017 and provided scholarships worth $5,900 to 9,600 low-income students.[68] In the fall of 2024, the state supreme court of South Carolina invalidated its scholarship program, citing a state constitutional provision against aid to private schools. The governor of North Carolina, a Democrat, vetoed new funding to expand eligibility for its voucher program, but the Republicans in the legislature immediately overrode his action. School choice went down to defeat in three statewide referenda (Colorado, Nebraska, and Kentucky) as Donald Trump walked across the finish line in the November 2024 election. Choice bound ballot measures remain unpopular with voters. Since 1978, thirteen straight referenda have been turned down in nineteen different states.[69]

In the meantime, the political climate across the nation remains favorable to school choice in the form of ESAs. These programs, by and large, neither target the most vulnerable students as the early voucher programs did, nor do they include strong accountability measures. As we enter a new era in the debate on school choice, Milton Friedman's market approach to choice is winning out over Jack Coons's progressive model.

What does this new groundswell for choice portend for the future of public schools? Is public education in danger? Let's look at the facts. According to the National Center for Education Statistics (NCES), between the fall of 2019 and the fall of 2021, public school enrollments decreased from 50.8 million to 49.4 million before rising again to 49.6 million in 2022. The steepest losses had been recorded in 2020, the first year of the COVID-19 pandemic.[70] NCES predicts a further enrollment loss to 46.9 million by 2031 due mostly to lower birthrates. This decline reverses the pattern that prevailed between 2012 and 2019, when enrollments increased by 2 percent.

NCES also reported that while public school (district) enrollment decreased 4 percent between 2019 and 2020, charter school enrollment rose 7 percent. Notably, between 2010 and 2021, charter school enrollment had more than doubled from 1.8 million to 3.7 million, underscoring the popularity of that newer public option. The number of students attending private schools remained steady between 2019 and 2021 (4.7 million). This represented a substantial increase since 2011 (4 million total) despite a significant loss at Catholic schools (from 1.9 million to 1.7 million). These data, however, do not capture the most recent acceleration of choice programs, how they will affect public school or charter enrollments or, more importantly, the students in our schools. At this point, nevertheless, it is a bit premature to declare the death of public schools.

Commenting on this data in *Education Week*, Thomas Dee, a Stanford University economist, estimated that approximately half the loss in public school enrollments is attributable to population changes, 20 percent to private school attendance, and 20 percent to homeschooling. He expressed particular concern with the latter, remarking, "Some of what exists as home schooling may be functionally equivalent to truancy."[71] To the extent that Dee's claims about homeschooling are true, it might better be described as subsidized truancy where ESA programs are propelling it. Citing data from NCES, Michael McShane of EdChoice offered the following reasons why parents abandon public schools for an at-home option: concerns about safety, drugs, and negative peer pressure; dissatisfaction with instruction; and desire for religious instruction.[72]

Let's take a closer look at where enrollment erosion is taking place. A recent study that Sofaklis Goulas of the Brookings Institution prepared for the Thomas Fordham Institute found that 12 percent of elementary schools (including district and charter) and 9 percent of middle schools have lost at least 20 percent of their enrollment between 2019 and 2023.[73] Goulas further observed that schools identified by their states as chronically low-performing (utilizing a variety of measures) were twice as likely to experience enrollment decline. Schools identified as urban, high-poverty, and charter were overrepresented among the latter.

It would not be a tragedy if such failing institutions were closed, whether district or charter, especially if resources were reinvested in schools more likely to flourish. Such a move would actually strengthen public education. Families, evidently, are already exercising the exit option. The question is: Where would the fleeing students from those shuttered institutions—a disproportionate number of whom are low-income and students of color—go? What real options are available to them?

A Sharp Right Turn

Although some ESA programs make accommodations for students with special needs and others provide more funding for academically vulnerable or low-income students (as indicated in Q9 of the addendum), they are by and large not designed in pursuit of a redistributive agenda. Increasingly popular universal programs do not target vulnerable students. The problem with the sudden growth of choice when viewed through a progressive lens is functionally one of supply and demand. With all the new programs, the number of students eligible for participation in choice programs by the end of 2024 was twenty-two million. That was twenty-two times the number currently enrolled.

As the demand for choice programs increases with broader eligibility, there simply aren't enough seats in private schools to accommodate more than a small fraction of those students who are eligible. This puts admissions officers at participating schools in a position to be more selective, passing up students who are in need of remediation. The problem is exacerbated when tuition amounts are allowed to exceed award levels, effectively excluding more needy families while subsidizing many who can pay tuition on their own. These cost dynamics provide an incentive for schools to raise tuition, pricing even more students out of market.

Notwithstanding the outcome, the scheme is not necessarily sinister in intent. It is a matter of parental disposition and capacity. James Coleman described it well in the foreword to Jack Coons's first major book, where the eminent sociologist explained why rich school districts spend more than poor ones. It is simply because they are able. He called the process a "continual struggle between two forces": those who strive to foster opportunity for all and those who indulge a natural instinct of parents to do the best for their own children.[74] Some are better equipped to do the latter than others. That is also how markets work, which is why government needs to intervene to level the playing field. With universal choice, more privileged families now enjoy a state subsidy while private school choice remains out of reach for those with more modest incomes.

Compared to other forms of private school choice, ESA programs impose little accountability for the expenditure of public funds. Private schools are subject to relatively few state and federal regulations to start.[75] According to the survey released at the beginning of 2024 by FutureEd, an independent think tank at Georgetown University (see Q14 in the Addendum), as of 2024 only three of the nation's fifteen ESA programs required students to take statewide standardized tests. Utah's and Arizona's new universal ESA programs require no student reporting.[76]

ESAs are especially difficult to monitor because they can be used for a wide variety of expenses, such as homeschooling and an array of educational support services like tutoring for which no minimum standards are set.[77] Increasingly popular microschools can serve no more than a handful of students and have no regulations.[78] Some parents have used the spending accounts to defray the costs of such questionable items as backyard trampolines, kayaks, greenhouses, pianos, and trips to Disneyland—all in the name of education. A state auditor in Arizona identified $700,000 worth of improper spending during the program's first year of operation.[79] The Grand Canyon Institute has estimated that a significant portion of the state's $1.3 billion deficit is attributable to ESA spending.[80] With twenty-one million (and growing) additional students eligible to join the ranks of the one million who have utilized school choice options around the country, this new pattern of spending is unsustainable in the long run.

Room for Negotiation

The school choice debate has brought us to an unusual point in our national discourse on education policy: Conservative Republicans have taken to spending with abandon, backing a no-strings-attached approach to their policies that bestow benefits on all, whether or not they need it; liberal Democrats have routinely opposed programs fashioned to uplift underresourced and underserved families and have used their influence to slash funding for such programs whenever they are enacted. What the two campaigns have in common is who suffers as a result of their respective bidding. The consequences are a systemic feature of our political process that can be measured in terms of race and class, in that order.

This wrangling between the left and the right has played out while President Trump's Secretary of Education Linda McMahon proceeds to dismantle the education department and a range of programs that originally were created to address the needs of our most vulnerable students.[81] Their clients include residents of high-poverty districts, children with special needs, English language learners, immigrants, racial and ethnic minorities, gender nonconforming students, preschoolers, and just about any young people who depend on human compassion to help them navigate their compromised circumstances. It remains to be seen how long it will take the Republican leadership in Congress to respond to growing public outrage and retrieve its legislative prerogatives to rebuke the callousness of the executive branch.

The continuing upsurge in universal choice programs, nevertheless, is fiscally unsustainable unless it is financed by either a significant infusion of new public funding or a dramatic redirection of spending away from public schools.[82] The former proposition is out of step with conservative priorities and is unfeasible politically; the latter will not be tolerated by the majority of Americans who continue to send their children to public schools. In the meantime, Democrats can no longer turn their backs on Black, Brown, and low-income children who struggle in chronically failing public schools for no other reason than keeping these institutions afloat.

According to a Pew survey released in early 2024, half of all Americans (51 percent) believe that K–12 public school education is moving in the wrong direction, compared to only 16 percent who believe it is moving in the right direction.[83] A more recent Gallup survey found that the percentage of Americans either somewhat or very dissatisfied with public education increased from 62% in 2019 to 73% in 2025. As indicated in the data cited in Q15 of the research addendum, about half of those Americans polled support school choice. That support could increase as more parents become familiar with its offerings; that support could erode if the rising costs for choice lead to higher taxes or divestment from public schools.

We need to do better. People on either side of the political divide need to talk, listen to each other, and come up with compromises that move the nation forward. Republicans and Democrats at both the federal and state levels need to get behind a choice program targeted at low-income children with clearly defined standards for participating private and religious schools that are regularly monitored for student progress with safeguards to protect the rights of students and professionals. Per-capita funding levels should be set to equal the amounts spent in local public schools. Charter school funding should be set at the same level as public schools and charters must remain secular. Allowing private and parochial schools to raise tuition rates to the same level of spending appropriated to local public schools will improve their capacity to serve academically challenged students and better share the burden with struggling school districts. Prohibiting schools from charging tuition above scholarship amounts will prevent abuses.

The goal of American education must be to provide reasonable alternatives for every parent whose child attends a failing public school. It is a matter of simple justice. There is nothing more oppressive than being told you have no choice. Every parent deserves an opportunity to dream.

Research Addendum

What We Know (and Don't) About School Choice

This addendum offers a deep dive into the facts about choice. The available data are simultaneously voluminous and incomplete. This section does not answer all the questions we have, but it gives us some understanding of what we know about the issue.

There are many forms of school choice beyond the modest offerings of public school districts that grant students more options within and beyond their residence-based boundaries. To the best that the available data allow, we examine each on the basis of questions prompted by the normative concerns mapped out earlier: How many programs are there? Who qualifies? Who participates? Are programs held accountable? Are students supported fairly? How well do they perform?

There are endless sources of data, some more reliable than others. I have drawn on those that, in my judgment, are the most credible based on the reputations of those who assemble and analyze them. Government sources are a good place to start, but are not always comprehensive or up to date. Where I depend on private sources, I acknowledge whom they represent. I note differences among the sources where they exist. Sometimes the differences are a result of how or when the data were collected, this being an ever-changing landscape. I present the work of respected scholars who analyze the data to draw empirically based conclusions about existing programs. This is hardly an exhaustive overview of the research. I tend to focus on more general literature reviews or meta-analyses rather than studies of particular programs. My own commentary appears in italics.

Charter Schools

As of 2024, charter schools exist in forty-six states and the District of Columbia. Kentucky passed a charter school law in 2017 but has not opened any schools. The existing charter schools serve 3.8 million students.[1] The data in this section are drawn from three sources: the National Center for Education Statistics (NCES) is the primary unit within the US Department

Radical Dreamers. Joseph P. Viteritti, Oxford University Press. © Oxford University Press (2025).
DOI: 10.1093/oso/9780197827109.003.0012

of Education responsible for collecting and analyzing education data. The Education Commission of the States (ECS) functions as a "partner to state policymakers by providing personalized support and helping education leaders come together to learn from one another."[2] The National Alliance for Public Charter Schools (NAPCS) describes itself as "the leading national nonprofit organization committed to advancing the charter school movement."[3]

Q1. Who may attend charter schools?

Charter schools do not typically have assignment zones, admission requirements, or entrance exams. When applications exceed available spaces, students are usually selected by lottery. In 2004, the US Department of Education issued a nonregulatory guidance pamphlet that held, "A charter school that is oversubscribed and consequently must use a lottery, generally must include in that lottery all eligible applicants for admissions."[4]

There are exceptions where enrollment preferences are given. According to the Education Commission of the States (ECS), five states do not give any enrollment preferences to students applying to charter schools: Alaska, Colorado, Kansas, Rhode Island, and Wyoming. The remaining forty-one states with charter laws and the District of Columbia all specify some enrollment preferences that either must or may be implemented in charter school admissions. Some common guidelines recorded by ECS are laid out below.[5]

Groups of students	# of states where preference must be granted	# of states where preference may be granted
Siblings of previously or currently enrolled students	11	20
Students previously enrolled at the school	10	8
Children of the school's founding or governing board, board of directors, full-time teachers, employees, and/or staff	1	23
Free or reduced-price lunch students	2	7
Homeless students	0	3
Students with limited English proficiency	0	5
At-risk students	0	6

According to my proposal, guidelines could have more redistributive effects if preferences were granted to low-income students or students who attend underperforming schools. That said, charter schools do attract a disproportionate number of Black and Latino students who are more likely to come from low-income families and have previously been assigned to underperforming public schools.

Q2. Who attends charter schools?

According to data provided by the National Center for Education Statistics (NCES), the racial/ethnic profile of charter school students (fall 2021) compared to regular public school students (2022), was as follows:[6]

Racial/ethnic demographic	Charter school students	Public elementary and secondary school students
Hispanic	36 percent	29 percent
White	29 percent	44 percent
Black	24 percent	15 percent
Two or more races	5 percent	5 percent
Asian	4 percent	5.5 percent
American Indian/Alaska Native	0.7 percent	1 percent
Pacific Islander	0.4 percent	<1 percent

According to the National Alliance for Public Charter Schools, the racial/ethnic profile of charter school students compared to regular public school students was as follows:[7]

Racial/ethnic demographic	Charter school students	Public school students
Hispanic	36.1 percent	28.1 percent
White	29.3 percent	46.2 percent
Black	24.4 percent	14.1 percent
Asian	4.3 percent	5.5 percent
Other	5.9 percent	6.1 percent

It is difficult to find specific income demographics for charter school students, but statistics are available on the percentage of charter school students who on the basis of family income are eligible to receive free or reduced-price lunch. According to the National Alliance for Public Charter Schools (NAPCS), 59 percent of charter school students are eligible for free or reduced-price lunch (FRPL). In contrast, the NAPCS reports that 50.3 percent of students in district public schools are eligible.[8]

Some opponents of charters claim that the overrepresentation of Black and Brown children at charters is a form of segregation. There is a significant difference between children attending a school of their choice and children attending a school because they have no choice.

Q3. Are there accountability standards that monitor charter schools based on student performance?

According to the Education Commission of the States (ECS), the grounds for termination of schools in the forty-five states and the District of Columbia with charter school laws are listed below:[9]

Grounds for termination of charter school	Number of states + DC *(out of 47)*
Failure to meet student performance / academic achievement standards	**26** AK, AZ, AR, CA, CT, DC, FL, IL, LA, MA, MI, MN, NV, NH, NM, NY, NC, OH, OK, OR, PA, RI, SC, VA, WI, WY
Failure to make progress toward "performance expectations"	**12** AL, GA, HI, ID, KY, ME, MS, MO, TN, TX, WA, WV
Failure to meet "educational goals"	**2** IA, IN
Failed to implement a turnaround plan or failure to make sufficient progress related to that turnaround plan	**1** CO
Failure to make progress in achieving the program goals contained in the charter	**1** KS
Failure to make adequate yearly progress under the No Child Left Behind Act	**1** UT
Failure to fulfill any condition imposed by the state commissioner of education	**1** NJ
Failure to comply with its charter; failure to satisfy, in its operation of the school, its approval criteria	**1** DE
None	**1** MD

Obviously, statutory standards for charter schools vary by state. The fact that all but one state has specific criteria for school closure suggests a higher level of accountability compared to regular public schools, where schools are rarely closed for failure to meet performance standards.

A report from 2023 by the Center for Research on Educational Outcomes (CREDO) at Stanford University, which we elaborate on further below, suggests that charter school board authorizers that require schools to undergo periodic performance reviews to remain in good standing are the "accountability side of the charter school equation" (in exchange for flexibility) in that they "evaluate performance and, if necessary, dictate remedies."[10]

Q4. Do charter school students receive equitable support compared to students in regular district run public schools?

The NCES reports that in fiscal year 2021, median current expenditure per pupil in independent charter districts was $11,745. Median current expenditure per pupil in noncharter and mixed districts (districts that include noncharter and charter schools) was $13,890, amounting to a $2,145 deficit in funding for independent charter districts.[11]

The NAPCS reports that charter schools in 2022 received on average 75 cents for every dollar that public schools receive. The authors caution that they were only able to obtain adequate data from twenty-seven states and are notably missing California, New York, and Florida.[12]

According to the University of Arkansas Department of Education Reform's August 2023 report on eighteen major US cities during the 2019–2020 school year, public charter schools received $7,147 less in per-pupil funding than traditional public schools (a 30 percent gap). The report also explains that, although the disparity has decreased 3 percent from the 2017–2018 academic year, the funding gap has remained consistent over seven of their reports. They attribute the largest portion of this funding inequality to an approximate $8,094 (67 percent) gap in local funds, noting that, in eleven out of the eighteen cities, charter schools do not receive any local revenue.[13]

If charter schools do receive less funding, as I believe they do, it can be considered another form of injustice imposed on the predominantly Black and Brown students who attend them. My proposal would at least require equal funding for all students.

Q5. How does student performance at charter schools compare to that of public schools and Catholic schools for which data are available?

As shown on pages 192–193 in the previous chapter, the most recent data published by the National Center for Education Statistics (NCES) indicate that charter school performance runs about even with public schools, except for the twelfth-grade level, where it lags behind.

Charters serve a population of students who very often have not done well in regular public schools and are in need of remediation to catch up with their public school peers. This is especially problematic for students who transfer to charter schools while in the upper grades. For that reason, snapshot comparisons taken at a particular point of time can be misleading measures of school effectiveness. Comparisons of performance between regular public schools and charter schools must also keep in mind disparities in funding that favor the former over the latter.

Research conducted by CREDO at Stanford University has addressed these methodological issues. Since 2000, CREDO has undertaken three major studies comparing the learning gains for charter students with those students in nearby traditional public schools (TPS) they would have attended if not for the availability of charter schools in their communities. Because students in charter schools often start out as underperformers, measuring student growth is a better indicator of the value added at the school. Led by Margaret Raymond, an economist, CREDO's charter school research has wide credibility across the scholarly community.

The most recent CREDO study published in 2023 involving 1,853,000 charter school students and their TPS peers used standardized testing data from twenty-nine states, the District of Columbia, and New York City.[14] It found that between 2014 and 2019, charter school students gained on average the equivalent of sixteen days of learning in reading and six days in math over their TPS peers. Eighty-three percent of charter schools performed the same or better than their TPS peers in reading, and 75 percent performed the same or better in math. Students who live in poverty at charters gained twenty-three days in reading and seventeen days in math, and English-language learners gained six days in reading and eight days in math. Overall, Black and Hispanic students in charters gain more than their TPS peers.

The report observes,

This growth represents accelerated learning gains for tens of thousands of students across the country. Each student and each school is a proof point that shows that it is possible to change the trajectory of learning for students at scale, and it is possible to dramatically accelerate growth for students who have traditionally been underserved by traditional school systems.[15]

The CREDO study also addresses claims that charter schools perform better because their students are a self-selected group whose parents are highly motivated or that the schools cherry-pick their students. CREDO's baseline data indicate that charter schools consistently enroll students who are lower achieving than those in the former TPS.

Comparing the results of CREDO's three major studies using a common methodology over time is also instructive in assessing their relative performance.[16] CREDO's first study spanning 2000–2001 through 2007–2008 found that charter school students lagged behind in reading and math. A second study spanning 2006–2007 to 2010–2011 showed that charter students broke even with their TPS peers. Most charter schools are relatively new institutions, and it takes time for them to realize their potential. The third study documents a positive long-term effect of charter schools. It reads, "Between the 2009 and 2023 studies, against the backdrop of flat performance for the nation as a whole, the trend of learning gains for students enrolled in charter schools is both large and positive."[17]

The CREDO study from 2023 also found that charter schools that belong to charter management organizations (CMOs) outperform standalone charter schools (SCS), even as the latter outperform typical public schools (TPS), suggesting that CMOs follow more clearly defined accountability standards. Students in schools that are part of CMO networks advanced twenty-seven additional days in reading and twenty-three days in math over their TPS peers; students attending SCS institutions grew ten additional days in reading and were the same in math compared to their TPS peers.[18]

In 2024, the Progressive Policy Institute (PPI) published a report designed to determine the "tipping point" at which a concentration of charter schools in an urban district began to close the performance gap evident among low-income students.[19] Focusing on ten districts during the period from 2010–2011 and 2022–2023, this analysis, as did the CREDO study, measured value added learning gains over time.[20] They found that in cities where at least one-third of the students were registered in charter or charterlike schools, low-income students were able to catch up to the statewide average. In four of these cities, there was a 50 percent growth on a normalized curve equivalent (NCE) where the state average was 80 points. The PPI report also cites several other studies that found a correlation between charter school enrollment and improved performance, including the cities of New Orleans, Washington, DC, and Denver.

Private School Choice

As mentioned earlier, a variety of programs are designed to relieve the economic burdens associated with attending nonpublic schools, which include independent and faith-based institutions. In addition to ECS, this section draws on data from EdChoice, which describes itself as a "nonprofit, nonpartisan organization committed to understanding and pursuing a K–12 education system that empowers every family to choose the schooling environment that fits their children's needs best."[21] Founded in 2016 to carry on the legacy of the Milton and Rose Friedman Foundation originally established by the Nobel laureate and his wife in 1996, EdChoice supports universal choice, which differs from a more progressive targeted model I have endorsed. That said, its website is the most comprehensive and up-to-date source of data available on private school choice programs, and I believe its information is reliable and sound. When reviewing the evidence on program effectiveness, I draw more broadly from the academic and research communities for analysis of our evolving experience with private school choice.

When considering the data presented here, note that institutions and organizations sometimes define these categories of programs differently, which can lead to different computational outcomes.[22] Time gaps in data collection may also contribute to differences among the various sources.

Let's explore some definitions of the various kinds of private choice programs, according to the Education Commission of the States (ECS):

- "School vouchers are state-funded programs—often called scholarship programs—that allow students to use public monies to attend a private school. The state provides a set amount of money, typically based on the state's per-pupil amount, for private school tuition."
- "Education Savings Accounts (ESA) are private savings accounts funded by a deposit from the state government and managed by a parent. The deposit amount varies from state to state and is typically based on the state's per-pupil amount. To use an ESA, parents purchase specified educational services, like tutoring, online courses or private school tuition."
- "Scholarship tax credit programs provide a tax credit to businesses and individual taxpayers for donating funds to scholarship granting organizations. Nonprofit organizations manage and distribute donated funds in the form of private school tuition scholarships to eligible students."[23]

EdChoice breaks down the offerings more specifically:

- "Vouchers give parents the freedom to choose a private school for their children, using all or part of the public funding set aside for their children's education. Under such a program, funds typically expended by a school district would be allocated to a participating family in the form of a voucher to pay partial or full tuition for their child's private school, including both religious and non-religious options."
- "Education savings accounts (ESAs) in K–12 education establish for parents a publicly funded, government-authorized savings account with restricted but multiple uses for educational purposes. Parents may use the funds to pay for expenses including: school tuition, tutoring, online education programs, therapies for students with special needs, textbooks or other instructional materials, and sometimes, save for college."
- "Tax-credit scholarships allow taxpayers to receive full or partial tax credits when they donate to nonprofits that provide private school scholarships. Eligible taxpayers can include both individuals and businesses. In some states, scholarship-giving nonprofits also provide innovation grants to public schools and/or transportation assistance to students choosing alternative public schools."
- "Individual tax credits and deductions allow parents to receive state income tax relief for approved educational expenses, which can include private school tuition, books, supplies, computers, tutors and transportation."
- "Tax-credit ESAs allow taxpayers to receive full or partial tax credits when they donate to nonprofit organizations that fund and manage parent-directed K–12 education savings accounts. Families may use those funds to pay for multiple education related expenses, including private school tuition and fees, online learning programs, private tutoring, community college costs, higher education expenses and other approved customized learning services and materials, and roll over unused funds from year to year to save for future educational expenses. Some tax-credit ESAs, but not all, even allow students to use their funds to pay for a combination of public school courses and private services."[24]

I would also mention "town tuitioning programs" in Maine, New Hampshire, and Vermont as a distinct category of school vouchers. In these rural jurisdictions where some towns do not have a sufficient population to maintain their own schools, the state assumes the costs for students to attend either private schools or public schools in neighboring towns. I would also highlight the voucher/scholarship programs in Milwaukee, Cleveland, and the District of Columbia as model programs that were originally designed to benefit low-income students. Because ESAs allow parents to apply money toward private school tuition, they can in effect function as vouchers. The varied tax-benefit programs support and enable parental choice in more indirect ways.

Q6. How many states have vouchers?

The number of voucher programs in the United States is listed below, as reported by ECS and EdChoice.

ECS (2024)[25]	EdChoice (2024)[26]
23 programs in 13 states plus DC DC, GA, IN, LA (2), ME, MD, MS (2), NH, NC, OH (5), OK, UT, VT, WI (4)	23 programs in 13 states plus DC DC, GA, IN, LA (2), ME, MD, MS (2), NH, NC, OH (5), OK, UT, VT, WI (4)

Q7. How many states have ESAs?

The number of ESA programs in the United States is listed below, as reported by ECS and EdChoice.

	ECS (2024)[27]	EdChoice (2024)[28]
Education savings account	15 programs in 13 states AZ, AR, FL (2), IN, IA, MS, MT, NH, NC, SC, TN (2), UT, WV	19 programs in 17 states AL, AZ, AR, FL (2), GA, IN, IA, LA, MS, MT, NH, NC, SC, TN (2), UT, WV, WY
Tax-credit education savings account	2 states FL, MO	3 states FL, MO, UT

Since 2022 there has been a sudden growth in ESAs across the country.

Q8. How many states have tax credit programs?

ECS only defines a scholarship tax credit category. EdChoice defines a scholarship tax credit category, individual tax credit/deduction program, and refundable tax credits.

	ECS (2024)[29]	EdChoice (2024)[30]
Scholarship tax credits	26 programs in 22 states AL, AZ (4), AR, FL, GA, IL, IN, IA, KS, LA, MT, NE, NV, NH, OH, OK, PA (2), RI, SC, SD, UT, VA	22 programs in 18 states AL, AZ (4), AR, GA, IN, IA, KS, LA, MT, NV, NH, OH, OK, PA (2), RI, SC, SD, VA
Individual tax credit/deduction programs	—	8 programs in 7 states IL, IN, IA, LA, MN, OH (2), WI
Refundable tax credits	—	4 programs in 4 states AL, MN, OK, SC

Q9. What are the criteria for eligibility for the various private school choice programs? (Are they targeted or universal in scope?)

ECS and EdChoice report on the limitations for each voucher program, ESA program, and tax credit program.

Voucher Limitations

	ECS[31]	EdChoice[32]
Geography limits	6	7
Limited to students in low-performing schools	2	1
Limited to students with special needs / Special needs pathway	8	9
Income limits	7	7
Town tuitioning programs	3	3
Universal (no limitations)	2	2

Education Savings Account and Tax-Credit ESA Limitations

	ECS[33]	EdChoice[34]
Geography limits	1	1 *(ESA)*
Limited to students in low-performing schools	1	0
Limited to students with special needs / Special needs pathway	7	5 *(ESA)* 1 *(tax-credit ESA)*
Income limits	5	9 *(ESA)* 1 *(tax-credit ESA)*
Universal (no limitations)	7	8 *(ESA)* 1 *(tax-credit ESA)*

Tax Credit Limitations		
	ECS[35]	EdChoice[36]
Geography limits	0	0
Limited to students in low-performing schools	3	2 *(scholarship)* 1 *(refundable credit)*
Limited to students with special needs / Special needs pathway	7	5 *(scholarship)* 1 *(refundable credit)*
Income limits	16	16 *(scholarship)* 1 *(refundable credit)*
Universal (no limitations)	3	2 *(scholarship)* 1 *(credit/deduction)* 1 *(refundable credit)*
Not specified	1	0

As per the above data, voucher programs are more likely to target more vulnerable students than other types of choice programs. A majority of voucher programs serve students who were previously from low-performing schools, students with disabilities, or students from families with limited income. Similarly, a majority of tax credit scholarships target students from families with limited income. Since 2022, efforts have been under way in many states to adopt universal choice programs in the form of ESAs that are not targeted at students with greater needs. This is steering both the purpose and the effects of the choice movement away from its more progressive roots.

Q10. What are the voucher amounts?

The voucher amounts as listed by ECS in 2024 and EdChoice in 2024 are as follows:

EdChoice data suggest a disparity in spending in most states disfavoring students in the voucher program. Any program that provides less per-pupil funding for students in voucher programs than that received by their public school peers violates a basic standard of equity. Programs that appropriate only the equivalent of state funding without an equivalent appropriation for the local funding public schools receive also violate a basic standard of equity. A voucher amount that is less than the full cost of tuition at a nonpublic school effectively excludes students who cannot afford the full cost of tuition. To be fair, any nonpublic school participating in a voucher program should be required to accept the voucher as full payment of tuition.

State (and program if multiple)	ECS Voucher Amounts (2024)[37]	EdChoice Voucher Value as a Percentage of Public School Per-Student Total Spending (2024)[38]
DC	$8,000 (K–8); $12,000 (9–12)	44 percent
GA	100 percent of state per-pupil funding in addition to the cost of services outlined in the student's Individual Education Program	54 percent
IN	90 percent of state per-pupil funding	51 percent
LA (Scholarships for Educational Excellence)	100 percent of state per-pupil funding	52 percent
LA (Choice Program for Certain Students with Exceptionalities)	50 percent of state per-pupil funding	18 percent
ME	The school district's per-pupil cost for the preceding year (public elementary); may not exceed the average per pupil cost of all elementary schools in the state for previous year (private elementary); the state's per-student amount or an amount determined by a statutory formula, whichever is less (public high school); the state's per-student amount or an amount determined by a statutory formula, whichever is less (private high school)	78 percent (maximum)
MD	May not be more than the state per-pupil amount or school tuition, whichever is less; determined by advisory board	18 percent
MS (Nate Rogers Scholarship)	100 percent of state per-pupil funding	60 percent
MS (Dyslexia Therapy Scholarship)	100 percent of state per-pupil funding	60 percent
NH	Current operating expenses, estimated by state BOE	88 percent

NC (Opportunity Scholarship)	100 percent of state per-pupil funding (at or below federal FRPL level); 90 percent of state per-pupil finding (between 100 and 200 percent of FRPL level); 60 percent of state per-pupil funding (between 200 and 450 percent of FRPL level); 45 percent of state per-pupil funding (above 450 percent of RFPL level);	50 percent
OH (Educational Choice Scholarship Program)	Students at or below 450 percent of the federal poverty line: $5,500 (K–8); $7,500 (9–12); Above 450 percent of the federal poverty level receive diminished rate	40 percent
OH (EdChoice Expansion Program / Income-Based)	Students at or below 450 percent of the federal poverty line: $5,500 (K–8); $7,500 (9–12) Above 450 percent of the federal poverty level receive diminished rate	36 percent
OH (Autism Scholarship Program)	The lesser of tuition or $32,445	193 percent
OH (Jon Peterson Scholarship)	The lesser of the cost of services provided by the school, 100 percent of state per-pupil funding plus disability services, or $30,000	72 percent
OH (Cleveland)	$6,165 (K–8); $8,407 (9–12)	42 percent
OK	The state's per-pupil amount or the amount of the private school's tuition and fees, whichever is less	80 percent
UT	The state's per-pupil amount times 2.5 or the cost of tuition and fees, whichever is less (students with 180 minutes per day of special education services); the state's per-pupil amount times 1.5 or the cost of tuition and fees, whichever is less (students with less than 180 minutes per day of special education services)	21 percent

Continued

Continued

State (and program if multiple)	ECS Voucher Amounts (2024)	EdChoice Voucher Value as a Percentage of Public School Per-Student Total Spending (2024)
VT	The state's per-pupil amount	79 percent
WI (Milwaukee)	$8,399 (K–8); $9,045 (9–12)	76 percent
WI (Racine)	$9,893 (K–8); $12,387 (9–12)	76 percent
WI (Statewide)	$9,893 (K–8); $12,387 (9–12)	76 percent
WI (Special Needs Scholarships)	$9,893 (K–8); $12,387 (9–12) Limit: $15,065	93 percent

Q11. What Is the ESA Amount?

The ESA and tax-credit ESA amounts listed by ECS in 2024 and EdChoice in 2024 are as follows:

State	ECS ESA Amounts (2024)[39]	EdChoice ESA Value as a Percentage of State-Level Public School Per-Student Spending (2024)[40]
AL	**Not listed by ECS as ESA	65 percent for students attending a participating school ($7,000); 19 percent for students not attending a participating school ($2,000)
AZ	90 percent of state per-pupil funding	90 percent (maximum)
AR	90 percent of state per-pupil funding	64 percent
FL (Family Empowerment Scholarship for Educational Options)	100 percent of state per-pupil funding and state categorical funding	72 percent (average)
FL (Family Empowerment Scholarship for Students with Unique Abilities)	100 percent of state per-pupil funding and state categorical funding	90 percent (maximum)

FL (tax-credit ESA)	100 percent of state per-pupil funding and state categorical funding	72 percent
GA	**Not listed by ECS as ESA	44 percent
IN	90 percent of state per-pupil funding	54 percent
IA	100 percent of state per-pupil funding	62 percent
LA	**Not listed by ECS as ESA	Not specified
MS	$6,500, adjusted annually	70 percent
MO (tax-credit ESA)	100 percent of state per-pupil funding	50 percent (maximum)
MT	Not specified, calculation utilizing payment rates	65 percent
NH	100 percent of state per-pupil funding	27 percent (average)
NC	$9,000 (full-time students); $4,000 (part-time students); $17,000 (full-time students with autism, hearing impairment, intellectual disability, orthopedic impairment, visual impairment); $8,500 (part-time students with autism, hearing impairment, intellectual disability, orthopedic impairment, visual impairment)	107 percent (average)
SC	$6,000	53 percent
TN (Education Savings Account Pilot Program)	100 percent of state and local per-pupil funding, including categorical funding	82 percent (maximum)
TN (Individualized Education Account Program)	100 percent of state and local per-pupil funding, including categorical funding	66 percent (average)

Continued

Continued

State	ECS ESA Amounts (2024)	EdChoice ESA Value as a Percentage of State-Level Public School Per-Student Spending (2024)
UT	$8,000, increased annually using average inflationary factor	84 percent
WV	100 percent of state per-pupil funding	34 percent (maximum)
WY	**Not listed by ECS as ESA	32 percent

Here also, ESA amounts do not usually equal per-capita amounts for regular public schools.

Q12. What is the scholarship tax credit amount?

The tax credit scholarship amounts listed by ECS in 2024 and EdChoice in 2024 are as follows:

State (program if multiple)	ECS Tax Credit Amounts (2024)[41]	EdChoice Tax Credit Scholarships Value as a Percentage of Public School Per-Student Total Spending (2024)[42]
AL	$10,000	63 percent
AZ (Original Individual Income Tax Credit Scholarship)	Not specified	20 percent (average)
AZ (Low-Income Corporate Income Tax Scholarship)	$6,00 (K–8); $7,900 (9–12)	31 percent
AZ (Lexie's Law)	90 percent of state per-pupil funding	39 percent
AZ ("Switcher" Scholarships)	Not specified	17 percent

AR	80 percent of state per-pupil funding (K–8); 90 percent of state per-pupil funding (9–12)	24 percent (maximum)
FL	100 percent of state per-pupil funding and state categorical funding	**Not listed by EdChoice as tax credit scholarship as of 2025
GA	100 percent of state and local per-pupil funding	36 percent
IL	The state's per-pupil amount or the cost of tuition, whichever is less; based on family income	**Not listed by EdChoice as tax credit scholarship
IN	Not specified in state policy	18 percent
IA	Determined by school tuition organizations, capped at full tuition	13 percent
KS	$8,000	25 percent
LA	80 percent of state's per-pupil funding (K–8); 90 percent of state's per-pupil funding (9–12)	53 percent
MT	May not exceed 100 percent of state's per-pupil amount	18 percent (average)
NE	75 percent of state per-pupil funding	Not specified
NV	$9,424	55 percent (average)
NH	$2,500 average	19 percent
OH	Not specified	Not specified
OK	$5,000 or 80 percent of state's per-pupil amount, whichever is greater; $25,000 (eligible special-needs students)	28 percent
PA (Educational Improvement Program)	Not specified	15 percent
PA (Opportunity Scholarship)	$8,500; $15,000 (students with IEP)	10 percent
RI	Not specified	16 percent
SC	$11,000	27 percent
SD	82.5 percent of state per-pupil funding	20 percent

Continued

Continued

State (program if multiple)	ECS Tax Credit Amounts (2024)	EdChoice Tax Credit Scholarships Value as a Percentage of Public School Per-Student Total Spending (2024)
UT	250 percent of state per-pupil funding (below 185 percent of federal poverty level); 200 percent of state per-pupil funding (above 185 percent of federal poverty level)	**Not listed by EdChoice as tax credit scholarship as of 2025
VA	100 percent of state per-pupil funding; 300 percent of state per-pupil funding (students with IEP)	23 percent

Although there are differences in the calculations presented by ECS and EdChoice, the data suggest, especially in the latter, a disparity disfavoring scholarship recipients compared to their public school peers, again violating a basic standard of equity.

Q13. How do students in private school choice programs perform compared to their public school peers?

This issue is complicated to resolve because there are so many varied programs in different locations, making comparisons difficult. Some studies are more rigorous than others, and some read more like polemics than objective analyses. It is not feasible to review the entire literature on performance—but we can take advantage of previous attempts at summarizing the evidence and then pay closer attention to a few particular studies that have gained credibility.

• **EdChoice** has done an excellent job identifying types of surveys available based on their quality, distinguishing between a Gold Standard (random assignment study), a Silver Standard ("matched" study method), and a Bronze Standard that is highly instructive and worth reading.[43] EdChoice then provides a review of the research literature on the basis of different variables that particular studies analyze to determine whether private choice programs had "Any Positive Effect" (Pos), "No Visible Effect" (None), or

"Any Negative Affect" (Neg). The first and third categories are not mutually exclusive:

> Compared to Public School Test Scores (17 total studies [Tot]): 11 Pos, 4 None, 3 Neg.
> High School Graduation, College Attendance (7 Tot): 5 Pos, 2 None, 0 Neg.
> Parent Satisfaction (33 Tot): 31 Pos, 1 None, 2 Neg.

The EdChoice literature review also cites studies that assess the impact of private choice programs on Public School Performance and School Spending:

> Public School Performance (29 Tot): 26 Pos, 1 None, 2 Neg.
> School Spending (74 Tot): 68 Pos, 5 None, 5 Neg.

The latter questions addressed in such studies are central to the assumptions inherent in Friedman's market model, which promises that robust competition will have an overall positive effect on school performance and reduce its costs.[44] They are not prioritized here. Although the improvement of public school performance would be a welcome outcome of more choice, I am wary of being backed into the position favored by choice opponents who evaluate its merits based on the impact it has on public schools. Should we assume that less choice is needed when public schools continue to fail? Let's first determine, as best we can, whether choice programs offer better opportunities for students stuck in failing schools. As far as the cost issue is concerned, more cost effectiveness is the key, with a focus on effectiveness. It's fine if we can do more with less; it would be better to do even more with more. Reduced spending for essential services like quality education is not a desirable societal goal in and of itself.

In the literature review that appears on its website, EdChoice refers to a meta-analysis conducted by M. Danish Shakeel, Kaitlin Anderson, and Patrick Wolf at the University of Arkansas. That report analyzed voucher participant test scores from nineteen studies of eleven different programs in the United States (8), India (2), and Colombia (1). It found that students who won voucher lotteries and used vouchers gained forty-nine more days in learning in math and twenty-eight more days in English.[45]

In an early study (2002), PatrickWolf collaborated with William Howell, David Campbell, and Paul Peterson to evaluate the effects of voucher programs in New York, Dayton, and Washington, DC. Conducting randomized field trials, they found that, after two years, African American students who transferred from public to private schools gained an average of 6.3 National Percentage Ranking points on the Iowa Test of Basic Schools relative to their public school peers.[46] Later, when Congress enacted a voucher program for the District of Columbia in 2004, Wolf was designated to lead the evaluation team

In 2021, Wolf posted a summary of his review of seventeen studies that were conducted between 1998 and 2017. He reported that seven studies found benefits for all participants, four found benefits for some students, four found no effects, and two found negative effects.[47]

Wolf collaborated with six other researchers preparing the Final Report of the District of Columbia Opportunity Scholarship Program (OSP) in 2010. They found that while there was no conclusive evidence that OSP affected student achievement, it significantly improved high school graduation rates.[48]

The Comprehensive Longitudinal Evaluation of the Milwaukee Parental Choice Program (MPCP) that Wolf completed in 2012 examined seven prior reports. Among his findings were the following:

- As participation in MPCP grows (from 17,749 in 2006–2007 to 20,996 in 2010–2011), it has contributed to the closure of or denial of funds to a substantial number of low-performing Milwaukee public schools).
- Enrolling in a private high school through MPCP increases the likelihood of graduating, enrolling in college, and persisting in college.
- When similar MPCP and MPS students are tracked over four years, achievement growth of MPCP is higher in reading, but similar in math.
- When a snapshot of all MPCP students who took the state accountability test is compared to a snapshot of MPS students with similar income disadvantages, the MPCP students are performing at higher levels in the upper grades in reading and science, but at lower levels in math at all grade levels examined and in reading and science in the fourth grade.
- When independent public charter students and MPS students are matched and tracked over four years, the achievement growth of the charter students compared to MPS students is similar in both reading

and math, though conversion charters that were once private schools clearly deliver higher achievement growth than MPS.[49]

Wolf coauthored an evaluation of the Louisiana Scholarship Program with Jonathan Millis in 2010. They found negative effects of voucher usage after four years, especially in math.[50]

In 2019, Wolf collaborated with Matthew Chingos, John Witte, and three other researchers for an Urban Institute study of college enrollment and completion of participants in the Florida, Milwaukee, and Washington, DC, private school choice programs. They found that Florida and Milwaukee students in choice programs were more likely to graduate from college than those who remained in public school. In Washington, DC, they found no significantly detectable difference between students who won the lottery and those who lost and remained in public schools.[51]

Wolf's literature review from 2021 parallels EdChoice's literature review from 2022 with findings that private school choice programs are more likely to improve student performance than to do harm. His meta-analysis summarized on the EdChoice website measures real learning gains in math and English for choice participants. His evaluations with colleagues of programs in specific locations (Washington, DC, Milwaukee, Louisiana, and Florida) produce more nuanced outcomes worthy of further comment. While their analysis of the Washington program in 2010 found no discernable impact on student test scores, they did observe a positive effect on high school graduation.

Their review of the Milwaukee evaluations provides a richer set of observations. Increased and growing opportunities for choice contributed to the closing of low-performing public schools. Some would argue that such school closings are a negative effect of choice, ignoring the fact that some students (disproportionately low-income students of color) would need to remain in those schools if they stayed open. Such arguments are especially unpersuasive in light of evidence that MPCP (choice) students who enrolled in private high schools were more likely to graduate, enroll in college, and continue their college studies for some time. MPCP students also experienced greater achievement growth after four years. Comparisons of MPCP and MPS performance on state accountability tests revealed more mixed outcomes. Interestingly, students at charter schools that had converted from private school status exceled over both MPS other charter schools, again underscoring the advantages of attending private schools. The Milwaukee results stand in bold contrast to Wolf's review of the Louisiana Scholarship Program, which found that participation in the program had a negative effect on student performance. The latter highlight the need for states to monitor choice programs and enforce high standards of accountability.

Notably, a study that Wolf completed with John Witte and three others in 2014 found substantial academic growth among voucher students in Milwaukee after Wisconsin, beginning in 2010–2011, enacted legislation requiring participating students in grades 3 to 8 to take the same standardized test in reading and math that public school students take.[52]

In a separate article written after twenty-five years of experience with the Milwaukee voucher program (1991–2015), Ford and Anderson found that 41 percent of the 247 private schools participating in the program failed and were shut down.[53] Startup schools, those created in response to increased demand (and consequential indirect aid through tuition), proved to be especially vulnerable, with a 67.8 percent failure rate. Schools affiliated with large supportive networks, especially religious schools, had lower failure risks (Lutheran 75 percent, Catholic 64 percent, independent Christian 45 percent).

An evaluation led by Matthew Chingos of the Urban Institute in 2019 again examined college attendance rates rather than test scores, focusing on Florida, Milwaukee, and Washington, DC. In its review of pertinent literature, the Urban Institute evaluation mentions negative effects of programs in Indiana, Louisiana, and Ohio that eventually dissipated over time.[54] As we saw with charter schools, students who leave underperforming schools to participate in choice programs need time to reverse their negative effects and catch up with their peers. The Urban Institute study itself found that choice students in Florida and Milwaukee were more likely to attend college, those in Washington were less so. If the latter finding seems to run contrary to the earlier evaluation of the Washington program completed by Wolf and colleagues,[55] it should be mentioned that the latter finding only focused on high school students who participated in the scholarship program.

In 2025, the Urban Institute released a study of college enrollment among students in the statewide Ohio voucher program.[56] At the time of the study, the program was limited to lo-income students attending failing schools. It found that program participants were more likely to enroll in college (64 percent vs 48 percent) than students who remained in public schools.

Let me close this review with another Urban Institute study completed by David Figlio at the end of 2021 finding that low-income students who attended Catholic schools as a result of choice opportunities gained more ground in academic achievement than students who attended other private schools under the auspices of choice programs.[57]

The latter study once again documents a positive Catholic school effect for low-income students that Coleman demonstrated four decades ago that were recently affirmed by national results on the NAEP tests.

Note also that most studies comparing the academic performance of choice participants with their public school peers do not take into account the funding disparities that have been recorded between the two. Equal funding would not only be fairer for the predominantly Black and Brown students utilizing choice opportunities, it would also provide a valid baseline for measuring the success of such programs.

Q14. Are there accountability standards that monitor student performance in private school choice programs?

In a recent survey, FutureEd, a research unit at Georgetown University's McCourt School of Public Policy, found that government-supported choice programs "vary widely in the degree of transparency and accountability they require of private schools." The standards are especially diverse among different types of choice programs.

As the survey reports, in all, eighteen of twenty-four voucher programs nationally require some kind of student testing. Most voucher programs that do not have testing requirements serve students with disabilities. Half of the voucher programs with testing requirements—such as those in Indiana, Louisiana, and Washington, DC—mandate the use of state tests allowing for comparisons between private and public school students. Others, including the voucher programs in Maryland and Arkansas, administer commercial tests that permit the tracking of student progress from year to year. Voucher programs in Milwaukee, North Carolina, Arkansas, and Washington, DC, have additional accountability features.

FutureEd reports that only ten of twenty-six tax-credit scholarship programs require testing, and only two of those require state testing. Only three of the nation's fifteen ESA programs require students to take state standardized tests, including Iowa's recently enacted universal choice program. Utah's and Arizona's new universal ESA programs require no student reporting.[58]

These data reported by FutureEd highlight an alarming pattern of little or no public accountability for the expenditure of public funds for private school programs, especially those structured in the form of tax-credit or ESA initiatives. This pattern appears to be growing as ESAs become more popular.

Q15. Is school choice popular in America?

In an article that appeared in *Education Next,* David M. Houston examined the results of three popular surveys conducted in 2024 to find that Americans are generally split on the question.[59]

When asked about their potential priorities for the next presidential administration, only 35 percent of the respondents to a PDK Poll of Public Attitudes Toward Public Schools said that they wanted to see a greater focus on charter schools, ranking charters as the last of eight possible priorities. Sixty-one percent indicated a preference for a candidate who supports increased public school funding. The PDK Poll did not query respondents on the issue of private school choice. The EdChoice Schooling in America Survey found that only 20 percent of the American public (25 percent of school parents) ranked parental choice among the top three education issues. The latter survey further revealed that 56 percent of the public (66 percent of parents) either somewhat or strongly support school choice generally. The survey found similar support for charter schools (55 percent public; 64 percent of parents), vouchers (51 percent public; 59 percent of parents), and ESAs (50 percent public; 58 percent of parents). Larger percentages supported tax credits (69 percent public; 79 percent of parents), interdistrict open enrollment (74 percent public; 81 percent of parents), and homeschooling (65 percent public; 69 percent of parents).

The Understanding America Survey conducted at the Center for Economic and Social Research at the University of Southern California included questions designed to determine whether respondents agreed with underlying arguments for and against choice. It found a fairly even split, asking whether private school students learn more than public school students (52 percent agree), whether competition for students makes public schools more careful about spending resources (51 percent agree), whether increased choice will make public school quality worse (50 percent agree), whether charter and private schools will drain off stronger students from public schools (48 percent agree), whether competition makes public schools better (41 percent agree), and whether choice increases segregation (40 percent agree). Seventy-three percent of the respondents preferred to see the federal government give money to improve public schools rather than provide funds for low-income families to attend private schools.

Q16. Who do the new universal school choice programs serve?

FutureEd at Georgetown University reports that the new universal choice programs have not sparked the expected shift from public to private education. Instead, early results show that universal choice programs are primarily serving children who already attend private school. In Arkansas, only 5 percent of recipients of the state's Education Freedom Account award came from public schools to private education in the program's first year. In Iowa, the number was 13 percent transitioning from public schools, with 66 percent of recipients already in private schools. These transition rates are much lower than lawmakers predicted. FutureEd points to Iowa data to attribute the low transition rate to geographic boundaries and private schools' admission processes.

In terms of income, FutureEd found that, in 2023–2024, every state that expanded eligibility for choice programs saw increased participation from higher-income families. In Florida, about one-third of the new ESA recipients were from FRPL households, while half came from families 400 percent above the poverty level. Low-income families' participation in Ohio's universal choice program dropped from 67 percent to just 17 percent in 2023–2024.

FutureEd also reports racial and ethnic data from Ohio's and Indiana's new programs. In Ohio, white participants in the choice program increased from 66 percent to 82 percent with the expansion, while Black and Hispanic recipients decreased. The increase in white recipients in Indiana went from 62 percent to 64 percent.[60]

Notes

Preface

1. *The ABCs of School Choice: The Comprehensive Guide to Every Private School Choice Program in America, 2025 Edition* (EdChoice, 2025), p. 3, https://www.edchoice.org/wp-content/uploads/2025/01/2025-ABCs-of-School-Choice.pdf. *The ABCs of School Choice: The Comprehensive Guide to Every Private School Choice Program in America, 2024 Edition* (EdChoice, 2024), p. 3, https://www.edchoice.org/wp-content/uploads/2023/11/2024-ABCs-of-School-Choice.pdf.
2. https://www.future-ed.org/legislative-tracker-2025-state-private-school-choice-bills/.
3. Jonathan Zimmerman, *Whose America? Culture Wars in the Public Schools*, 2nd ed. (University of Chicago Press, 2022), pp. 237–257.
4. "Mathematics Scores Declined for Both Fourth- and Eighth-Graders in Nearly All Districts and States," news release, National Center for Education Statistics, October 24, 2022.
5. "Results for the 2024 NAEP Reading and Mathematics Assessments at Grades 4 and 8," news release, National Assessment of Educational Progress, January 29, 2025.
6. Sarah Schwartz, "Reading Scores Fall to a New Low on NAEP, Fueled by Declines for Struggling Students," *Education Week,* January 29, 2025.
7. "Results for the 2024 NAEP Reading and Mathematics Assessments at Grades 4 and 8."
8. *Brown v. Board of Education*, 347 U.S. 493 (1954).
9. *The ABCs of School Choice, 2025 Edition*, p. 3.
10. Donald J. Trump, "Executive Order: Expanding Educational Freedom and Opportunity for Families," January 29, 2025, https://www.whitehouse.gov/presidential-actions/2025/01/expanding-educational-freedom-and-opportunity-for-families/.

Chapter One

1. *Espinoza v. Montana* 591 U.S. __ (2020).
2. Joseph P. Viteritti, *Choosing Equality: School Choice, the Constitution and Civil Society* (Brookings Institution Press, 1999); Joseph P. Viteritti, "Blaine's Wake: School Choice, the First Amendment, and State Constitutional Law," *Harvard Journal of Law & Public Policy*, Vol. 21, No. 3 (Summer, 1998).
3. Viteritti, *Choosing Equality*, pp. 219–223.
4. *Zelman v. Simmons-Harris*, 536 U.S. 639 (2002).
5. Conversation with John Ross, November 14, 2019.
6. Ronald Edmonds et al., "A Black Response to Christopher Jencks's *Inequality* and Certain Other Issues," *Harvard Educational Review*, Vol. 43, No. 1 (1978).
7. Ronald R. Edmonds, "You Can Get Hurt Waiting for the Bus," *The Journal of Intergroup Relations*, Vol. 2, No. 2 (October, 1972); Ronald R. Edmonds, "Advocating Inequity: A Critique of the Civil Rights Attorney in Class Action Desegregation Suits," *The Black Law Journal*, Vol. 3 (1974).
8. Ronald Edmonds, "Effective Schools for the Urban Poor," *Educational Leadership*, October, 1979.
9. *Serrano v. Priest*, 18 Cal. 3d.728, 557 P. 2d. 929 (1976).
10. John E. Coons, William H. Clune, and Stephen D. Sugarman, *Private Wealth and Public Education* (Harvard University Press, 1970).
11. John E. Coons and Stephen D. Sugarman, *Education by Choice: The Case for Family Control* (University of California Press, 1978).
12. Christopher Jencks, "Education Vouchers: A Report on Financing Education by Payments to Parents," Center for the Study of Public Policy, 1970. See also Theodore Sizer and Philip Whitten, "A Proposal for a Poor Children's Bill of Rights," *Psychology Today*, August, 1968.

13. Diane Ravitch, *The Death and Life of the Great American School System: How Testing and Choice Are Undermining Education* (Basic Books, 2010).
14. Diane Ravitch, *Left Back: A Century of Failed School Reform* (Simon & Schuster, 2000).
15. See Howard Fuller, with Lisa Frazier Page, *No Struggle, No Progress: A Warrior's Life from Black Power to Education Reform* (Marquette University Press, 2014).

Chapter Two

1. Joseph P. Viteritti, *Across the River: Politics and Education in the City* (Holmes and Meier, 1983).
2. Viteritti, *Across the River*, pp. 335–346.
3. Joseph P. Viteritti, "Agenda Setting: When Politics and Pedagogy Meet," *Social Policy*, Vol. 15 (Autumn, 1984).
4. Ronald R. Edmonds, "Advocating Inequity: A Critique of the Civil Rights Attorney in Class Action Desegregation Suits," *The Black Law Journal*, Vol. 3, No. 2 (1974), p. 178.
5. Edmonds, "Advocating Inequity," p. 179.
6. Edmonds, "Advocating Inequity," p. 179.
7. Ronald Edmonds, "A Theory and Design of Social Service Reform," *Social Policy*, Vol. 15, No. 2 (Autumn, 1984), p. 63.
8. *Brown v. Board of Education*, 347 U.S. 483 (1954).
9. For an excellent update on the efficacy of judicial intervention since *Brown*, see R. Shep Melnick, *The Crucible of Desegregation: The Uncertain Search for Educational Equity* (University of Chicago Press, 2023).
10. Adam Taylor, "Low and High Income Schools Now Receive Equal Funding," Fordham Institute, July 13, 2023.
11. See Janis Sarra and Cheryl L. Wade, *Predatory Lending and the Destruction of the African-American Dream* (Cambridge University Press, 2020).
12. Conversation with Karen Edmonds, July 10, 2022.
13. See, for example, Richard Delgado and Jean Stefancic, *Critical Race Theory: An Introduction*, 4th ed. (New York University Press, 2023); Kimberle' Crenshaw et al., eds., *Critical Race Theory: Key Writings That Formed a Movement* (New Press, 1996); Richard Delgado and Jean Stefancic, eds., *The Derrick Bell Reader* (New York University Press, 2005).
14. Derrick A. Bell Jr., *Race, Racism and American Law* (Little Brown, 1973).
15. See also Derrick Bell, *And We Are Not Saved: The Elusive Quest for Racial Justice* (Basic Books, 1987).
16. Diane Ravitch, email, May 11, 2023.
17. Bell, *Race, Racism and American Law*, p. 574.
18. Bell, *Race, Racism and American Law*, p. 574.
19. John E. Coons, William H. Clune, and Steven D. Sugarman, *Private Wealth and Public Education* (Harvard University Press, 1970); Coons, Clune, and Sugarman, "Educational Opportunity: A Workable Constitutional Test for State Financial Structures," *California Law Review*, Vol. 57 (1969); Coons, "Fairness in the Distribution of Education," *University of Illinois Law Forum* (1972).
20. Derrick A. Bell Jr., "Serving Two Masters: Integration Ideals and Client Interests in School Desegregation Litigation," *Yale Law Journal*, Vol. 85, No. 4 (March 1976).
21. "Freedom House Response to Boston's Desegregation Plan," Freedom House Institute on Schools and Education, February 3, 1975, preface.
22. Freedom House Institute on Schools and Education, "Critique of the Boston School Committee Plan," 1975, at 2, quoted in Bell, "Serving Two Masters," p. 470.
23. Derrick A. Bell Jr., "The Remedy in Brown Is Effective Schooling for Black Children," *Social Policy*, Vol. 15 (Fall, 1984).
24. Bell, "Serving Two Masters," p. 483.
25. Bell, "Serving Two Masters," pp. 484–492.
26. Bell, "Serving Two Masters," p. 490.
27. Bell, "Serving Two Masters," p. 512.
28. Derrick A. Bell Jr., "Brown v. Board of Education and the Interest Conversion Dilemma," *Harvard Law Review*, Vol. 93, No. 3 (January, 1980).

29. Bell, "Brown v. Board of Education and the Interest Conversion Dilemma," p. 518. For a critical commentary on Bell's essay, see Justin Driver, "Rethinking the Interest-Convergence Thesis," *Northwestern University Law Review*, Vol. 105, No. 1 (2011), pp. 149–197.

30. Bell, "Brown v. Board of Education and the Interest Conversion Dilemma," p. 523.

31. Bell, "Brown v. Board of Education and the Interest Conversion Dilemma," p. 523.

32. Derrick Bell, *Silent Covenants: Brown v. Board of Education and the Unfulfilled Hopes for Racial Reform* (Oxford University Press, 2004), p. 69.

33. Bell, "Serving Two Masters," p. 474.

34. *Brown v. Board of Education*, 349 U.S. 294 (1955). In 2007, the court placed further restrictions on the use of race as a criterion for student assignments when it struck down desegregation plans in Seattle and Louisville (*Parents Involved in Community Schools v. Seattle District 1*, 551 U.S. 701 [2007]) .

35. Derrick Bell, *Faces at the Bottom of the Well: The Permanence of Racism* (Basic Books, 1992), pp. 197–242.

36. Bell, *And We Are Not Saved*.

37. Bell, *Silent Covenants*, pp. 20–28.

38. Bell, *Silent Covenants*, pp. 160–179.

39. Ronald Edmonds, "Judicial Assumptions on the Value of Integrated Education for Blacks," Proceedings, National Policy Conference on Education for Blacks, pp. 140–144 (1972).

40. Bell, *Race, Racism and American Law*, pp. 574–598.

41. Charles Hamilton, "Race and Education: A Search for Legitimacy," *Harvard Educational Review*, Vol. 38 (1968), quoted in Bell, *Race, Racism and American Law*, p. 578.

42. Hamilton, "Race and Education," quoted in Bell, *Race, Racism and American Law*, p. 580.

43. Stokely Carmichael and Charles Hamilton, *Black Power: The Politics of Liberation in America* (Vintage, 1967).

44. Diane Ravitch, *The Great School Wars: New York City, 1805–1973* (Basic Books, 1974), pp. 251–404. See also Richard D. Kahlenberg, *Tough Liberal: Albert Shanker and the Battles over Schools* (Columbia University Press, 2007), pp. 67–124.

45. Ravitch, *The Great School Wars*, p. 334.

46. Bell, *Race, Racism and American Law*, p. 603.

47. *Serrano v. Priest*, 5 Cal. 3d. 584 (1971).

48. *San Antonio Independent School District v. Rodriguez*, 411 U.S. 1 (1973).

49. *Brown v. Board of Education*, at 493.

50. Bell, *Race, Racism and American Law*, pp. 599–600.

51. Bell, *Race, Racism and American Law*, pp. 601–602.

52. Gail Foster, "Historically Black Independent Schools," in Diane Ravitch and Joseph P. Viteritti, eds., *City Schools: Lessons from New York* (Johns Hopkins University Press, 2000).

53. Bell, *Silent Covenants*, p. 167.

54. Bell, *Silent Covenants*, pp. 171–172.

55. *Bell, Silent Covenant*, p. 174.

56. I am not suggesting that Forman speaks for Bell or anyone else. He speaks for himself, and that is sufficient for me to pay attention to what he has to say.

57. James Forman Jr., *Locking Up Our Own: Crime and Punishment in Black America* (Farrar, Straus and Giroux, 2018).

58. James Forman Jr., "The Secret History of School Choice: How Progressives Got There First," *Georgetown Law Journal*, Vol. 93 (2005).

59. See also Forman's less optimistic essay on the future of school choice, "The Rise and Fall of School Vouchers: A Story of Religion, Race and Politics," *UCLA Law Review*, Vol. 54 (2007).

60. Bell, *Silent Covenants*, p. 176.

61. Bell, *Silent Covenants*, p. i.

Chapter Three

1. Data and sources in this paragraph are cited in Joseph P. Viteritti, *Across the River: Politics and Education in the City* (Holmes & Meier, 1983), pp. 5–6.

2. David Rogers, *110 Livingston Street: Politics and Bureaucracy in the New York City School System* (Random House, 1968), p. 267.

3. James S. Coleman et al., *Equality of Educational Opportunity* (Office of Education, National Center for Educational Statistics, 1966).

4. See, for example, Frederick Mosteller and Daniel P. Moynihan, eds., *On Equality of Educational Opportunity* (Vintage, 1972).

5. Christopher Jencks et al., *Inequality: A Reassessment of the Effect of Family and Schooling in America* (Basic Books, 1972).

6. Arthur Jensen, "How Much Can We Boost IQ and Scholastic Achievement," *Harvard Educational Review* (Winter, 1969).

7. "Perspectives on *Inequality: A Reassessment of the Effect of Family and Schooling in America*," *Harvard Educational Review*, Vol. 43 (Winter, 1973).

8. The group, as listed in the symposium, included Ronald Edmonds (Harvard), Andrew Billingsley (Howard University), James P. Comer (Yale), James M. Dyer (Carnegie Corporation), William Hall (Princeton), Robert B. Hill (National Urban League), Nan E. McGehee (University of Illinois, Chicago), Lawrence Reddick (Temple University), Howard F. Taylor (Syracuse University), and Stephen J. Wright (College Entrance Examination Board).

9. Ronald Edmonds et al., "A Black Response to Christopher Jencks's *Inequality* and Certain Other Issues," *Harvard Educational Review*, Vol. 43 (Winter, 1973), p. 77.

10. Edmonds, "A Black Response to Christopher Jencks' *Inequality* and Certain Other Issues," pp. 76–91.

11. Edmonds, "A Black Response to Christopher Jencks," p. 77.

12. Edmonds, "A Black Response to Christopher Jencks," p. 79.

13. Edmonds, "A Black Response to Christopher Jencks," p. 79.

14. Edmonds, "A Black Response to Christopher Jencks," p. 79

15. Edmonds, "A Black Response to Christopher Jencks," p. 88.

16. Edmonds, "A Black Response to Christopher Jencks," pp. 80–81.

17. Edmonds, "A Black Response to Christopher Jencks," p. 81.

18. Kenneth B. Clark, "Social Policy, Power, and Social Science Research," *Harvard Educational Review* (Winter, 1973), p. 114.

19. Clark, "Social Policy, Power, and Social Science Research," p. 116.

20. Christopher Jencks, "*Inequality* in Retrospect," *Harvard Educational Review* (Winter, 1973), 138.

21. Jencks, "*Inequality* in Retrospect," p. 145.

22. Diane Ravitch, "Inequality, by Christopher Jencks," *Commentary*, February, 1973.

23. Ronald R. Edmonds et al., "Desegregation Planning and Equity," *Theory into Practice*, Vol. 17, No. 1 (February, 1978), p. 13.

24. Edmonds et al., "Desegregation Planning and Equity," p. 14.

25. Derrick Bell, "*Brown v. Board of Education* and the Interest Conversion Dilemma," *Harvard Law Review*, Vol. 93, No. 3 (January, 1980), p. 525.

26. The biographical material in this and the following paragraph is based on a personal note I received from Ron's children on July 2, 2022. Daniel Edmonds-Walters and Kristin Edmonds, "Ron Edmonds Origin Story," n.d.

27. Jan Stucker, "School Human Relations Director Appointed," *Ann Arbor News*, October 13, 1968.

28. "School Equity Unit Urged," *Ann Arbor News*, February 19, 1970.

29. George Weber, "Inner City Children Can Be Taught to Read: Four Successful Schools" (Council for Basic Education, 1971).

30. See Ronald Edmonds, "Effective Schools for the Urban Poor," *Educational Leadership*, October 1979; Edmonds, "Some Schools Work and More Can,"*Social Policy*, March/April 1979; Edmonds, "A Discussion of the Literature and Issues Related to Effective Schools," unpublished draft, n.d. Edmonds had shared the latter forty-five-page draft with me while he was working on it. See also, New York State Office of Education Performance Review, "School Factors Influencing Reading Achievement: A Case Study of Two Inner-City Schools," Albany, NY, March 1974; J. V. Madden, D. R. Lawson, and D. Sweet, "School Effectiveness Study" (State of California Department of Education, 1976).

31. Wilbur Brookover and Lawrence Lezotte, "Changes in School Characteristics Coincident with Changes in Student Achievement" (Michigan State University, College of Urban Development, 1977).

32. Christopher Jencks, "Education Vouchers: A Report on Financing Education by Payments to Parents" (Center for the Study of Public Policy, 1970).

33. Ronald R. Edmonds, *Search for Effective Schools: The Identification and Analysis of City Schools That Are Instructionally Effective for Poor Children* (Harvard University Press, 1977).
34. Lawrence Lezotte, Ronald R. Edmonds, and George Ratner, "Remedy for School Failure to Equitably Deliver Basic School Skills" (Center for Urban Studies, 1975).
35. John Frederiksen, "School Effectiveness and Equality of Educational Opportunity" (Center for Urban Studies, 1975).
36. Ronald R. Edmonds and John Frederiksen, "Search for Effective Schools: The Identification and Analysis of City Schools That Are Instructionally Effective for Poor Children." (Center for Urban Studies, 1978).
37. Ronald R. Edmonds, "Effective Education for Minority Pupils: Brown Confounded and Confirmed," in Derrick Bell, ed., *Shades of Brown: New Perspectives on School Desegregation* (Teachers College Press, 1980), p. 110.
38. Edmonds, "Effective Education of Minority Students," p. 121.
39. Joseph P. Viteritti, *Across the River: Politics and Education in the City* (Holmes & Meier, 1983), pp. 18–19.
40. Memorandum from Ron Edmonds to the Chancellor's Staff, n.d.
41. Ronald R. Edmonds and Charles V. Willie, *Black Colleges in America: Challenges, Development and Survival* (Teachers College Press, 1978).
42. Robert Reinhold, "25 Years After Desegregation, North's Schools Lag," *New York Times*, May 17, 1979.
43. See Ronald R. Edmonds, "Simple Justice in the Cradle of Liberty: Desegregating the Boston Public Schools," *Vanderbilt Law Review*, Vol. 31, No. 4 (May, 1978).
44. See Viteritti, *Across the River*, pp. 215–265.
45. For more detailed description of Ron Edmonds's initiatives in New York, see Viteritti, *Across the River*, pp. 99–156. All quotes in this section and the next are taken from there.
46. "Statement of Chancellor Frank J. Macchiarola on the New York State Regency Competency Testing Program," January 11, 1979.
47. *New York Newsday*, January 10, 1980.
48. Alfred Melov, private interview, April 30, 1981.
49. "Editorial," *New York Times*, December 31, 1979.
50. For a detailed analysis of the data, see Viteritti, *Across the River*, pp. 140–149. (Check numbering. Erased Note 53)
51. Joseph P. Viteritti, "Transition Report to the Superintendent, Boston Public Schools," September 14, 1981.
52. "Superintendent Robert R. Spillane's Speech to Principals, Headmasters, and Other Key Personnel at West Roxbury High School," August 26, 1981.
53. Peter Baker, "Robert Spillane, Who Retooled Boston's Schools, Dies at 80," *New York Times*, July 20, 2015.

Chapter Four

1. John E. Coons, William H. Clune, and Stephen D. Sugarman, *Private Wealth and Public Education* (Harvard University Press, 1970); John E. Coons and Stephen D. Sugarman, *Education by Choice: The Case for Family Control* (University of California Press, 1978).
2. John Chubb and Terry Moe, *Politics, Markets, and America's Schools* (Brookings Institution Press, 1990).
3. Nicole Stelle Garnett, Richard W. Garnett, and Ernest Morrell, eds., John E. *Coons: The Case for Parental Choice: Parent, God, Family and Educational Liberty* (University of Notre Dame Press, 2023).
4. See, for example, Margaret F. Brinig and Nicole Stelle Garnett, *Lost Classroom, Lost Community: Catholic Schools' Importance in Urban America* (University of Chicago Press, 2014).
5. Ansley T. Erickson and Ernest Morrell, eds., *Educating Harlem: Schooling and Resistance in a Black Community* (Columbia University Press, 2019).
6. John E. Coons, *School Choice and Human Good: Why All Parents Must Be Empowered to Choose*, ed. Ron Matus (BALBOA Press, 2021).
7. John Coons, "Jack Coons: Law, Ethics and Educational Finance Reform," interviews conducted by Martin Meeker, Oral History Center, the Bancroft Library, University of California, Berkeley, 2015 (hereafter "oral history).

8. Coons, "An Informal Bibliography of Parental Choice," in Garnett, Garnett, and Morrell, *John Coons*, pp. 253–269.
9. Coons, oral history.
10. John Coons, personal phone conversation, January 31, 2021.
11. Coons, oral history.
12. James S. Coleman, Sara D. Kelly, and John A. Moore, *Trends in School Segregation: 1968–1973* (Urban Institute, 1975).
13. James Coleman, "Integration, Yes: Busing, No," *New York Times*, August 24, 1975.
14. See, for example, Nancy St. John, *School Desegregation: Outcomes for Children* (John Wiley, 1975).
15. James S. Coleman et al., *High School Achievement: Public, Private and Catholic Schools Compared* (Basic Books, 1982).
16. James S. Coleman and Thomas Hoffer, *Public, Private and Catholic Schools: The Impact of Community* (Basic Books, 1987).
17. Arthur Wise, *Rich Schools, Poor Schools: The Promise of Equal Educational Opportunity* (University of Chicago Press, 1968).
18. John E. Coons, William H. Clune, and Stephen D. Sugarman, "Educational Opportunity: A Workable Constitutional Test for the State Financial Structures," *California Law Review*, Vol. 57, No. 2 (1969).
19. *Serrano v. Priest*, 5 Cal.3d 584 (1971).
20. *Brown v. Board of Education*, 347 US 483, 493 (1954) (italics added).
21. *San Antonio Independent School District v. Rodriguez*, 411 US 1, 24 (1973).
22. *San Antonio Independent School District v. Rodriguez*, at 43.
23. *San Antonio Independent School District v. Rodriguez*, at 43.
24. *Brown v. Board of Education*, 349 US 294 (1955).
25. Over time, appeals for "equity" were replaced in school finance litigation by appeals for "adequacy," a term that could be applied to describe a minimum funding needed to abide by state constitutional standards that would not necessarily result in an equitable or equal distribution. See Joseph P. Viteritti, "The Inadequacy of Adequacy Guarantees: A Historical Commentary on State Constitutional Provisions That Are the Basis for School Finance Litigation," *University of Maryland Law Journal of Race, Religion, Gender, and Class*, Vol. 7, No. 1 (2007).
26. See, generally, Coons, "School Choice and Sheer Bad Luck," in Coons, *School Choice and Human Good*, p. 105.
27. John Coons, "The Too Modest Milton," in Coons, *School Choice and Human Good*, pp. 13–15.
28. Coons, personal phone conversation, January 31, 2021.
29. Milton Friedman, "The Role of Government in Education," in Robert A. Solo, ed., *Economics and the Public Interest* (Rutgers University Press, 1955).
30. Milton Friedman and Rose Friedman, *Free to Choose: A Personal Statement* (Harcourt Brace, 1980), p. 172, citing Kenneth Clark, "Alternative Public School Systems," *Harvard Educational Review* (Winter, 1968), p. 111.
31. Coons, "Introduction: Values in Collision," in Coons, Clune, and Sugarman, *Private Wealth and Public Education*, p. 1.
32. Coons, "Preface," in Coons, Clune, and Sugarman, *Private Wealth and Public Education*, pp. xvii, xviii.
33. Derrick A. Bell Jr., *Race, Racism and American Law* (Little Brown, 1973), p. 665, citing Coons, in Coons, Clune, and Sugarman, *Private Wealth and Public Education*, p. 30.
34. Coons, in Coons, Clune, and Sugarman, *Private Wealth and Public Education*, p. 3.
35. Coons, "Our School Deportation Problem" in Coons, *School Choice and Human Good*, pp. 95–97.
36. Coons, in Clune, Coons, and Sugarman, *Private Wealth and Public Education*, p. 4.
37. James S. Coleman, "Foreword," in Coons, Clune, and Sugarman, *Private Wealth and Public Education*, p. vii.
38. Coleman, "Foreword," in Coons, Clune, and Sugarman, *Private Wealth and Public Education*, p. ix.
39. Coons and Sugarman, *Education by Choice*; John Coons and Stephen Sugarman, *Family Choice in Education: A Model State System of Vouchers* (Institute of Government Studies, 1971).
40. Coleman, "Foreword," in Coons and Sugarman, *Education by Choice*, p. xiii.
41. Coleman, "Foreword," in Coons and Sugarman, *Education by Choice*, p. xii.

42. See Derrick A. Bell Jr., "*Brown v. Board of Education* and the Interest Convergence Dilemma," *Harvard Law Review*, Vol. 93, no. 3 (January, 1980).

43. Coons, "Introduction," in Coons and Sugarman, *Education by Choice*, p. 2.

44. Coons, "School Choice and Sheer Bad Luck," in Coons, *School Choice and Human Good*, pp. 106–107.

45. John E. Coons and Patrick M. Brennan, *By Nature Equal: The Anatomy of a Western Insight* (Princeton University Press, 1999), p. 13.

46. Coons and Sugarman, *Education by Choice*, p. 53.

47. See Coons, "School Choice as Simple Justice," in Garnett, Garnett, and Morrell, *John E. Coons*, pp. 54–70. (Originally in *First Things*, April 1992.)

48. Coons, "School Choice as Simple Justice," p. 63.

49. Coons, "School Choice as Simple Justice," p. 57.

50. Terry M. Moe, *Special Interests: Teachers Unions and America's Public Schools* (Brookings Institute Press, 2011), p. 93, quoted in Garnett, Garnett, and Morrell, *John E. Coons*, p. viii.

51. The others were Scott Jensen (American Federation of Children), Doug Tuthill (Step Up for Children), John Witte (University of Wisconsin), and Patrick Wolf (University of Arkansas).

52. Joseph P. Viteritti, "The Federal Role in School Reform: Obama's Race to the Top," *Notre Dame Law Review*, Vol. 87, no. 5 (June, 2012).

53. Richard W. Garnett, "Review Essay, Brown's Promise, Blaine's Legacy," *Constitutional Commentary*, Vol. 17, no.3 (2000).

Chapter Five

1. Edward N. Costikyan, *Behind Closed Doors: Politics in the Public Interest* (Harcourt Brace, 1966).

2. For an overview of this period in New York City political history, see Joseph P. Viteritti, *The Pragmatist: Bill de Blasio's Quest to Save the Soul of New York* (Oxford University Press, 2017), pp. 106–122.

3. See Joseph P. Viteritti, "The Tragic Self-Immolation of Rudy Giuliani," *Think: Opinion, Analysis, Essays*, NBC News, March 30, 2018.

4. Diane Ravitch, *The Great School Wars: A History of the New York City Public Schools* (Basic Books, 1988), p. xiv.

5. Diane Ravitch, "Somebody's Children: Educational Opportunity for All America's Children," in Diane Ravitch and Joseph P. Viteritti, eds., *New Schools for a New Century: The Redesign of Urban Education* (Yale University Press, 1997).

6. Ravitch, "Somebody's Children," p. 252.

7. Ravitch, "Somebody's Children," p. 253.

8. Ravitch, "Somebody's Children," p. 267, n. 21, citing Lawrence H. Tribe, *American Constitutional Law* (Foundation Press, 1988), p. 1223.

9. Ravitch, "Somebody's Children," p. 254.

10. James S. Coleman, Sara D. Kelly, and John A. Moore, *Trends in School Segregation, 1968–1973* (Urban Institute, 1975).

11. Diane Ravitch, "Busing: The Solution That Has Failed to Solve," *New York Times*, December 21, 1975.

12. Diane Ravitch, "The White Flight Controversy," *Public Interest*, Vol. 51 (Spring, 1978), p. 146.

13. Ravitch, "Busing."

14. Nathan Glazer, *We Are All Multiculturalists Now* (Harvard University Press, 1998).

15. Nathan Glazer, *Affirmative Discrimination: Ethnic Inequality and Public Policy* (Harvard University Press, 1987).

16. "About Diane," Diane Ravitch, 2023, https://dianeravitch.com/about-diane/.

17. Diane Ravitch, *The Revisionists Revised: A Critique of the Radical Attack on the Schools* (Basic Books, 1978).

18. These days, the Trump phenomenon complicates political labeling further. If one were to concede his capability of having a cultivated idea of political philosophy, it would fit more neatly under such labels as narcissist or autocrat. Many or most of his supporters identify as conservative, but to equate Trumpism with conservatism is not fair to many philosophical conservatives who want nothing to do with him.

19. Diane Ravitch, "On the History of Minority Group Education in the United States," reprinted in Ravitch, *The Schools We Deserve: Reflections on the Educational Crises of Our Time* (Basic Books, 1985), p. 204.

20. Diane Ravitch, "Integration, Segregation, Pluralism," reprinted in Ravitch, *The Schools We Deserve*, p. 223.

21. Ravitch, *The Schools We Deserve*, p. 224.

22. See, generally, Diane Ravitch, *The Troubled Crusade: American Education 1945–1980* (Basic Books, 1983), pp. 114–181.

23. Derrick Bell, *And We Are Not Saved: The Elusive Quest for Racial Justice* (Basic Books, 1987).

24. Diane Ravitch, "Honesty on Critical Race Theory," *New York Daily News*, June 29, 2021.

25. Diane Ravitch, "Desegregation: Varieties of Meaning," in Derrick Bell, ed., *Shades of Brown: New Perspectives on School Desegregation* (Teachers College Record, 1980), p. 44.

26. Ronald R. Edmonds, "Effective Education for Minority Pupils: *Brown* Confounded or Confirmed," in Bell, *Shades of Brown*, pp. 110–111.

27. Ravitch, "The Meaning of the New Coleman Report," reprinted in Ravitch, *The Schools We Deserve*, p. 104.

28. Diane Ravitch, "The Coleman Reports and American Education," in Aage B. Sorensen and Seymour Spilerman, eds., *Social Theory and Social Policy: Essays in Honor of James S. Coleman* (Praeger, 1993), p. 137.

29. Ravitch, "The Coleman Reports and American Education," p. 136.

30. Fred M. Hechinger, "About Education: New Coleman Study Adds Controversy over Tuition Tax Credit," *New York Times*, April 7, 1981; Edward B. Fiske, "New School Dispute Stirred by Coleman," *New York Times*, April 12, 1981.

31. Ravitch, "The Coleman Reports and American Education," p. 136.

32. See Diane Ravitch, "The Uses and Misuses of Tests," *College Board Review* (Winter, 1983–1984)

33. Diane Ravitch, *National Standards in American Education: A Citizens Guide* (Brookings Institution, 1995).

34. Ravitch, *National Standards in American Education*, p. 3.

35. Diane Ravitch and Joseph Viteritti, "A New Vision for City Schools," *Public Interest* (Winter, 1996).

36. Ravitch and Viteritti, "A New Vision for City Schools," p. 5.

37. Ravitch and Viteritti, *New Schools for a New Century*.

38. Ravitch and Viteritti, "New York: The Obsolete Factory," in Ravitch and Viteritti, *New Schools for a New Century*, p. 17.

39. Ravitch and Viteritti, "New York: The Obsolete Factory," p. 33.

40. Ravitch and Viteritti, "New York: The Obsolete Factory," p. 34.

41. Ravitch and Viteritti, "New York: The Obsolete Factory," p. 36.

42. James Traub, "What Can Public Schools Learn?" *New York Times Book Review*, November 9, 1997.

43. Diane Ravitch and Joseph P. Viteritti, *City Schools: Lessons from New York* (Johns Hopkins University Press, 2000).

44. Gail Foster, "Historically Black Independent Schools," in Ravitch and Viteritti, *City Schools*. See Derrick Bell, *Silent Covenants: Brown v. Board of Education and the Unfulfilled Hopes for Racial Reform* (Oxford University Press, 2004), pp. 166–170.

45. Paul E. Peterson and William G. Howell, "When Low-Income Students Move from Public to Private Schools," in Ravitch and Viteritti, *City Schools*.

46. See Jack Schneider and Jennifer Berkshire, *A Wolf at the Schoolhouse Door: The Dismantling of Public Education and the Future of the School* (New Press, 2020); Mercedes Schneider, *School Choice: The End of Public Education?* (Teachers College Press, 2016); Josh Cowan, *The Privateers: How Billionaires Created a Culture War and Sold School Vouchers* (Harvard Education Press, 2024). Cara Fitzpatrick suggests the same with the provocative title of her book, but she never completes the argument: *The Death of Public School: How Conservatives Won the War over Education in America* (Basic Books, 2023).

47. "CFS: A Story Worth Telling," Children's Scholarship Fund, 2023–2024 Annual Report.

48. Diane Ravitch and Joseph P. Viteritti, eds., *Making Good Citizens: Education and Civil Society* (Yale University Press, 2001). Contributors included, William Damon, Jean Bethke Elstain, Nathan Glazer, Charles Glenn, Gerald Grant, D. Sunshine Hillygus, Mark Holmes, Norman

Nie, Warren Nord, Robert Putnam, Rosemary Salomone, and Alan Wolfe. See Gary Rosen, "Advanced Civics," *New York Times Book Review*, November 18, 2001.

49. Alan Wolfe, ed., *School Choice: The Moral Debate* (Princeton University Press, 2003). Contributors, excluding respondents, were Charles Glenn, Amy Gutmann, Meira Levinson, Sanford Levinson, Stephen Macedo, Martha Minow, Joseph O'Keefe, SJ, Michael Perry, Nancy Rosenblum, Rosemary Salomone, and myself.

50. Diane Ravitch, *Left Back: A Century of Failed School Reforms* (Simon & Schuster, 2000).

51. Diane Ravitch, *The Language Police: How Pressure Groups Restrict What Students Learn* (Knopf, 2003).

52. Diane Ravitch and Joseph P. Viteritti, eds., *Kid Stuff: Marketing Sex and Violence to America's Children* (Johns Hopkins University Press, 2003).

Chapter Six

1. Joseph P. Viteritti, "Unapportioned Justice: Local Elections, Social Science, and the Evolution of the Voting Rights Act," *Cornell Journal of Law and Public Policy*, Vol.4, no. 1 (Fall, 1994).

2. Joseph P. Viteritti, "Choosing Equality: Religious Opportunity and Educational Opportunity Under Constitutional Federalism," *Yale Law & Policy Review*, Vol. 15, no. 1 (1996). The article examined the laws of New York, Washington, Massachusetts, Pennsylvania, Wisconsin, and Puerto Rico.

3. Joseph P. Viteritti, "Blaine's Wake: School Choice, the First Amendment and State Constitutional Law,"*Harvard Journal of Law & Public Policy*, Vol. 21, no. 3 (Summer, 1998).

4. Mark Edward DeForrest, "An Overview and Evaluation of State Blaine Amendments: Origins, Scope and First Amendment Concerns," *Harvard Journal of Law and Public Policy*, Vol. 26 (Spring, 2003).

5. *Espinoza v. Montana Department of Revenue*, 591 US ___ (2020).

6. Affidavit of Joseph P. Viteritti, *Simmons-Harris v. Zelman*, United States Court of Appeals for the Sixth Circuit, Case No. 99-4048, October 7, 1999.

7. The group included Michael McConnell, Douglas Kmiec, Michael Heise, Eugene Volokh, Phil Murrin, and Mark Snyderman. See, generally, Clint Bolick, *Voucher Wars: Waging the Legal Battle over School Choice* (Cato Institute, 2003), pp. 109–124, 167–199.

8. *Zelman v. Simmons-Harris*, 546 US 639 (2002).

9. For an analysis of the decision, see Joseph P. Viteritti, "Reading Zelman: The Triumph of Pluralism and its Effects on Liberty, Equality and Choice," *Southern California Law Review*, Vol. 76, no. 5 (July, 2003).

10. Linda Greenhouse, "Win the Debate, Not Just the Case," *New York Times*, July 14, 2002.

11. Greenhouse's commentary is also mentioned in Justin Driver's treatise on law and education, *The School-House Gate: Public Education, the Supreme Court and the Battle for the American Mind* (Pantheon Books, 2018), pp. 533–534, n. 149.

12. The opening paragraph began,

> Nearly half a century has passed since the parents of a little black girl from Topeka, Kansas, entered a federal court room to argue that every child in America has an equal right to a decent education. Since then the political process has conjured up a remarkable array of schemes to demonstrate the nation's commitment to that ideal, but the results have been unimpressive. We have sent children on long bus rides into hostile environments; we have poured tons of money into faltering programs; we have tinkered on the edges of institutional reform; and we have even experimented with several forms of school choice—some to promote racial integration and others to improve the academic opportunities available to disadvantaged children. Notwithstanding Linda Brown's courageous efforts to fulfill the promise of equality and a range of well-intentioned government actions, race and class remain the most reliable predictors of educational achievement in the United States.

> Joseph P. Viteritti, *Choosing Equality: School Choice, the Constitution and Civil Society* (Brookings Institution Press, 1999), p. 1.

13. Joseph P. Viteritti, *The Last Freedom: Religion from the Public School to the Public Square* (Princeton University Press, 2007).

Chapter Seven

1. "Race is permanent. We must fight, but I don't see the possibility of racial equality in this country. I get this from Derrick Bell. Read *Faces at the Bottom of the Well* and *Silent Covenants.*" Conversation with Howard Fuller, October 27, 2021.
2. Derrick A. Bell Jr., "Brown v. Board of Education and the Interest Conversion Dilemma," *Harvard Law Review*, Vol. 93 (January, 1980).
3. Howard Fuller, with Lisa Frazier Page, *No Struggle, No Progress: A Warrior's Life from Black Power to Education Reform* (Marquette University Press, 2014).
4. Unless otherwise stated, material quoted in the following paragraphs is taken from my phone conversation with Howard Fuller, January 15, 2020.
5. Phone conversation with Howard Fuller, January 15, 2020.
6. Phone conversation with Howard Fuller, October 27, 2021.
7. Unless otherwise stated, this biographical section is drawn from Fuller and Frazier, *No Struggle*, pp. 9–57.
8. Fuller and Frazier, *No Struggle*, p. 10.
9. Fuller and Frazier, *No Struggle*, p. 54.
10. Fuller and Frazier, *No Struggle*, p. 54.
11. Unless otherwise indicated, this biographical section is drawn primarily from Fuller and Frazier, *No Struggle*, pp. 57–159, although his story shows up in other literature also.
12. For more details on Fuller's leadership development efforts, see Charles W. McKinney Jr., *Greater Freedom: The Evolution of the Civil Rights Struggle in Wilson, North Carolina* (Rowman & Littlefield, 2010), pp. 155–158.
13. McKinney, *Greater Freedom*, p. 157. This assessment of Fuller is corroborated in Devin Fergus, *Liberalism, Black Power, and the Making of American Politics, 1965–1980* (University of Georgia Press, 2009), pp. 20–28.
14. Quoted in, Fergus, *Liberalism, Black Power and the Making of American Politics*, p. 41.
15. For more details on the African Liberation Day event and Fuller's role in organizing it, see Cedric Johnson, *Revolutionaries to Race Leaders: Black Power and the Making of African American Politics* (University of Minnesota Press, 2007), pp. 139–145.
16. See Patrick D. Jones, *The Selma of the North: Civil Rights Insurgency in Milwaukee* (Harvard University Press, 2009), focusing on the 1960s and 1970s.
17. Howard Fuller, "The Impact of the Milwaukee Public School System's Desegregation Plan on Black Students and the Black Community (1976–1982)" (PhD dissertation, Marquette University, 1985).
18. Cited in Bill Dahlk, *Against the Wind: African Americans and the Schools in Milwaukee* (Marquette University Press, 2010), p. 369.
19. See Dahlk, *Against the Wind*, pp. 351–357.
20. For background on the history of magnet schools in Milwaukee, see James K. Nelson, *Educating Milwaukee: How One City's History of Segregation and Struggle Shaped Its Schools* (Wisconsin Historical Society, 2015), pp. 65–141.
21. Jack Dougherty, *More Than One Struggle: The Evolution of Black School Reform in Milwaukee* (University of North Carolina Press, 2004), p. 171.
22. Howard Fuller, "Enough Is Enough," audio tape, n.d.
23. "Enough Is Enough: Save North Division High School," campaign document, Coalition to Save North Division High School, n.d.
24. Dougherty, *More Than One Struggle*, p. 178.
25. Derrick Bell, ed., *Shades of Brown: New Perspectives on School Desegregation* (Teachers College Press, 1980).
26. Dougherty, *More Than One Struggle*, p. 176. See also Dahlk, *Against the Wind*, pp. 358–364.
27. Cited in Dahlk, *Against the Wind*, p. 383.
28. Fuller and Frazier, *No Struggle*, p. 194.
29. Dahlk, *Against the Wind*, p. 392.
30. Dahlk, *Against the Wind*, p. 386.
31. Conversation with Howard Fuller, January 21, 2022.
32. Howard Fuller and Robin Harris, "Opinion: Ahead of Betsy DeVos's Confirmation Hearings, Some Thoughts on Why the Face of School Choice Belongs to Parents, Not Politicians," *Hechinger Report*, January 8, 2017.

Chapter Eight

1. Bill Dahlk, *Against the Wind: African Americans and the Schools in Milwaukee* (Marquette University Press, 2010, pp. 424–425.

2. Dahlk, *Against the Wind*, p. 461.

3. George A. Mitchell, "An Evaluation of State Financed School Integration in Metropolitan Milwaukee" (Wisconsin Policy Research Institute, June 1989).

4. Dahlk, *Against the Wind*, p. 403.

5. Dahlk, *Against the Wind*, p. 403.

6. Dahlk, *Against the Wind*, p. 462.

7. Michael Rutter et al., *Fifteen Thousand Hours: Secondary Schools and Their Effects on Children* (Harvard University Press, 1979).

8. Cited in Sarah Barber, "Never Stop Working: Examining the Life of and Activism of Howard Fuller" (master's thesis, University of Wisconsin, Milwaukee, 2012).

9. Howard Fuller, "A Manifesto for New Directions in the Education of Black Children in the City of Milwaukee," August 8, 1987.

10. Cited in James K. Nelson, *Educating Milwaukee: How One City's History of Segregation and Struggle Shaped Its Schools*, (Wisconsin Historical Society, 2015) p. 132.

11. Cited in Nelson, *Educating Milwaukee*, pp. 132–133.

12. Conversation with Howard Fuller, January 21, 2022.

13. Derrick Bell, "Control, Not Color: The Real Issue in the Milwaukee Manifesto," *Milwaukee Journal*, September 30, 1997.

14. Karen J. Putnam, "The Milwaukee Manifesto: Is a Separate Black School District Constitutional? Is It a Good Idea," March 1988.

15. Correspondence from Derrick Bell to Howard Fuller, April 6, 1988.

16. Putnam, "The Milwaukee Manifesto," pp. 3–4.

17. Nelson, *Educating Milwaukee*, p. 133.

18. Robert S. Peterkin and Janice E. Jackson, "Transforming Schools for African Americans: How Well Are We Doing?" *Journal of Negro Education* (Winter, 1994), p. 130.

19. Peterkin and Jackson, "Transforming Schools for African Americans," p. 126.

20. Peterkin and Jackson, "Transforming Schools for African Americans," p. 135.

21. Nelson, *Educating Milwaukee*, pp. 134–136, on Peterkin's early initiatives in Milwaukee.

22. See Christine H. Rossell, "Controlled Choice Desegregation Plans: Not Enough Choice, Too Much Control," *Urban Affairs Review* (September, 1995), tracing the evolution of this discussion.

23. See Robert S. Peterkin, "What's Happening in Milwaukee?" *Educational Leadership* (December, 1990), p. 52.

24. On the legislative banter and its consequences, see Paul E. Peterson and Chad Noyes, "School Choice in Milwaukee," in Diane Ravitch and Joseph P. Viteritti, eds., *New School for a New Century: The Redesign of Urban Education* (Yale University Press, 1997).

25. Conversation with Howard Fuller, October 27, 2021.

26. Quoted in Dahlk, *Against the Wind*, p. 518.

27. Seventy-three percent of the participants were African American and 21 percent were Hispanic. John Witte, *The Market Approach to Education: An Analysis of America's First Voucher Program* (Princeton University Press, 1999), p. 59.

28. There were only twenty-three secular private schools in Milwaukee at the time, and only half chose to participate. More than one hundred religious schools were excluded. Witte, *The Market Approach to Education*, pp. 55–56.

29. Conversation with Deborah McGriff, April 6, 2022.

30. Quoted in Cedric Johnson, *Revolutionaries to Race Leaders: Black Power and the Making of African American Politics* (University of Minnesota Press, 2007), p. 191.

31. Quoted in Johnson, p. 191.

32. Quoted in Coleman, *Long Way to Go*, p. 158.

33. Quoted in Coleman, *Long Way to Go*, p. 192.

34. Coleman, *Long Way to Go*, p. 191.

35. Quoted in Coleman, *Long Way to Go*, p. 194.

36. Dahlk, *Against the Wind*, p. 586.

37. Coleman, *Long Way to Go*, p. 191.

38. For an elaboration of this model, see Ravitch and Viteritti, eds., *New Schools for a New Century*.

39. See David Tyack, *The One Best System: A History of American Urban Education* (Harvard University Press, 1974). See also Raymond Callahan, *Education and the Cult of Efficiency* (University of Chicago Press, 1962).
40. For a more detailed treatment of this plan and the resulting controversy, see Dahlk, *Against the Wind*, pp. 565–568; Coleman, *Long Way to Go*, pp. 333–335.
41. Dahlk, *Against the Wind*, p. 568.
42. Witte, *The Market Approach to Education*, p. 56.
43. Dahlk, *Against the Wind*, p. 534.
44. Quoted in Nelson, *Educating Milwaukee*, p. 151.
45. Quoted in Dahlk, *Against the Wind*, p. 540.
46. Quoted in Dahlk, *Against the Wind*, p. 541.
47. Brent Staples, "Showdown in Milwaukee: How Choice Changes Public Schools," *New York Times*, May 15, 1997.
48. Brent Staples, *Parallel Time: Growing Up in Black and White* (Pantheon, 1994).
49. *Zelman v. Simmons-Harris*, 536 US 639 (2002).
50. Dahlk, *Against the Wind*, p. 550.
51. Material in this and the next two paragraphs is based on two conversations I had with Howard Fuller (April 26, 2022; August 11, 2022) and an internal document that Fuller shared with me prepared by Assembly Majority Leader Scott Jensen with no title or date on it.
52. John Tierney, "Let Your People Stay," *New York Times*, February 21, 2006.
53. Information in this paragraph is based on conversations I had with Fuller (April 26, 2022; August 11, 2022). See also Fuller and Frazier, *No Struggle*, pp. 269–270.
54. To Governor Scott Walker and Others, "Statement on the Milwaukee Parental Choice Program," January 5, 2011.
55. Wisc. Stat. Sec. 119.25 (2) (6) b, created by Act 32 Sec. 2536c.
56. For additional background on the formation of BAEO, see Jeanette Mitchell, "Fighting the Inequalities in Education for African Americans: A Comparative Analysis of Two Leaders' Stories" (dissertation in partial fulfillment of EdD, Cardinal Stritch University, April 2001), pp. 216–277.
57. Quoted in Mitchell, "Fighting the Inequalities in Education for African Americans," p. 217.
58. Conversation with Howard Fuller, August 11, 2022.
59. "Planning Document for the Establishment of the Black Alliance for Educational Options," n.d.
60. Albert O. Hirschman, *Exit, Voice and Loyalty: Responses to Decline in Firms, Organizations and States* (Harvard University Press, 1972).
61. Albert O. Hirschman, *Rival Views of Market Society and Other Essays* (Harvard University Press, 1992, p. 89.
62. Conversation with Howard Fuller, August 11, 2022.
63. Conversation with Howard Fuller, August 11, 2022.

Chapter Nine

1. Terri N. Watson, "A Love Letter to Babette Edwards: Harlem's Othermother," The Gotham Center for New York City, April 19, 2019. See Patricia H. Collins, "Shifting the Center: Race, Class, and Feminist Theorizing about Motherhood," in Evelyn Nakano Glen, Grace Chang, and Linda Rennie Forcey, eds, *Mothering: Ideology, Experience and Agency* (Routledge, 1994).
2. Watson, "A Love Letter to Babette Edwards," pp. 5–6.
3. Cited in Gregory B. Bodwell, "Grassroots, Inc.: A Sociopolitical History of the Cleveland Voucher Battle, 1992–2002 (PhD dissertation, Case Western Reserve University, June 2006).
4. For a more detailed discussion of the bill and its passage, see Bodwell, "Grassroots, Inc.," pp. 59–90; Joseph P. Viteritti, *Choosing Equality: School Choice, the Constitution and Civil Society* (Brookings Institution Press, 1999), pp. 108–113; John Witte, *The Market Approach to Education: An Analysis of America's First Voucher Program* (Princeton University Press, 1999), pp. 74, 75, 170, 171; Jay P. Greene, William C. Howell, and Paul E. Peterson, "Lessons from the Cleveland Scholarship Program," in Paul E. Peterson and Bryan C. Hassel, eds., *Learning from School Choice* (Brookings Institution Press, 1998).
5. The three papers were the *Cleveland Plain-Dealer, Columbus Post Dispatch*, and *Cincinnati Enquirer*.

6. Drew Lindsay, "Wisconsin, Ohio, Back Vouchers for Religious Schools," *Education Week*, July 12, 1995.

7. Linda Greenhouse, "Cleveland's School Vouchers Weighed by Supreme Court," *New York Times*, February 21, 2002.

8. See Babette Edwards Education Reform in Harlem Collection (1964–1966), "Biographical/Historical Information," Archives and Manuscripts, Call no. Sc MG 809, http://catalog.nypl.org/record=b20800432.

9. For more detailed analysis of this episode and its significance, see Clarence Taylor, *Knocking at Our Own Door: Milton A. Galamison and the Struggle to Integrate New York City Schools* (Columbia University Press, 1997), esp. pp. 176–207.

10. E. Babette Edwards, "Why a Harlem Parents Union?" in James S. Coleman, ed., *Parents, Teachers, and Children: Prospects for Choice in American Education* (Institute for Contemporary Studies, 1977).

11. Brittney Lewer, "Pursuing 'Real Power to Parents': Babette Edwards's Activism from Community Control to Charter Schools," in Ansley T. Erickson and Ernest Morrell, eds., *Educating Harlem: A Century of Schooling and Resistance in a Black Community* (Columbia University Press, 2019), p. 277. Morrell was also an editor of the Notre Dame collection of Jack Coons's work. See Nicole Stelle Garnett, Richard W. Garnett, and Ernest Morrell, eds., *John E. Coons: The Case for Parental Choice: Parent, God, Family and Educational Liberty* (University of Notre Dame Press, 2023).

12. Lewer, "Pursuing 'Real Power to Parents,'" p. 280.

13. "Boycotting Parents Want Funds Used for Private Schools," *New York Times*, January 22, 1976.

14. Basil A. Smikle Jr., "Regimes, Reform and Race: The Politics of Charter School Growth and Sustainability in Harlem" (PhD dissertation, Columbia University, 2019), p. 196.

15. Charter School Institute, State University of New York. newyorkcharters.org

16. "NYC Charter School Facts: 2024–25," New York City Charter School Center.

Chapter Ten

1. Diane Ravitch, *The Death and Life of the Great American School System: How Testing and Choice Are Undermining Education* (Basic Books, 2010).

2. Jane Jacobs, *The Death and Life of Great American Cities* (Random House, 1961).

3. Diane Ravitch, *Reign of Error: The Hoax of the Privatization Movement and the Danger to America's Public Schools* (Random House, 2013).

4. Diane Ravitch, *Slaying Goliath: The Passionate Resistance to Privatization and the Fight to Save America's Public Schools* (Knopf, 2020).

5. Diane Ravitch, "Why I Changed My Mind About School Reform," *Wall Street Journal*, March 9, 2010. See also Ravitch, "Why I Changed My Mind," *The Nation*, June 14, 2010.

6. Chester Finn was the other. See Finn, *Trouble Maker: A Personal History of School Reform Since Sputnik* (Princeton University Press, 2008).

7. Ravitch, *The Death and Life of the Great American School System*, pp. 97–98.

8. For fuller treatment of my own thinking on this evolution in federal policy, see Joseph P. Viteritti, "The Federal Role in School Reform: Obama's Race to the Top," *Notre Dame Law Review*, Vol. 87, No. 5 (June, 2012).

9. Diane Ravitch, *National Standards in American Education: A Citizens Guide* (Brookings Institution Press, 1995).

10. Ravitch, *The Death and Life of the Great American School System*, p. 13.

11. Ravitch, *The Death and Life of the Great American School System*, pp. 135, 240–241.

12. Ravitch, *The Death and Life of the Great American School System*, p. 127.

13. Diane Ravitch, "Somebody's Children: Educational Opportunity for All Americans," in Ravitch and Joseph P. Viteritti, eds., *New Schools for a New Century: The Redesign of Urban Education* (Yale University Press, 1997).

14. Glen C. Altschuler, "The 'Great American School System' Flunks Out," NPR, book review, March 16, 2010.

15. Chester E. Finn Jr., "School's Out," *Forbes*, March 3, 2010.

16. Alan Wolfe, "The Education of Diane Ravitch,"*New York Times Book Review*, March 14, 2010.

17. Alan Wolfe, ed., *School Choice: The Moral Debate* (Princeton University Press, 2003).

18. See Jonathan Zimmerman, *Whose America? Culture Wars in the Public Schools* (University of Chicago Press, 2022).

19. Michael W. Apple, "Challenging One's Own Orthodoxy: Diane Ravitch and the Fate of American Schools," *Educational Policy*, Vol. 24, no. 1 (July, 2010), p. 690.

20. Joseph Featherstone, "Resisting Reforms: On Diane Ravitch," *The Nation*, August 12, 2010.

21. James P. Spillane, "Book Review," *Journal of Policy Analysis and Management*, Vol. 30, No. 3 (2011), pp. 669–673.
22. Carl B. Anderson, "Book Review," *Educational Studies*, Vol. 47 (2011).
23. Ben Wildavsky, "Education's Tea Party," *The New Republic*, March 15, 2010.
24. Ben Wildavsky, "Is Education on the Wrong Track?" *The New Republic*, March 10, 2010.
25. Andrew J. Rotherham, "Is Education on the Wrong Track?" *The New Republic*, March 17, 2010.
26. Kevin Carey, "Is Education on the wrong track?" *The New Republic*, March 16, 2010.
27. Richard Rothstein, "Moment of Clarity," *The New Republic*, March 16, 2010.
28. Diane Ravitch, "Is Education on the Wrong Track?" *The New Republic*, March 17, 17, and 21, 2010.
29. Ravitch, *Reign of Error*, p. 14.
30. Ravitch, *Reign of Error*, p. 19.
31. Ravitch, *Reign of Error*, p. 36
32. Ravitch, *Reign of Error*, p. 49.
33. Ravitch, *Reign of Error*, p. 55.
34. Ravitch, *Reign of Error*, p. 92.
35. Jonathan Kozol, "This Is Only a Test," *New York Times*, September 29, 2013.
36. T. Rees Shapiro, "Reign of Error, by Diane Ravitch," *Washington Post*, October 18, 2013.
37. Trevor Butterworth, "Book Review: 'Reign of Error' by Diane Ravitch," *Wall Street Journal*, September 20, 2013.
38. Jay P. Greene, "Historian Trades Fact for Fiction," *Education Next*, November 7, 2013.
39. Paul E. Peterson and William G. Howell, "When Low-Income Students Move from Public to Private Schools," in Diane Ravitch and Joseph P. Viteritti, eds., *City Schools: Lessons from New York* (Johns Hopkins University Press, 2000).
40. Michael J. Petrilli, "Rain of Errors," *Education Next*, October 18, 2013.
41. In a more recent essay in the same publication, Petrilli rejects the notion that "genetic differences drive racial achievement gaps" as "morally and empirically dubious" and compliments advocates on the political left who call for improved pre- and post-natal healthcare, the elimination of environmental; pollutants and direct aid to families. Michael J. Petrilli, "The Biggest Enemy of Equity Isn't Excellence," *Education Next* (Spring, 2023), p. 5.
42. Ravitch, *Slaying Goliath*.
43. Ravitch, *Slaying Goliath*, p. 30.
44. Ravitch, *Slaying Goliath*, p. 5.
45. Ravitch, *Slaying Goliath*, p. 28.
46. Ravitch, *Slaying Goliath*, p. 193.
47. Ravitch, *Slaying Goliath*, p. 77.
48. Ravitch, *Slaying Goliath*, p. 137.
49. Ravitch, *Slaying Goliath*, pp. 273–274.
50. Annie Murphy Paul, "Diane Ravitch Declares the Education Reform Movement Dead," *New York Times Book Review*, January 21, 2020.
51. Diane Ravitch, blog, March 13, 2020.
52. Melanie McCabe, "An Indictment of Education Reformers, and a Call to Fight Back," *Washington Post*, January 30, 2020.
53. Rob Boston, "Welcome to the Resistance: Diane Ravitch's New Book Is a Powerful Defense of Public Education," *Church and State*, Vol. 73, No. 4 (April, 2020).
54. Frederick M. Hess, "A Voice of the 'Resistance,' Breathless and Crude," *Education Next*, Vol. 20, No. 3 (Summer, 2020).
55. See, especially, Richard J. Herrnstein and Charles Murray, *The Bell Curve: Intelligence and Class Structure in American Life* (Free Press, 1994).
56. Viteritti, "The Federal Role in School Reform," pp. 2109–2111.

Chapter Eleven

1. Ashley Jochim, *In Search of Opportunity: Can Families Use Education Choice to Secure More of What They Want?* (Center for Reinventing Public Education, Mary Lou Fulton Teachers College, Arizona State University, December 2024).
2. Adam Taylor, "Low- and High-Income Schools Now Receive Equal Funding," Fordham Institute, July 13, 2024.
3. https://www.nationsreportcard.gov/ltt/?age=9.
4. "Mathematics Scores Declined for Both Fourth- and Eighth- Graders in Nearly All Districts and States," news release, National Center for Education Statistics, October 24, 2022.

5. "NAEP Data Explorer," *The Nation's Report Card,* 2024 mathematics and reading, grades 4 and 8, race ethnicity used to report trends, school-reported, https://www.nationsreportcard.gov/ndecore/xplore/NDE.

6. "NAEP Report Card: Mathematics: Performance by Student Group," *The Nation's Report Card,* January 2025. https://www.nationsreportcard.gov/reports/mathematics/2024/g4_8/performance-by-student-group/?grade=4.

7. "NAEP Report Card: Reading: Performance by Student Group," *The Nation's Report Card,* January 2025. https://www.nationsreportcard.gov/reports/reading/2024/g4_8/performance-by-student-group/?grade=8.

8. In his *Notes on Virginia,* Jefferson wrote, "I advance it, therefore, as a suspicion only that the blacks, whether originally a distinct race, or made distinct by time or circumstances, are inferior to whites in the endowments both of body and mind." Cited in Garrett Ward Sheldon, *The Political Philosophy of Thomas Jefferson* (Johns Hopkins University Press, 1991), p. 130.

9. Kareem Weaver, "NAACP Resolutions on Literacy as a Civil Right Are a Wakeup Call," *The74,* September 22, 2024.

10. Lauren Wagner, "St. Louis NAACP Files Federal Complaint over Black Students' Low Reading Scores," The74, August 28, 2024.

11. "In Conversation with Betsy DeVos and Howard Fuller, The Future of Education," Tommy G. Thompson Center for Public Leadership, University of Wisconsin, Oshkosh, October 11, 2022.

12. "NAEP Data Explorer," *The Nation's Report Card,* 2024 mathematics and reading, grades 4 and 8, NAEP SES index 3 components, categorized, https://www.nationsreportcard.gov/ndecore/xplore/NDE.

13. John Creamer et al., "Poverty in the United States: 2021," US Census Bureau, September 13, 2022.

14. A study published by the Fordham Institute recently estimated that socioeconomic factors explain 34 percent to 64 percent of the performance between Blacks and whites and 51 percent to 77 percent of the gap between Hispanics and whites. See Eric Hengyu Hu and Paul L. Morgan, *Explaining the Achievement Gap: The Role of Socio-Economic Factors* (Thomas Fordham Institute, August, 2024), https://fordhaminstitute.org/national/research/explaining-achievement-gaps-rolesocioeconomic-Factors.

15. Percentages are considerably higher in urban areas and in elementary grades. "NCEA Data Brief 2023–2024," National Catholic Education Association, January 2025, https://ncea.org/common/Uploaded percent20files/Who percent20We percent20Are/Data/2023-2024-NCEA-Data-Brief.pdf.

16. "NAEP Data Explorer," *The Nation's Report Card,* 2024 mathematics and reading, grades 4 and 8, school identified as charter, public or nonpublic school, 5 categories, https://www.nationsreportcard.gov/ndecore/xplore/NDE.

17. This observation for 2024 replicates and analysis conducted in 2022 in Kathleen Porter-Magee, "Amid the Pandemic, Progress in Catholic Schools," *Wall Street Journal,* October 27, 2022.

18. "NAEP Data Explorer," *The Nation's Report Card,* 2024 mathematics and reading for grades 4 and 8; 2019 mathematics and reading for grade 12; race ethnicity used to report trends (school-reported); school identified as charter; public or nonpublic school (5 categories), https://www.nationsreportcard.gov/ndecore/xplore/NDE.

19. James S. Coleman et al., *High School Achievement: Public, Private and Catholic Schools* (Basic Books, 1982).

20. Nationally, 40 percent of the student body at Catholic schools identify as either minority or Latino/Hispanic. Percentages are considerably higher in urban areas and in elementary grades. "NCEA Data Brief 2023–2024," National Catholic Education Association, January 2025, https://ncea.org/common/Uploaded percent20files/Who percent20We percent20Are/Data/2023-2024-NCEA-Data-Brief.pdf.

21. "Charter School Data Dashboard," National Alliance for Public Charter Schools, 2024, https://data.publiccharters.org/.

22. "Public Charter School Enrollment," National Center for Education Statistics, May 2023, https://nces.ed.gov/programs/coe/indicator/cgb/public-charter-enrollment; "Racial/Ethnic Enrollment in Public Schools," National Center for Education Statistics, May 2024, https://nces.ed.gov/programs/coe/indicator/cge.

23. "Charter School Data Dashboard," *National Alliance for Public Charter Schools,* 2022, https://data.publiccharters.org/.

24. Margaret E. Raymond et al., *As a Matter of Fact: The National Charter School Study III 2023* (Center for Research on Educational Outcomes, 2023), p. 5, https://ncss3.stanford.edu/wp-content/uploads/2023/06/Credo-NCSS3-Report.pdf.

25. See Ted Kolderie, "Beyond Choice to New Public Schools: Withdrawing the Exclusive Franchise," Progressive Policy Institute, Policy Report no. 8 (November 1990). See also Joe Nathan, *Charter Schools: Creating Hope and Opportunity for American Education* (Jossey Bass, 1999). Nathan, a former public school teacher, had worked closely with Kolderie in Minnesota to enact the nation's first charter school law.

26. S. Q. Cornman, O. Ampadu, K. Hanak, and S. Wheeler, *Revenues and Expenditures for Public Elementary and Secondary School Districts: FY 21* (NCES 2024–303), US Department of Education, National Center for Education Statistics, https://nces.ed.gov/pubsearch/pubsinfo.asp?pubid=2024303.

27. Yueting "Cynthia" Xu and Jamison White, "How Are Charter Schools Financed?" National Alliance for Public Charter Schools, December 6, 2022, https://data.publiccharters.org/digest/charter-school-data-digest/how-are-charter-schools-financed/.

28. Alison Heape Johnson et al., *Charter School Funding: Little Progress Toward Equity in the City* (University of Arkansas, August 2023), p. 4, https://cpb-us-e1.wpmucdn.com/wordpressua.uark.edu/dist/9/544/files/2018/10/charter-school-funding-inequity-surges-in-the-cities.pdf.

29. Erica L. Green, "New Biden Administration Rules for Charter Schools Spur Bipartisan Backlash," *New York Times,* May 13, 2022.

30. *The ABCs of School Choice: The Comprehensive Guide to Every Private School Choice Program in America, 2025 Edition* (EdChoice, 2025), https://www.edchoice.org/wp-content/uploads/2025/01/2025-ABCs-of-School-Choice.pdf.

31. See John F. Witte, *The Market Approach to Education: An Analysis of America's First Voucher Program* (Princeton University Press, 2000), 112–151, finding notable parent satisfaction, but negligible academic outcomes; Jay P. Greene, Paul Peterson, and Jiangtao Du, "School Choice in Milwaukee: A Randomized Experiment," in Paul E. Peterson and Bryan C. Hassel, eds., *Learning from School Choice* (Brookings Institution Press, 1998), finding measurable academic gains among participants. Because of its limited scope, this research is not cited in the addendum.

32. Matthew M. Chingos, David N. Figlio, and Krzysztof Karbovnik, The Effects of Ohio's EdChoice Voucher Program on College Enrollment and Graduation. Urban Institute, April 2025.

33. Organisation of Economic Co-operation and Development, Income Inequality (indicator), 2022, doi: 10.1787/459aa7flen. The G6 includes Canada, France, Germany, Italy, Japan, the United Kingdom, and the United States.

34. "The United States of America: Income Inequality in the United States," Economic Policy Institute, https://www.epi.org/multimedia/unequal-states-of-america/.

35. Matthew Desmond, *Poverty, by America* (Crown, 2023).

36. *Citizens United v. Federal Election Commission*, 200 U.S. 321 (2010).

37. Sarah Bryner and Brendan Glavin, "Total 2024 Election Spending Projected to Exceed Previous Record," Open Secret, October 8, 2024.

38. "Billionaire Clans Spent Nearly $2 billion on 2024 Elections," Americans For Tax Fairness, October 10, 2024.

39. See, for example, Thomas Piketty, *Capital in the Twenty-First Century* (Harvard University Press, 2014); Paul Pierson and Jacob Hacker, *Winner-Take-All Politics: How Washington Made the Rich Richer—and Turned Its Back on the Middle Class* (Simon & Schuster, 2010); Robert B. Reich, *The System: Who Rigged It, How We Fix It* (Knopf, 2020); Emmanuel Saez and Gabriel Zucman, *The Triumph of Injustice: How the Rich Dodge Taxes and How to Make Them Pay* (Norton, 2019); Tim Wu, *The Curse of Bigness: Antitrust in the New Gilded Age* (Columbia Global Reports, 2018).

40. Anand Giridharadas, *Winners Take All: The Elite Charade of Changing the World* (Knopf, 2018).

41. Elizabeth Collins, "Tech CEOs Take Their Place as Power Shifts," *Wall Street Journal,* January 21, 2025.

42. See Joseph P. Viteritti, *The Last Freedom: Religion from the Public School to the Public* Square (Princeton University Press, 2007), pp. 114–144; Joseph P. Viteritti, *Choosing Equality: School Choice, the Constitution and Civil Society* (Brookings Institution Press, 1999), pp. 117–179.

43. See, especially, John E. Coons, "School Choice as Simple Justice," *First Things* (April 1992).

44. See Joseph P. Viteritti, "A Truly Living Constitution: Why Educational Opportunity Trumps Strict Separation on the Voucher Question," *New York University Annual Survey of American Law*, Vol. 57 (2000).

45. *Zelman v. Simmons-Harris*, 536 U.S. 639 (2002).

46. See Joseph P. Viteritti, "Reading Zelman: The Triumph of Pluralism, and Its Effects on Liberty, Equality and Choice," *Southern California Law Review*, Vol. 76 (July 2003).

47. See Joseph P. Viteritti, "Choosing Equality: Religious Freedom and Educational Opportunity Under Constitutional Federalism," *Yale Law and Policy Review*, Vol. 15 (1996); Joseph P. Viteritti, "Blaine's Wake: School Choice, the First Amendment and State Constitutional Law," *Harvard Journal of Law and Public Policy*, Vol. 21 (Summer, 1998).

48. *Locke v. Davey*, 540 U.S. 712 (2004).

49. Joseph P. Viteritti, "Davey's Plea: Blaine, Blair, Witters and the Protection of Religious Freedom," *Harvard Journal of Law and Public Policy*, Vol. 27 (Fall, 2003).

50. *Trinity Lutheran Church v. Comer*, 582 U.S. ___ (2017).

51. *Espinoza v. Montana Department of Revenue*, 591 U.S. ___ (2020).

52. *Carson v. Makin*, 596 U.S. ___ (2022).

53. The head for this section plays on the title of Alexander M. Bickel's widely debated book *The Least Dangerous Branch: The Supreme Court at the Bar of Justice* (Yale University Press, 1986).

54. *Dobbs v. Johnson*, 597 U.S. ___ (2002).

55. *Roe v. Wade*, 410 U.S. 113 (1973).

56. *Trump v. U.S.*, 603 U.S. ___ (2024). For a revealing analysis on how the chief justice shaped this and other relevant decisions, see John Kantor and Adam Liptak, "How the Chief Justice Shaped Trump's Supreme Court Winning Streak," *New York Times*, September 15, 2024.

57. *Our Lady of Guadalupe School v. Morrissey-Berru*, 591 U.S. ___ (2020).

58. *Hosanna-Tabor Evangelical Lutheran Church and School v. EEOC*, 565 U.S. 171 (2012).

59. See also Bryce Covert, "License to Discriminate," *The Nation*, October 31–November 7, 2022.

60. "Victory for Public Education in Oklahoma," National Alliance for Public Charter Schools, June 25, 2024, https://publiccharters.org/news/victory-for-public-education-in-oklahoma/.

61. *St. Isidore of Seville Virtual Catholic School* v. Drummond, ___S.Ct.___, 2025 WL 1320000 (Mem).

62. See, Starlee Coleman, "High Court Could Crush Charter Schools," *Wall Street Journal*, April 30, 2025.

63. Editorial, "The School Choice Drive Accelerates," *Wall Street Journal*, January 28–29, 2023.

64. "Arizona: Empowerment Scholarship Accounts," *EdChoice*, December 18, 2023, https://www. edchoice.org/school-choice/programs/arizona-empowerment-scholarship-accounts/.

65. These states were Arizona, Arkansas, Florida, Indiana, North Carolina, Ohio, Oklahoma, Utah, Virginia, and West Virginia. Mike McShane, "Oh, What a Year (for School Choice)," *Forbes*, December 19, 2023.

66. *The ABCs of School Choice: The Comprehensive Guide to Every Private School Choice Program in America, 2025 Edition* (EdChoice, 2025), p. 3, https://www.edchoice.org/wp-content/uploads/2025/01/2025-ABCs-of-School-Choice.pdf.

67. Travis Pillow, "Florida Leads the Nation in 2023," *Next Steps*, June 12, 2024.

68. A state-commissioned evaluation of the program found that program participants registered few academic gains compared to their public school peers, but the assessment was flawed because it failed to compare participants' scores with those of public school students at the same income level and whose parental satisfaction was extremely high. See D. Bugler et al., *Evaluation of Invest in Kids Act: Final Report* (WestEd, 2024), https://www.isbe.net/Documents/Invest-in-Kids-Act-Evaluation-Report.pdf.

69. Parker Baxter, Michael Hartney, and Vladimir Kogan, "Voters Reject Vouchers — Again," *Education Next*, Vol. 25.2 (Spring, 2025).

70. National Center for Education Statistics, nces.ed.gov.

71. Mark Lieberman, "What's Going On with Public School Enrollment? All Big Questions Answered," *Education Week*, June 27, 2024.

72. Michael McShane, "Why Do Parents Homeschool?" *Forbes*, September 27, 2024.

73. Sofoklis Goulas, *Underachieving and Underenrolled: Chronically Low-Performing Schools in the Post-Pandemic Era* (Thomas B. Fordham Institute, September, 2024).
74. James S. Coleman, "Foreword," in John E. Coons, William H. Clune, and Stephen D. Sugarman, *Private Wealth and Public Education* (Harvard University Press, 1970) p. vii.
75. See Michael McShane, "Introducing the School Starter Checklist," *EdChoice*, June 12, 2024, https://www.edchoice.org/engage/introducing-the-school-starter-checklist/.
76. Bella DiMarco and Liz Cohen, "The New Wave of Public Funding of Private Schooling, Explained," *FutureEd*, January 19, 2024, https://www.future-ed.org/the-new-wave-of-public-funding-of-private-schools-explained/.
77. According to EdChoice, sixteen programs allow broad flexibility in the use of funds with no priority given to tuition. Ann Marie Miller, "The *2025 ABCs of School Choice* Is Now Available," *EdChoice*, January 22, 2025, https://www.edchoice.org/engage/the-2025-abcs-of-school-choice-is-available-now/.
78. Dana Goldstein, "A School with 7 Students: Inside Microschools," *New York Times,* June 17, 2024.
79. Caroline Hendrie, "As Many More States Enact Education Savings Accounts, Implementation Challenges Abound," *Education Next*, Vol. 23 (Fall, 2023), pp. 11, 22–23.
80. Christian M. Wade, "Capless School Choice Squeezes State Budgets," *CNHI News*, August 29, 2024, https://www.cnhinews.com/article_a95997c6-65ed-11ef-bdf2-43cc582f733a.html.
81. Michael C. Binder, "Funds for K-12 Students Are on the Chopping Block," *New York Times*, May 2, 20225.
82. After Indiana expanded eligibility for its voucher program in 2023, the percentage of students receiving funding in half its participating schools was at 90% percent compared to only 11% percent the previous year. Aleksandra Appleton and Mia Hollie, "Vouchers Nearly Universal at Half the Private Schools tThat Take Them," *Chalkbeat Indiana,* September 24, 2024.
83. Another 32% percent are not sure. Rachel Minkin, "About Half of Americans Say Public K—12 Eeduucation iIs Moving in the Right Direction," Pew Research Center," April 4, 2024.

Research Addendum

1. "Charter School Data Dashboard," National Alliance for Public Charter Schools, 2024.
2. "Who We Are," Education Commission of the States, https://www.ecs.org/who-we-are-2/.
3. "Our Work," National Alliance for Public Charter Schools, https://www.publiccharters.org/our-work. April, 2025.
4. Charter Schools Program, "Title V, Part B: Non-Regulatory Guidance," US Department of Education, July 2004, p. 12, https://www2.ed.gov/policy/elsec/guid/cspguidance03.pdf.
5. "Charter School Policies: Does the State Specify the Students Who May Be Given Enrollment Preference?" Education Commission of the States, January 2020, https://reports.ecs.org/comparisons/charter-school-policies-04.
6. "Public Charter School Enrollment," National Center for Education Statistics, May 2023, https://nces.ed.gov/programs/coe/indicator/cgb/public-charter-enrollment; "Racial/Ethnic Enrollment in Public Schools," National Center for Education Statistics, May 2024, https://nces.ed.gov/programs/coe/indicator/cge.
7. "Who Attends Charter Schools?" National Alliance for Public Charter Schools, December 22, 2023, https://data.publiccharters.org/digest/charter-school-data-digest/who-attends-charter-schools/
8. "Who Attends Charter Schools?"
9. "Charter School Policies: Does the State Specify the Grounds for Terminating or Not Renewing a School's Charter," Education Commission of the States, January 2020, https://reports.ecs.org/comparisons/charter-school-policies-15.
10. Margaret E. Raymond et al., *As a Matter of Fact: The National Charter School Study III 2023* (Center for Research on Educational Outcomes, 2023), p. 13, https://ncss3.stanford.edu/wp-content/uploads/2023/06/Credo-NCSS3-Report.pdf
11. S. Q. Cornman, O. Ampadu, K. Hanak, and S. Wheeler, *Revenues and Expenditures for Public Elementary and Secondary School Districts: FY 21* (NCES 2024-303) (US Department of Education, : National Center for Education Statistics), https://nces.ed.gov/pubsearch/pubsinfo.asp?pubid=2024303.

12. Yueting "Cynthia" Xu and Jamison White, "How Are Charter Schools Financed?" National Alliance for Public Charter Schools, December 6, 2022, https://data.publiccharters.org/digest/charter-school-data-digest/how-are-charter-schools-financed/.

13. Johnson et al., *Charter School Funding*, p. 4.

14. Raymond, *As a Matter of Fact*, p. 5.

15. Raymond, *As a Matter of Fact*, p. 5.

16. See Libby Stanford, "Charter Schools Now Outperform Traditional Public Schools, Sweeping Study Finds," *Education Week*, June 14, 2023.

17. Raymond, *As a Matter of Fact,* p. 12.

18. Raymond, *As a Matter of Fact,* p. 7.

19. Tessa Pankovits, "Searching for the Tipping Point: Scaling Up Public School Choice Spikes Citywide Gains," Progressive Policy Institute, October 2024.

20. The cities included Camden, Indianapolis, Kansas City, Washington, DC, Detroit, St. Louis, Philadelphia, Dayton, Newark, NJ, and St. Paul, January 2025.

21. "Who We Are," EdChoice, https://www.edchoice.org/who-we-are/.

22. Another relatively new source of data and research on private school choice is FutureEd, an independent think tank based at Georgetown University's McCourt School of Public Policy. Bella DiMarco and Liz Cohen, "New Wave of Public Funding of Private Schooling, Explained," FutureEd, Georgetown University McCourt School of Public Policy, January 19, 2024, https://www.future-ed.org/the-new-wave-of-public-funding-of-private-schools-explained/.

23. Ben Erwin, Emily Brixey, and Eric Syverson, "50-State Comparison: Private School Choice," Education Commission of the States, March 24, 2021, https://www.ecs.org/50-state-comparison-private-school-choice/.

24. *The ABCs of School Choice: The Comprehensive Guide to Every Private School Choice Program in America, 2024 Edition* (EdChoice, 2024), pp. 4–5, https://www.edchoice.org/wp-content/uploads/2023/11/2024-ABCs-of-School-Choice.pdf.

25. Ben Erwin, "50-State Comparison: Private School Choice," Education Commission of the States, January 24, 2024, https://www.ecs.org/50-state-comparison-private-school-choice-2024/.

26. *The ABCs of School Choice: The Comprehensive Guide to Every Private School Choice Program in America, 2025 Edition* (EdChoice, 2025), pp. 180–181, https://www.edchoice.org/wp-content/uploads/2025/01/2025-ABCs-of-School-Choice.pdf.

27. Erwin, "50-State Comparison."

28. *The ABCs of School Choice, 2025 Edition,* pp. 178–195.

29. Erwin, "50-State Comparison."

30. *The ABCs of School Choice, 2025 Edition,* pp. 174–195.

31. Erwin, "50-State Comparision."

32. *The ABCs of School Choice, 2025 Edition,* pp. 180–181.

33. Erwin, "50-State Comparison."

34. *The ABCs of School Choice, 2025 Edition,* pp. 178–179.

35. Erwin, "50-State Comparison."

36. *The ABCs of School Choice, 2025 Edition,* pp. 182–185.

37. Erwin, "50-State Comparison."

38. "School Choice in America Dashboard," EdChoice, modified June 7, 2024.

39. Erwin, "50-State Comparison."

40. "School Choice in America Dashboard," EdChoice, modified June 7, 2024.

41. Erwin, "50-State Comparison."

42. *The ABCs of School Choice, 2024 Edition,* pp. 102–155.

43. *EdChoice Study Guide: A Review of the Research on Private School Choice, 2023 Edition* (Indianapolis: EdChoice, 2023), https://www.edchoice.org/wp-content/uploads/2023/07/2023-EdChoice-Study-Guide-WEB.pdf.

44. See also Patrick J. Wolf et al., *Education Freedom and Student Achievement: Is More School Choice Associated with Higher State-Level Performance on the NAEP?* (Fayetteville University of Arkansas, March 2023), assessing the effects of choice-induced competition on public school performance; Martin F. Leuken, *Fiscal Effects of School Choice: Analyzing the Costs and Savings of Private School Choice Programs in America* (EdChoice, November 2021), assessing the fiscal effects of choice. See also David Griffith, "The Case for Urban Charter Schooling," *National Affairs,* Fall 2020.

45. M. Danish Shakeel, Kaitlin P. Anderson, and Patrick J. Wolf, "Working Paper Series: The Participant Effects of Private School Vouchers Across the Globe: A Meta-Analytic and Systemic Review" (University of Arkansas, May 10, 2016), https://doi.org/10.1080/09243453. 2021.1906283. Cited in *EdChoice Study Guide,* p. 6.

46. William G. Powell et al., "School Vouchers and Academic Performance: Results from Three Randomized Field Trials," *Journal of Policy Analysis and Management*, Vol. 21, No. 2 (2002).

47. Patrick J. Wolf, *The Academic Effects of Private School Choice: Summary of Final-Year Results from Experimental Studies* (University of Arkansas, 2021), https://scdp.uark. edu/the-academic-effects-of-private-school-choice-summary-of-final-year-results-from-experimental-studies/.

48. Patrick Wolf et al., *Evaluation of the DC Opportunity Scholarship Program: Final Report* (US Department of Education, National Center for Education Evaluation and Regional Assistance, Institute of Education Sciences, 2010), https://scdp.uark.edu/evaluation-of-the-impact-of-the-dc-opportunity-scholarship-program-final-report/.

49. Patrick J. Wolf, *The Comprehensive Longitudinal Evaluation of the Milwaukee Parental Choice Program: Summary of Final Reports* (University of Arkansas, 2012), p. 4, https://scdp. uark.edu/the-comprehensive-longitudinal-evaluation-of-the-milwaukee-parental-choice-program-summary-of-final-reports/.

50. Jonathan N. Mills and Patrick J. Wolf, *The Effects of the Louisiana Scholarship Program on Student Achievement After Four Years* (University of Arkansas, 2019), https://scdp.uark.edu/ the-effects-of-the-louisiana-scholarship-program-on-student-achievement-after-four-years/.

51. Matthew M. Chingos et al., *The Effects of Means-Tested Private School Choice Programs on College Enrollment and Graduation* (Urban Institute, July 2019), https://www.urban.org/ sites/default/files/publication/100665/the_effects_of_means-tested_private_school_choice_ programs_on_college_enrollment_and_graduation_2.pdf.

52. John F. Witte et al., "High-Stakes Choice: Achievement and Accountability in the Nation's Oldest urban Voucher Program," *Educational Evaluation and Policy Analysis*, Vol. 36, No. 4 (December, 2014).

53. Michael R. Ford and Fredrik O. Andersson, "Determinants of Organizational Failure in the Milwaukee School Voucher Program," *Policy Studies Journal*, Vol. 47, no. 4 (2019).

54. Chingos et al., *The Effects of Means-Tested Private School Choice,* p. 1.

55. Wolf et al., *Evaluation of the DC Opportunity Scholarship Program.*

56. Matthew Chingos, David Figlio and Krzysztof Karbovnik, The Effects of Ohio's EdChoice Voucher Program on College Enrollment and Graduation, Urban Institute, April 2025.

57. David Figlio, *Evidence of a Catholic School Advantage in Nonpublic Scholarship Programs for Low-Income Families* (Urban Institute, 2021), https://www.urban.org/sites/default/files/ publication/105270/evidence-of-a-catholic-school-advantage-in-nonpublic-scholarship-programs-for-low-income-families.pdf.

58. DiMarco and Cohen, "New Wave of Public Funding of Private Schooling, Explained."

59. David M. Houston, "The Year in Public Opinion on US K–12 Education Policy," *Education Next*, (Winter, 2025).

60. Liz Cohen and Bella DiMarco, "Early Returns: First Results from the New Wave of Public Funding of Private Schooling," FutureEd (Georgetown University McCourt School of Public Policy, October 7, 2024), https://www.future-ed.org/early-returns-first-results-from-the-new-wave-of-public-funding-of-private-schooling/#:~:text=expanded   percent20ESA percent20program.-,How   percent20is   percent20the   percent20Money   percent20Spent percent3F,-The percent20states percent20we.

Index

For the benefit of digital users, indexed terms that span two pages (e.g., 52–53) may, on occasion, appear on only one of those pages.